our de l'argent on donne à tous   *Cette boutique à des delices,*
Des maccarrons, des darioles,   *Qui charment en mille façons*
Des gasteaux diuers des rissoles   *Les filles les petits garçons,*
Du biscuit, et de petits chous.   *Les seruantes et les Nourrices.*

du Palais, sur le Quay qui regarde la Megisserie, à l'Asphere auec Priuilege du Roy.

The Delectable Past

THE JOYS OF THE TABLE—FROM ROME TO THE RENAISSANCE,
FROM QUEEN ELIZABETH I TO MRS. BEETON. THE MENUS,
THE MANNERS—AND THE MOST DELECTABLE
RECIPES OF THE PAST, MASTERFULLY RE-CREATED
FOR COOKING AND ENJOYING TODAY.

BY ESTHER B. ARESTY

SIMON AND SCHUSTER

DESIGNED BY EVE METZ
LIBRARY OF CONGRESS CATALOG CARD NUMBER: 64-22415
MANUFACTURED IN THE UNITED STATES OF AMERICA
PRINTED BY THE MURRAY PRINTING COMPANY, FORGE VILLAGE, MASS.
BOUND BY H. WOLFF MFG. CO., INC., NEW YORK

*To the memory of
my mother*

Contents

IL TRINCIANTE

DI M· VINCENZO

CERVIO,

AMPLIATO, ET RIDOTTO A PERFETTIONE

DAL CAVALIER REALE FVSORITTO

DA NARNI,

Trinciante dell'illuſtriſsimo , & Reuerendiſsimo
Signor Cardinal Farneſe .

CON PRIVILEGIO.

IN VENETIA.   M. DC. IIII.

Appreſſo Aleſſandro Vecchi.

*Illustrated title page of an early book on carving, Il Trinciante (The Carver),
by Vincenzo Cervio. The carver is shown at work in one scene. From the
1604 edition.*

Introduction

FOR THE PAST TWENTY YEARS, it has been my rewarding hobby to collect old and rare cookbooks. This book is the result of my adventuring through their pages. The more I wandered around in those precious volumes, the more I wanted to share them with others, and so *The Delectable Past* came about. It does not pretend to be a complete history of cooking. Nor does it claim to be a definitive work on old cookbooks and their recipes. It does grow out of a long acquaintance with them, however; most of the books referred to are in my collection and a partial list of my treasures follows the final chapter of this book.

I am often asked what started me on this absorbing occupation. Well, until twenty years ago, I was an average bibliomaniac buying any interesting old book that beckoned from a dealer's shelves or book catalogue, and leaning rather heavily to nineteenth-century English novelists. Quite by accident I acquired a battered eighteenth-century cookbook, *The Queen's Royal Cookery* by T. Hall, in a lot of six books bought at an auction sale. I browsed through it, smiled at the quaint, flowery language and howled over the recipes. A peck of flour and twenty eggs in a cake? Life was certainly different then. And what on earth was a Taffety Tart? Why, a frosted apple pie, of all things. That seemed good enough to try on my pie-loving family. Instant success.

I began to look for more old cookbooks and tried more recipes. In no time, "Cookery" was the first category I turned to in catalogues and soon it was the *only* one. I had become a cookbook collector.

I found that cookbooks were rarely more than a pinch of seasoning in the fattest catalogue and touched off hot contests at auction
sales. Cookbook collectors seemed to be as numerous as beans in
Boston: gastronomes; prominent restaurateurs; collectors who suspected cookbooks might be good investments (they are); doctors
who found cookbooks interesting because of the medical advice so
many contain; ardent bibliophiles who wanted those rare books that
also happened to be cookbooks, such as *Le Pastissier François,* the
seventeenth-century work on pastry-making and the most sought-
after imprint of the Elzevir press. With only twenty-nine copies
accounted for, securing that little pastry book was quite a feat. It
was even harder to lay hands on an Elizabethan cookbook. Imagine
cornering six of them in twenty years! I gloat over them like a miser.

Age is not the only determinant of rarity. I have yet to find the
undated 1896 edition of the *Boston Cookbook* that Fannie Farmer
paid to have printed, though early in my collecting days I acquired
the first of all cookbooks to be set in type: *De Honesta Voluptate,*
printed in 1475, still in its original boards and its pages as crisp as
a starched napkin.

I am giving you a limited view of cookbook collecting, however,
if I create the impression that only rare cookbooks are worth the
game. Regional American cookbooks, pamphlets compiled by church
and club groups, the little recipe folders issued by baking powder,
gelatin and chocolate companies at the turn of the century are
eagerly sought today and worth collecting. Books by such influential
late nineteenth-century authors as Juliet Corson, Mrs. Sarah Rorer,
Marion Harland, Sara Van Buren, to name a few, are still available
at modest prices and are sure to be rarities some day.

I am often asked how I find my books. Most are bought from
dealers who know my special interests and are generous in calling
books to my attention or in looking for books that I specially want.
Some are bought from catalogues that arrive casually in the mail.
(Book catalogues are an education in themselves, studded with morsels of fascinating erudition.) Some books were found as far from
their original homes as I was from mine when I discovered them:
Le Pâtissier Royal Parisien, by Carême, in Malaga, Spain; Mrs.

Lincoln's *Boston Cookbook* (it preceded Fannie Farmer's) in Goteborg, Sweden; and the *Chicago Edgewater Beach Hotel Salad Book* in Paris.

One of my luckiest finds appeared in my own backyard one day, like Maeterlinck's bluebird. Massialot's *Nouvelle Instruction Pour Les Confitures*, the 1692 first edition, was tucked away in a stack of nondescript second-hand books in a Trenton bookstore. It was mine for less than four dollars, but I had no idea of what a prize I had really captured until I returned home and peeled off the brown cloth that shrouded the covers. With this outer husk gone, an absolutely beautiful book was revealed, bound in white leather and stamped with golden fleurs-de-lis. I suspect it may have belonged to Jérôme Bonaparte, who lived for a while in near-by Bordentown, New Jersey, was married briefly to Elizabeth Patterson of Baltimore, and later became king of Westphalia.

I know for certain that my rare Elizabethan *Dyets Dry Dinner* was once part of the famous nineteenth-century library of the English bibliophile Henry Huth; the Huth bookplate is still in the book.

Some of my warmest attachments are formed for books with a personal inscription. "Mr. Swarbick to Mrs. Swarbick, in hopes of personal profit" is penned on the flyleaf of Soyer's *Modern Housewife*. Now, who could help wondering about the Swarbicks? Were they young, old, newly wed? Was Mrs. Swarbick a good cook?

Mary J. Lincoln, original compiler of the *Boston Cookbook*, was, I know. Her bold signature in my copy of *American Cookery* by Amelia Simmons also reveals Mrs. Lincoln as the forceful executive who made the Boston Cooking School so great.

Manuscript cookbooks are the most interesting of all, with their personal asides. "My own mother's way with a hogg's pudding." "My sister's cake, the best that ever was eat." Hopestill Brett's dowry list was still pinned to a page of her handwritten cookbook, dated 1678, when I acquired it. It starts with "45 payer of sheets and a od one." It concludes with "One gray horse," and in between are enough itemized possessions to reveal Hopestill's careful, thorough nature. She counted every pin, I'm sure, including the one I found in her book.

Old cookbooks make delightful reading. And I found old recipes easier to follow than some modern ones, once I'd learned to ignore the quantities that were obviously meant to serve huge households. (As for all those eggs in a cake, they were necessary to provide leavening, before baking powder was invented.) I've tried to adapt the recipes in the simple style that made them such a delight to read and follow. A few have been included as colorful oddities. (I don't really expect you to make a tart using the brains of cock sparrows.)

The "serious" recipes are intended to offer fresh and new ideas to the imaginative and sophisticated cook of today. With few exceptions, they are all easy to prepare, and rely on a subtle twist, or nuance, or combination, rather than laborious preparation. Though canned soups and other commercially prepared products have not been specified, they may be substituted wherever you deem proper.

A favorite shortcut in my kitchen is to keep leftover homemade soups and gravies in frozen cubes, and use them as needed. (Sometimes, when several liquid leftovers have been combined and poured into a freezing tray, a unique blend results; like the lost chord, it can never again be duplicated, but makes for some wonderful effects.)

You may arrive at some individual effects of your own while using the recipes in *The Delectable Past*. All have been tested in my kitchen, but your imagination can take over in many of them. After all, the same recipe will produce varying though equally good results in different hands. Yours may be better than mine.

I must add thanks to my angel-editors, Pat Read and Evelyn Gendel, who snipped, tucked and tailored the material of this book until it fitted properly.

My deepest gratitude to Bob Gottlieb for being unsparing in his criticism, and teaching me some valuable lessons.

And thanks to Jules, who tasted everything—and to Bob and Jane, who ate their share.

—E. B. A.

1

Antiquity

to the Middle Ages

THE DELICIOUS BEGINNINGS

THE ART OF COOKERY" has been a favorite title for cookbooks through the centuries, and with good reason. Close your eyes, sniff reminiscently, recall a superb meal where compatible flavors and textures were blended with the sure touch of knowledge and experience, and you'll agree—to cook like that *is* an art.

Moreover, it is an art that touches everyone and can be understood by all. The educated palate of the gastronome can recognize genius at work in the kitchen, but even a laborer knows if the meat has been seasoned competently. Because everyone must eat, the art of cooking is also, in a way, the art of living. Consequently, it is a subject of universal interest and has produced immortals, memorable masterpieces, and a long and delectable past stretching back to the earliest cooking records of antiquity.

I have explored this past with delight through my collection of old cookbooks, and found sparkling ideas for modern tables even among the ancient Greeks. A delicious shrimp recipe was inspired by a passage from one of the oldest books in my collection, *The Deipnosophists* (Banquet of the Learned). The passage is a quotation from a Greek poet on the gastronomic merits of various ancient fishes. Two of these fish are strangers to me, but the third begins many modern dinners.

> For spring the chromius is best;
> The anthias in winter;
> But of all fish the daintiest
> Is a young shrimp in fig leaves

Petit triclinium (*a little dining area*) *in a Pompeian home. From* Les Classiques de la Table. *1844.*

What a delightful idea. By simply substituting canned grape leaves for fig leaves, we dine on shrimp as the poet Ananius did. The ancient Greeks deserve our gratitude for this one.

Shrimp in Leaves

Raw jumbo shrimp, shelled and vein removed
Canned grape leaves (1 leaf per shrimp)
A marinade of 2 parts vinegar to 1 part oil
  (for 20 shrimp: 2 tablespoons oil and 4 tablespoons vinegar)
Pinch of orégano in the marinade

Wash the grape leaves to remove all the brine. Slit the shrimp down the back (vein side) and flatten them with your hand as for butterfly shrimp. Place a shrimp, split side down, on a leaf and lap the leaf around the shrimp. It is not necessary to tuck in the leaf ends. Arrange the shrimp close together in a shallow baking dish, preferably one that can come to the table. The lapped side of the leaf should be at the bottom, to guard against opening during cooking. Pour the marinade over the shrimp and bake in a preheated oven (375°) for 20 to 25 minutes, basting once or twice.

Garnish each shrimp with a thin half-slice of lemon crossed with a thin strip of pimiento. The diner will press the lemon juice into his leaf-wrapped shrimp with his fork if you demonstrate and lead the way —the leaves are edible, of course. A superb first course; serve it with sesame wafers.

The shrimp enthusiast was but one of many ancient writers quoted in *The Deipnosophists*. This remarkable anthology, compiled around 230 A.D., is regarded as one of the chief sources of information about ancient times.

Athenaeus, the compiler, was as interested in *his* past as we are in ours; he reached back five hundred years for some of the quotations he preserved. Most of them, as it happens, are concerned with cooking and dining. The subject obviously fascinated Athenaeus, and he found many ancient writers who shared his enthusiasm.

Among them was the Greek poet, Archestratus, who had written an entire work on gastronomy way back in 350 B.C. The original of this earliest known work of its kind has not been found, but Athenaeus obligingly provided many excerpts in *The Deipnosophists*. This one indicates the Greek bard's preference for good plain cooking.

> Many are the ways and many the recipes
> For dressing hares; but this is best of all,
> To place before a hungry set of guests,
> A slice of roasted meat fresh from the spit,
> Hot, season'd only with plain simple salt,
> Not too much done. And do not you be vex'd
> At seeing blood fresh trickling from the meat,
> But eat it eagerly. All other ways
> Are quite superfluous, such as when cooks pour
> A lot of sticky clammy sauce upon it,
> Parings of cheese, and lees, and dregs of oil,
> As if they were preparing cat's meat.

If the words of Archestratus sound like an order in a modern steak house, "And please omit the sauce," consider these lines by the poet Antiphanes. His advice for a hangover is *still* recommended to heavy imbibers.

> Take the hair, it well is written,
> Of the dog by whom you're bitten.
> Work off one wine by his brother,
> And one labour with another.

Many passages in *The Deipnosophists* have this surprisingly modern ring; others re-create amusing and interesting pictures of life in ancient times. In verse, a husband complains because his negligent wife feeds him boiled cabbage and pulse of peas when he hungers for melon, lamb stuffed with forcemeat, and cheesecake.

The poor man probably hungered most for cheesecake. It was by far the favorite item of food mentioned in *The Deipnosophists*. An entire section of the book is devoted to cheesecakes, and almost every poet took a fling at praising them. Cooks molded the cakes in the shape of a woman's breast, and the island of Samos devised so

ATHENAEVS

ΑΘΗΝΑΙΟΥ δειπνοσοφιστοῦ τὴν πολυμαθεστάτην πραγματείαν τῶν ἔξισι σοι φιλολόγε μικροῦ
πριαμένῳ πολλῶν τε καὶ μεγάλων καὶ ἀξιομνημονεύτων καὶ θαυμαστῶν καὶ ποικίλων καὶ δαι-
δάλων καὶ γλαφυρῶν καὶ ὧν ἴσως πρότερον οὐκ ἤδεις, ἐς γνῶσιν ἐλθεῖν· καὶ ὅλως τῶν τῆς
ἑλληνικῆς παιδείας ἀρρήτων κὴ δυσευρέτων κειμηλίων ἐγκρατεῖ γενέσθαι· τῶν
δὲ βιβλίων πεντεκαίδεκα τὸν ἀριθμὸν ὄντων, τὰ μὲν τελοσκαίδεκα, ὁλοσχερῶς·
τὸ δέ τοι πρῶτον κὴ δεύτερον ἐπιτετμημένα σοι παρέχομεν· ἀκέφαλον
σώματι κεφαλὴν ἀνεγκαδήντες ἐπιθεῖναι κολοβῶ· ἀπορῶν οὖν
ἔτι εὐγνωμόνων τὸ παντὶ τὰ συγγράμματ' ἀσκλεγομέ-
νους, μάλιστα μὴ τοῖς πολλοῖς ἀλλὰ τὸν πολύαθλον
τε καὶ πολυγράμματον εὐχαριστεῖν· οὐχ ἥ-
κιστα δὲ καὶ μουσουργῷ τῷ διδασκάλῳ.
τῷ εἰ καὶ μὴ παντάπασιν ἴσοια-
μένῳ ἀντίγραφον τῶνδε
τῶν τύπων ἀνῃκί-
στοις ἕλκεσι
πολλα-
χῆ
διεφθο-
ρός,
ἀλλ' εἴω
πολλὰς μὲν μυ-
ριάδας διορθώσαντι
σφαλμάτων πολλοῦς δὲ στί-
χους τῶν παρεισαγομένων καὶ τὰ
λοιάδην πρότερον ἀνηγνωσμομένους
καὶ χύδην, εἰς τὴν προσήκουσαν τῆς ἑμμέτρου
τάξεως εὐκρίνειαν ἀποκαταστήσαντί τι, χάριν εἰδέναι.

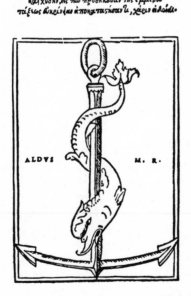

ALDVS   M. R.

Title page of The Deipnosophists by Athenaeus. The first printed version
of this book, text in Greek, printed by the notable Aldine Press. 1514.

17

many varieties that it became known as the cheesecake-making is-land. Here is a recipe that borrows its inspiration directly from the ancients.

Almond Cheesecake

Honey and almonds, ingredients much used in ancient times, give this cheesecake an unusual texture. Bake it in a well-buttered 9-inch spring form—no need to line the spring form with a crumb crust beforehand. However, if you prefer, a crumb crust may be used.

⅞ cup sugar
¼ cup butter
1 pound cream cheese
¼ cup pastry flour (sifted before measuring)
2 tablespoons honey
5 eggs, separated (whites beaten stiff but not dry)
½ cup light cream
¼ teaspoon almond extract
1 teaspoon vanilla extract
½ cup finely chopped blanched almonds, measured after chopping
   (these may be done in the blender)

TOPPING:
¼ cup light brown sugar
1 teaspoon cinnamon
¼ cup finely chopped almonds

Cream the butter and sugar together until well mixed, add the cheese, and cream until mixture is fluffy. Blend in flour and honey, then the egg yolks. Beat well after adding egg yolks. Add cream and extracts, then lightly fold in the beaten egg whites. Last, fold in the chopped almonds with a few deft strokes, distributing them through the batter. Pour into the well-buttered spring form, sprinkle with topping mixture, set on a low rack in a preheated oven (325°) and bake for 1 hour. Turn off heat and allow to cool in oven for 1 hour.

THE EARLIEST COOKBOOK in the strict sense of recipes is *De Re Coquinaria* or, as it is sometimes spelled, *De Re Culinaria*. In either case, it means "Of Culinary Matters," and is supposed to have been

First page of an early 15th-century manuscript attributed to Apicius. Incipit Foeliciter: begins happily. The two recipes are: Conditum Paradoxum—Fine Spiced Wine; Conditum Melixomum—Honey Refresher.

APICII·CELII· Diligentia EPIMELES·LIBER·PRIMVS. INCIPIT·FOELICITER

CAPITVLA

Cinnatum in hostrea & conchilis
Lasericum
Oenogarum in tubera
Oxiporium
Hypotrimma
Oxigarum digestibile·
Mortaria·

CONDITVM·PARADOXVM

ONDITI Paradoxi compositio mellis p·xv· in aeneū
uas mittit' proemissis uini sextarijs dubus: ut in coctura
mellis vinū decoquas quod igni lento & aridis li-
gnis·calefactū comutū ferula dū coquit': si efferuere coe-
perit vini rore copescat' pret' quod subtracto igni in se
redit cū pfrixerit rursus hoc accendit' hoc secundo aut t'tio
fiet actū·Demū remotum a foco post pdie despumatur in
piperis vncijs quatuor iam trit mastichis scrupulis·iii·folii·
et croci Dragme singule dactiloz ossibz torridis qnque dac-
tilis ni mollitis intercedente prius suffusione vini de suo modo
ac numero ut tritura lenis habeat· his omibz paratis supnic-
tas uini lenis sextaria·xviii·carbones perfecto addere duo milia

CONDITVM·MELIXOMVM

iatorum conditū melixomū perpetuū quod subministrat'
per uiam peregrinanti·piper tritū cū melle despumato in

written by the Roman gourmet Apicius, in the first century A.D. However, there is considerable doubt that Apicius had anything to do with *De Re Coquinaria,* or even that it was written in his day. Athenaeus, who lived at least a hundred years later, knew all about Apicius as a gourmet but seemed unaware of a cookbook by him. And the only known copies of the so-called Apicius cookbook date from the eighth and ninth centuries.

In any case, the Roman antecedents of the recipes are unmistakable. The book abounds in sausages and spicy meat loaves, and these were as Roman as Caesar. So was the enthusiasm for vegetables that *De Re Coquinaria* reflects. Some noble Roman families even took their names from vegetables: Fabius from faba (beans); Lentulus from lenticula (lentils); and even Cicero from cicer arietinum (peas). With few exceptions, most of the vegetables we know today are mentioned in *De Re Coquinaria.*

The style of cooking ran to heavy spicing, and meats combined with sweet syrups or with honey and vinegar. The recipes make strange reading until one recognizes that many sweet-and-sour dishes enjoyed today are roundabout descendants of this same Apician cookery. Baked hams are prepared today with brown sugar, basted with sweet juices, and garnished with glazed fruits. In view of this, a recipe for ham and figs in *De Re Coquinaria* seemed worth a try and turned out to be a combination that tasted as good as it looked.

Apician Ham and Figs

A canned or precooked ham
¼ cup brown sugar (add a pinch of ground cloves)
Canned figs (or dried figs, steamed for 20 minutes or soaked in hot water for the same length of time)
¼ cup canned fig juice

If a canned ham is used, remove all gelatin and bake for 20 minutes before adding sugar, to enable any remaining gelatin to ooze out and be drained off.

Coat the top of the ham with the brown sugar and cloves mixture.

Bake in a shallow pan at 325°, allowing 18 to 20 minutes per pound. When the sugar on the ham begins to melt, pour over it the canned fig juice. Baste at 20-minute intervals; if juice begins to stick at bottom of the pan, add a small quantity of orange juice.

Forty-five minutes before ham is to be removed from oven, decorate it with figs, as follows: If canned figs are used, cut them nearly in half, spread them open, and arrange over the top of the ham. If dried figs are used, nip off the little hard end and cut the fig nearly into quarters. Open it and flatten out on the ham in the appearance of a four-leaf clover. The decoration is enhanced if a small hole is made in the uncut center of the fig and a green grape forced halfway through it. (The canned fig is too soft for this and really needs nothing to enhance it.)

The recipes in *De Re Coquinaria* are little more than a list of ingredients. From that point on, it was evidently up to the cook. The ingredients for a boiled chicken in a "rough sauce" had all the makings for a delicious dish, if one omitted the asafoetida, a pungent flavoring not to modern tastes. I omitted it. And here is the recipe:

Apician Dilled Chicken

[IN PULLO ELIXO IUS CRUDUM]

THE APICIAN INGREDIENTS:	MODERNIZED, WITH EXACT QUANTITIES:
One chicken	1 *frying chicken, left whole*
Dill	¼ *cup (feathery part, fresh, chopped)*
Vinegar	1 *tablespoon*
Fig wine	½ *cup (any dry white wine)*
Asafoetida	1 *teaspoon Worcestershire (optional)*
Oil	*Used in browning chicken; make this equal parts oil and margarine*
Mustard	½ *teaspoon dry mustard*
Dried mint	½ *teaspoon*
	Salt and pepper

The Apician recipe is for boiled chicken. I find that braised is tastier. So braised this is. The chicken is left whole. Season it to your taste with salt and pepper, inside and out. Brown in a Dutch oven or any pan with a tight-fitting lid. (Less spattering if you keep chicken covered while browning, lifting lid only to turn chicken.)

When nicely browned on all sides, transfer to a covered casserole or roaster. Mix together all the following ingredients and pour over the chicken: vinegar, dill, mint, wine, mustard. Bake *covered* in a moderate oven (375°) for about 1 hour and 15 minutes. (Halfway through the cooking, turn the chicken from its back onto its breast; beyond this there is no need for basting since braising is a self-basting method.)

Before serving, strain the sauce to remove any bits of swimming dill and mint. Serve with rice, noodles or some starch accompaniment that will be enhanced by a sauce, for this one is a winner.

THOUGH NO PROOF EXISTS of the date of *De Re Coquinaria's* first appearance, there is no doubt that it was in use until the fifteenth century: my collection includes a hand-written copy made around 1400. All books were hand-written until printing began in the middle of the fifteenth century, and in general books were for the privileged few. As for cookbooks, only kings and princes had need of them for their households.

Around 1390 a royal cookbook was compiled by the cooks who served England's Richard II, a monarch noted for zestful living. The book was called *The Forme of Cury,* "cury" being the Old English word for cooking, and the title a Chaucerian way of saying "The Art of Cookery." Macraw (macaroni) was served at King Richard's table, and apparently he enjoyed a crisp green "salat" with his meals, as this recipe from *The Forme of Cury* would indicate.

King Richard's Salat

Take *parsel, sawge, garlec, chibollas, onyons, leeks, borage, myntes, fenel,* and ton *tressis, rew, rosemarye, purslayre.* Lave, and waishe hem clene; pike hem, pluk hem small with thyn hande and myng hem wel with *rawe oile.* Lay one *vynegar* and *salt,* and serve it forth.

[Take *parsley, sage, garlic, small onions, onions, leeks, borage, mint, fennel, cress, rue, rosemary, purslain.* Rinse and wash them clean; pick them over, tear them with your hands and mix them well with oil. Add *vinegar* and *salt,* and serve it forth.]

The recipes are written in the blunt language of medieval England and sometimes sound as violent as the events that were transpiring there.

· ffor to make cyalbmenny ———————————— xx· ix·xiij·

[facsimile of medieval manuscript text]

Facsimile recipe for Mawmenny (a hash of capon) from the ancient Forme of Cury, 1390. Reproduced in the translation by Samuel Pegge, The Forme of Cury. 1780.

"Take hares and hew them to gobbets . . ." one recipe begins. "Take conies (rabbits) and smite them to pieces; seeth them in grease . . ." commands another.

But from such an unpromising beginning as "Take chickens and ram them together, serve them broken . . ." emerged a delicious recipe.

Chicken Hash Fit for a King

3½- to 4-pound stewing chicken
1 pound mushrooms, sliced, sautéed in butter, then chopped fine
2 cups rich cream sauce (add 1½ tablespoons excellent dry sherry)
Grated cheese (combine two kinds, Swiss and Romano, for example)
Butter

Stew the chicken in a broth flavored with celery tops and one small onion. Add salt during last half hour of cooking. Chill chicken thoroughly before cutting into bite-size cubes (a nicer result is obtained).

For the cream sauce: Melt 1 tablespoon butter; add 1 tablespoon flour, and stir until free from lumps and well blended. Pour in 1 cup scalded milk and stir until mixture thickens. Cool slightly, add 1 cup light cream and the sherry. Add salt and a dash of white pepper.

Carefully combine the chicken and mushrooms in an ample bowl, using a large spoon. The object is not to tear up the chicken any more than necessary. Pour the cream sauce over it, combine with a few more tosses, then transfer to a baking-serving dish. With a rubber scraper, gather up every scrap of sauce that adheres to the bowl and add it to the chicken. Sprinkle with cheese, dot with butter and, if mixture is cool, warm briefly in the oven, then place under broiler until cheese begins to melt and run.

The cheese, cream sauce, and chicken follow *The Forme of Cury*, but I must admit the mushrooms are my own addition. They must be chopped fine.

Serve this delicious hash with Buttered Noodles Polonaise (noodles topped with fried bread crumbs). The recipe for the bread crumbs follows:

Fried Bread Crumbs

[POLONAISE]

For these, *day-old white bread* should be pulled by hand into tiny crumbs. Discard all crust and use only the white part. One slice of bread will provide ½ cup of cooked crumbs, enough to top an 8-inch (2-quart) casserole. Use the smallest skillet you have. (A 6-inch iron skillet is handy for this purpose.) Heat it until butter will sizzle in it. Melt 1 tablespoon of *butter* in the hot skillet, and promptly dump in all the crumbs, stirring quickly to make them absorb all the butter. Promptly add another tablespoon of butter, stirring all the while. From this point on, add butter less generously—only enough to keep the crumbs cooking as they grow crisp and golden. Stir constantly—the whole process takes only a few minutes—and remove skillet from fire as crumbs reach the desired golden hue.

They are delicious over a casserole of plain noodles that have been tossed with butter. Equally good served with brown butter sauce over hot asparagus tips.

WHILE RICHARD PLANTAGENET's cooks were smiting and hewing their way through royal menus, a more gently phrased cookery manuscript had been prepared in the kingdom across the Channel. *Le Viandier* was compiled by Guillaume Tirel (Taillevent) about 1375 for the cooks of Charles V, also a monarch with a taste for the better things. A "viandier" is a meat cook, and the manuscript had a special section on roasts which included—along with mutton, kid and venison—pigeons roasted with their heads intact.

Among the potages (soup-stews), one recipe employed mustard as a seasoning for the broth. Using Taillevent's ingredients, a delicious soup emerges that may be served hot or cold. Either way, its lovely green color is as refreshing as its taste.

Mustard Soup

2 *tablespoons butter*
3 *tablespoons prepared yellow mustard*
2 *tablespoons flour*
2½ *cups thoroughly skimmed chicken stock, heated*
1¼ *cups rich milk, heated*
½ *teaspoon salt and a dash of white pepper*
½ *teaspoon onion juice*
2 *egg yolks*
2 *to 3 tablespoons sweet cream*

Melt the butter, stir in the flour and blend smoothly. Add the hot chicken stock and milk, and whisk until smooth. Add salt, pepper and onion juice. Simmer for 10 to 15 minutes. Cool slightly. Combine egg yolks and cream and add to the soup, custard style—that is, temper first with a few spoonfuls of the warm broth. Last, add the mustard.

If served cold, garnish with a dab of whipped cream. If hot, garnish with pancake shreds or green peas.

In spite of the differences of language and approach, *Le Viandier* and *The Forme of Cury* had many similarities. In both cookbooks the dominant line was heavy spicing. Most foods were minced or hashed in order to be eaten with a spoon, and often combined with Blank Manng (Blancmange), the classic almond mixture which is today a dessert, but in those days was used like a cream sauce.

The two cookbooks also shared a number of dishes with common names that show how the languages intermingled. Jellied aspics of fish and meat were "galantines" to the French, "galyntynes" to the English. A gruel of bread and milk was "brewis" in English, "brouet" in French. But veal was "veel" in both books; the French had not yet adopted "veau." A creamy tart called "Darioll" by the

French was "Daryols" in *The Forme of Cury,* and given here exactly as it appeared in the manuscript.

Daryols

Take creme of cowe mylke, (or) almandes. Do thereto ayren (eggs), with sugar, safron, and salt. Medle it ifere (mix it together). Do it in a coffyn of two ynche depe; bake it wel, and serve it forth.

The recipe for Daryols is an excellent example of a recipe that started its career in medieval days and made its way down through the centuries. The delicate tarts continued to be "served forth" long after their medieval origins had been forgotten, and eventually became a standard recipe in cookbooks. (You will encounter them later in this book; for those who cannot wait, the expanded recipe is listed in the Index.) However, for centuries Daryols were known only to the tables of the nobility, just as cookbooks were to be found only in royal kitchens. To eat like a prince meant just that—you had to be one.

An engraved illustration from Antiquitates Culinariae, *by the Reverend Richard Warner. 1791.*

2

The

Renaissance

PRINTED COOKBOOKS BEGIN

Between the medieval manuscript cookbooks and the first printed cookbook in 1475, a hundred years elapsed. By that time, the Renaissance was flourishing in Italy and the first printed book, the Gutenberg Bible, had appeared (twenty years earlier) in Germany.

The story of printed books and their role in spreading the enlightenment of the Renaissance is a fascinating subject. As a bibliophile, it grieves me to pass it by so lightly, but we must concern ourselves only with cookbooks here. However, cookbooks were an important part of the story of books from the start. Along with Bibles, they shared the distinction of being the earliest books printed.

Quite naturally, with Italy the spring from which the Renaissance was gushing, the first cookbook was printed there. Besides, the Italians had a culinary past that went back to the splendors of Roman Empire days. One might have expected the first printed cookbook to be a reprint, or at least a rehash, of the well-known Roman manuscript cookbook, *De Re Coquinaria,* but instead it was an original work, far surpassing that ancient manuscript. The identity of the author, the noted Renaissance humanist and Vatican librarian, Bartolomeo de' Sacchi, better known as Platina (the Latinized version of his name), shows that cookery was one of the arts revived by the Renaissance.

The title of Platina's cookbook—*De Honesta Voluptate*—is a clue to its contents. Freely translated, it means Permissible Pleasures, an appropriate title at a time when the pursuit of pleasure was a way of life and the senses were catered to as never before.

Actually, *De Honesta Voluptate* was only in part a cookbook; it was also a philosophical guide to good health. Eat like a prince, but know when and what to eat, was Platina's theme as he ranged from Apple Fritters to Insomnia with stopovers for such topics as How Bears Cohabit. Because of its medical interest, Platina's book is in many medical libraries; the United States Medical Library in Washington owns several editions. (My collection has two, including the first edition.)

PLATINA ON PLAY AND PLEASURE

At times, when a worried mind impedes good digestion, it is a good idea to find distraction in play and pleasure. Games of chess, of cards of various kinds are good, so long as they are played without anger and indignation which are bad for digestion, whereas hearty laughter is good. Above all, there must be no cheating or avarice which deprive the game of all liberality and are to be detested, and arguments also produce no pleasure. Both the fear of losing and the immense desire to gain can provoke quarrels. If you must quarrel, let it not be soon after dinner, but only after you have enjoyed it. The stomach needs natural warmth, little motion and little mental agitation; otherwise it becomes weak and unable to produce its digestive juices.

PLATYNAE DE HONESTA VOLVPTATE:
ET VALITVDINE AD AMPLISSIMVM AC
DOCTISSIMVM.D.B.ROVERELLAM.S.CLE
MENTIS PRAESBITERVM CARDINALEM
LIBER PRIMVS.

RRABVNT Et quidem uehemētes Amplif/
fime pater.B.Rouerella qui hanc noſtram ſu/
ſceptionem nequaq̄ dignam quæ tuo nomini
aſcriberetur putarint:q̄ & uoluptatis & ualitu
dinis titulum præſeferat. Veꝝ quū mihi atq; omnibus
eruditis ſpectata ſit ingenii tui ais:& acumen moꝝ: &
honeſtiſſimæ uitæ cōſtantia:doctrinæ ac eruditionis ma
gnitudo:malui te uigiliaꝝ meaꝝ patronum ac iudicem
ſiqd peruerſe ſcriptū ineſt facere:q̄ alium quempiam.
Inſtabūt acriter maleuoli(ſat ſcio):de uoluptate ad ui/
rum optimum & continentiſſimum non fuiſſe ſcriben/
dum.Sed dicant quæſo ii ſtoicide:qui elatis ſuperciliis
non de ui ſed de nominum uocibus tantummodo diiu/
dicant:quid mali in ſe habeat conſiderata uoluptas?Eſt
enim huius ut ualitudinis uocabulum mediū. De uolu
ptate quam intemperantes & libidinoſi ex luxu & uarie
tate ciborum:ex titillatione reꝝ uenerearū percipiunt.
Abſit ut Platyna ad uiꝝ ſanctiſſimum ſcribat.De illa uo
lupate quæ ex contmentia uictus:& eaꝝ reꝝ quas huma
na natura appetit loquor.Neminem enim adhuc uidi
adeo libidinoſum & incontinentem:qui non aliqua tan
geretur voluptate:ſi quando a rebus pluſq̄ ſatis ē cōcu
pitis declinauiſſ&.Valet apud hos (ut video)Ciceronis
auctoritas:qui quidem ut Ariſtoteles Platonem:Pytha
goram:zenonem:Democritum:Chryſippum: Parmeni
dem:Heraclitum:ſic Epicuꝝ ſegetem & materiam eru
ɔnis ac doctrinæ ſuæ facit:quo cū.n.tutius congre/

Title page of the first printed cookbook, De Honesta Voluptate, by Barto-lomeo de' Sacchi (Platina). Printed in Venice by Aquila and Umber. 1475.

Any doctor today would agree with Platina that recreation and laughter have their share in maintaining good health.

The recipes in *De Honesta Voluptate* differed considerably from those in the earlier manuscript cookbooks. Platina wrote with style and grace, and the recipes are more precise, some of them even specifying exact ounces. The recipe formulas are supposed to be the work of a chef named Martino, then in the employ of the Patriarch of Aqueleia, one of Italy's foremost churchmen. Although many of the earlier minced and hashed preparations are to be found in Platina's pages, there are also many innovations, especially pies and pastries. Several of these suggest the quiche we know today. Platina's Torta of Chestnuts and Cheese makes an interesting starch substitute or an ample first course.

Chestnut Torta

1 *cup loosely packed riced chestnuts*
¾ *cup riced pot cheese*
2 *tablespoons melted butter*
½ *cup cream*
2 *eggs*
2 *bulb ends of scallions, finely minced*
⅛ *teaspoon salt*
Dash of white pepper
8-inch pie shell, baked for 5 minutes at 400°

Beat the eggs, add the cream, the scallions and seasonings. Combine the chestnuts, cheese and melted butter and add to the egg mixture. Pour into partially baked pie shell. Place in a preheated oven (375°) and bake for 25 to 30 minutes.

Serve hot as an accompaniment to meats that have a gravy or sauce.

Fish, always a prominent article in the Italian diet, was dealt with in many of Platina's recipes. His Pesce in Gelatina will make a handsome appearance on a buffet table, or will start off a sit-down dinner in style.

Pesce in Gelatina
[FISH IN ASPIC]

For this, use a *fish suitable for boiling.* Striped bass, pike or a large trout are recommended. Have it scaled and cleaned, and delivered to you with head and tail intact. If you do not have a fish boiler, use a long shallow baking pan or the bottom of a roaster. Prepare the stock as follows:

STOCK:
2 *quarts water*
¼ *cup vinegar*
½ *cup white wine*
1 *tablespoon salt*
1 *onion, sliced*
1 *bay leaf*
¼ *teaspoon each: whole allspice, peppercorns, ground thyme*

Bring these ingredients to the boil and simmer for 10 minutes. Cool slightly before adding fish. Wrap fish tightly in cheesecloth and tie ends. The stock should be just below the boiling point during the cooking; a gentle bubble is the proper pace. Cooking time will depend on the weight and thickness of the fish, as well as its texture. In general, 12 to 15 minutes per pound is the rule. The fish should be thoroughly cooked, but firm. When it has reached this stage, remove it from broth and allow to cool slightly.

Strip off the cheesecloth and carefully pull off all skin that adhere to the cheesecloth. Strain the fish stock, add ¼ *teaspoon saffron,* then cook gently for another 30 minutes. Strain the fish stock and prepare aspic as below.

ASPIC:
1 *tablespoon gelatin softened in* ¼ *cup cold water*
Add:
1½ *cups hot fish broth to gelatin to dissolve it*
¼ *cup white wine, added when gelatin mixture begins to cool*

If you wish the aspic to sparkle like a jewel, set stock aside to grow quite cold after you remove the fish. Then place the cold stock in a
(*Continued on next page*)

31

clean saucepan and add *1 slightly beaten egg white.* (The crushed shell may also be added.) Whisk the stock steadily as you bring it gently to the boiling point. When bubbles appear, promptly lower heat and simmer stock very, very gently for 20 to 25 minutes, uncovered. Do not stir it. The egg white will collect on the surface and act as a filter. It should be carefully strained off through a thin tea towel, or through a fine strainer covered with cheesecloth. (The same method will clarify a meat stock, but every particle of fat must first be removed.) Now proceed with the aspic.

To apply aspic: Lay fish on a strip of wax paper extending 2 inches beyond each end of the fish. Under wax paper use a sheet of foil of similar length. Lay the fish thus prepared on a flat cookie sheet, or anything from which you can later transfer it when congealed.

For garnish, slit *cooked shrimp* in half and alternate with *thin half slices of lemon* on top of the fish. When aspic begins to thicken (you can hasten this process by placing bowl in cracked ice), carefully spoon it over the garnish to set it firmly in place. When aspic is at point of setting, spoon it around the sides of the fish. Bend foil around sides and ends of fish to keep the aspic in place.

When thoroughly set, trim away all excess aspic (use it for garnish) and gently ease fish off the paper and onto its serving platter. *Cucumber cups filled with horseradish sauce,* interspersed with mounds of the sparkling aspic, will make an effective garnish to surround the fish.

Other countries did print cookbooks, although none comparable to Platina's was written until much later. Germany's first printed cookbook, *Kuchenmeistrei,* appeared in 1485; the French put the hundred-year-old manuscript *Le Viandier* into print around 1490; in 1500 the English printed *The Boke of Cokery* "for a Pryncis Household"; and Roberto de Nola, chef to Spanish nobility, wrote a cookbook in 1526. All the books could have been labeled "For a prince's household."

The slim, small volumes, each containing a few dozen recipes, differed chiefly in their tongues. The recipes were similar and followed the casual style of the early manuscript cookbooks: spices were applied with a heavy hand to thick concoctions of meat, fish and the ubiquitous pounded almonds. Among the meats, bear, squirrel and even beaver were mentioned, but beef was conspicuously absent and considered fit only for peasants. Gentlemen—especially noble gentlemen—preferred meat captured in the chase.

Platina's cookbook was translated into French and German, and in Italy many of his recipes were included in the cookbook, *Epulario* (*The Italian Banquet*), published in 1516. Epulario outdid Platina, however, in the following outsize version of a pie that released live birds when it was cut open: (This recipe is from the 1598 English translation.)

To Make Pies That the Birds May Be Alive in Them, and Flie Out When It Is Cut Up

Make the coffin of *a great pie or pasty,* in the bottome thereof make a hole as big as your fist, or bigger if you will, let the sides of the coffin bee somewhat higher then ordinary pies, which done put it full of *flower* and bake it, and being baked, open the hole in the bottome, and take out the flower. Then having *a pie of the bigness of the hole in the bottome of the coffin aforesaid,* you shal put it into the coffin, withall put into the said coffin round about the aforesaid pie *as many small live birds as the empty coffin will hold,* besides the pie aforesaid. And this is to be done at such time as you send the pie to the table, and set before the guests: where uncovering or cutting up the lid of the great pie, all the birds will flie out, which is to delight and pleasure shew to the company. And because they shall not bee altogether mocked, you shall cut open the small pie, and in this sort you may make many others, the like you may do with a tart.

THE MOST IMPORTANT and elaborate of the Renaissance cookbooks appeared in 1570—*Cooking Secrets of Pope Pius V* by Bartolomeo Scappi. (My copy is still in its original vellum cover.) The book is two inches thick, and bulges with recipes, menus and instructions for management of the kitchen and dining room. Its many detailed illustrations of the Pope's kitchens and household effects make it virtually a culinary documentary of Renaissance Italy. Women apparently had no place in Renaissance kitchens; only men are shown at work.

Scappi recommended that the kitchens be separated from the

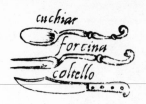

The first picture of a fork (as far as I know) for use in dining. From Cvoco Secreto di Papa Pio Quinto (Cooking Secrets of Pope Pius V) by Bartolomeo Scappi. 1570.

main house, not because of cooking odors but to guard against poisoners. You may be sure that the Pope's meals were prepared under top security and that the foods which reached his table were absolutely fresh. One illustration shows a tub of water in the kitchen stocked with live fish.

Of all the illustrations in Scappi's book, the most significant is of a place setting: a knife, fork and spoon. This is the first printed picture of a fork, and tells us much about the advanced manners of the Italians. In other countries even kings still ate with their hands.

We know from Scappi that it was now the custom to divide the meal into several courses. Everything to be eaten during the course was placed on the table at one time, except foods to be kept warm or to be carved. The diners sat down to a table that provided a visual feast: platters of game birds, fish, salads, fanciful pastries, cold hams, melons, baskets of fruits. The platters were handed around by one group of servants, while others brought hot foods from the kitchens, and the carvers performed with dazzling precision at the credenza, or sideboard.

To judge from this menu in *Cooking Secrets of Pope Pius V*, the company must have spent the better part of the day at table for such a banquet.

Pranzo Alli XV D'Ottobre

Dinner for the fifteenth of October, with two services from the sideboard and two from the kitchen, Served with four changes of plates by four Stewards and four Carvers.

FIRST SERVICE FROM THE CREDENZA
Pieces of marzipan
Neapolitan spice-cakes
Marzipan balls

34

A scene in a Renaissance kitchen. One of 28 pages of copperplate illustrations in Cooking Secrets of Pope Pius V, *by Bartolomeo Scappi. 1570.*

Camera propinqua alla Cucin̄

tauole confitare

forno

Conserua

pozzo

murello

si passa giclo

Candelier

lauorano de Pasta

passano sapori

penelo p indorar pastici

a magnar fresco

2

Malaga wine in glasses, with Pisan biscuits

Plain puff pastries, made with milk and eggs

Prosciutto cooked in wine, and then sliced, served with capers, strained grapes and sugar

Salted pork's tongues cooked in wine and cut in slices

Songbirds roasted on the spit, served cold, with the tongues sliced over them

Sweet mustard for seasoning

Fresh grapes

Spanish olives

FIRST SERVICE FROM THE KITCHEN

Fried sweetbreads and liver of veal, served with a sauce of eggplant, salt, sugar and pepper over it

Skylarks roasted on the spit, served with lemon sauce over it

Quails roasted on the spit, served with sliced eggplant over it

Partridges larded and roasted on the spit, served with slices of lemon over it

Puff pastries filled with minced veal sweetbreads, and slices of prosciutto

Our own well-seasoned poultry, served with slices of lemon and sugar over it

Stuffed pigeons roasted on the spit, served with sugar and capers over it

Rabbits roasted on the spit, covered with sauce, served with crushed pine-nuts over it

Slices of veal, of 5 ounces each, roasted on the spit, served with its juices over it

Legs of goat roasted on the spit, served with its juices over it

Soup of almond paste, with the flesh of 3 pigeons in it for each serving

Meat jelly cut into squares

SECOND AND LAST SERVICE FROM THE KITCHEN

Stuffed fat geese boiled in Lombard style, covered with sliced almonds, served with cheese, sugar and cinnamon

Stuffed breast of veal, boiled, served with flowers over it

Very young calf, boiled, served with parsley over it

Almonds in garlic sauce

Rice in Turkish style with milk, served with sugar and cinnamon over it

Stewed pigeons with mortadella sausage and whole onions

Soup of chopped cabbage with pieces of sausage in it
Pies of poultry with 2 chickens per pie, served hot
Fricasseed breast of goat, with fried onions over it
Large pies filled with custard cream
Boiled calf's feet, with cheese and egg

SECOND AND LAST SERVICE FROM CREDENZA

Tarts of beans
Tarts of pears in marzipan
Quince pastries with 1 quince per pastry
Pears, and apples of various kinds
Parmesan cheese in slices
Riviera cheese
Fresh pitted almonds, served on vine leaves
Chestnuts roasted over the coals, served with salt, sugar and pepper
Milk curds, served with sugar over it
Wafers made of ground corn
Ring-shaped cakes

When the table is cleared and water provided for the hands, the napkins are changed for clean ones.

Stalks of sweet, fresh fennel
Toothpicks in dishes of rose water
Bunches of scented flowers
Sweets and confections

FAMILIAR DISHES rise from the pages of Scappi and read so temptingly one can almost sniff their tantalizing odors. Parmesan is strewn freely through the recipes and often is combined with other varieties of cheese, Romano, for example. Scappi's practice of combining cheeses is one to heed. Try Gruyère with Parmesan, Cheddar with Edam, or any two gratable cheeses you choose.

Scappi also combined varieties of fish and inspired me to mate smoked salmon with fresh crab meat. I call this elegant seafood appetizer Scappicini.

Scappicini

Use back fin (large lump) fresh crab meat and Nova Scotia salmon; 3 parts crab meat to 1 part salmon. Cut the salmon into narrow shreds about 1 inch long. Combine the two seafoods with a few tosses, using a large spoon so as not to tear up the crab meat. Add a mere *pinch of salt* and a fairly generous quantity of *freshly ground black pepper* before tossing. Serve with the dressing, which can be passed at the table, along with *hot, buttered rye melba toast.* The cold seafood and hot toast contrast deliciously.

For the dressing: Combine 4 *tablespoons chili sauce; 3 tablespoons mayonnaise; 1 tablespoon lemon juice; 1 tablespoon Worcestershire sauce; 1 tablespoon finely minced chives or scallion ends, and ¼ teaspoon curry powder.* This quantity will amply top 6 servings of Scappicini.

A recipe by Scappi for something resembling a boiled doughnut had to be read twice before its meaning became clear. It turned out that the "doughnuts" were really ring cookies—first boiled, then dipped in beaten egg and baked in the oven. This adapted recipe produces a buttery cookie that may be baked without prior boiling.

Ciambellette

½ *cup butter*
½ *cup sugar*
2 *egg yolks*
1 *teaspoon almond extract*
1 *cup bread flour*
½ *cup cornstarch (sifted with the flour)*
Jelly or preserves

Cream the butter and sugar until fluffy. Add the egg yolks, the extract, and last the flour mixed with the cornstarch. The dough should be stiff enough to handle without rolling. Traditionally, a piece of dough should be pinched off, rolled into the shape of a string bean and formed into a circle. However, we prefer to roll the dough into ¾-inch balls, place them on a lightly greased cookie sheet, and press each one down firmly in the center. Into this little well, drop a dab of jelly or preserves, or a split almond. Less work, and a more attractive result. Bake in a preheated oven (375°) for 12 to 15 minutes. Check at 12 minutes. They may be finished. (Recipe makes about 40 2-inch cookies.)

If you wish to duplicate Scappi's recipe exactly, you may drop each cookie into boiling water; count to ten; fish out the cookie, drain it, then dip it in beaten egg yolk. If boiled first, the cookies will be less crisp.

No Italian meal was complete without fruit, which was usually eaten fresh. A favorite fruit, however, was the quince, and as anyone knows who has tried it, a quince cannot be eaten uncooked. Scappi had many ways of preparing this astringent fruit; a favorite method was to bake it. Baked quinces are delicious as a side dish with pot roast, pork or fowl, and may also be served as a dessert. Hot or cold, the handsome deep color they acquire when cooked adds sparkle to any meal.

Baked Quinces

Peel, core, and cut the *quinces* into quarters or sixths. Place them in a shallow baking pan and sprinkle with *sugar* (1 tablespoon per quince). Add enough *water* to cover the bottom of the quinces. Cover the dish itself tightly, and bake the fruit in a slow oven (325°) for 2 hours, or until quite tender. Serve hot or cold.

In Scappi's day the quinces were baked whole, wrapped in buttered paper and buried in hot ashes for the better part of a day. The above method is more practical for modern kitchens.

In the menus that Scappi devised, stewed quinces were often used as a filling for tart shells or served as a fruit compote.

Quince Compote

Select *large, smooth, ripe quinces*. Peel, core and slice them. Cook in *water* and *lemon juice* until they begin to grow tender. (For each cup of water, allow 1 tablespoon lemon juice.) Add the *lemon rind,* and a *dash of salt* as well. When the fruit is somewhat soft, remove it from the liquid. Measure liquid and add an equal proportion of *sugar:* 1 cup liquid; 1 cup sugar. Bring syrup to the boil and simmer gently for 5 minutes. Return quinces to this syrup and simmer them for 20 to 30 minutes, or until they are quite tender. Serve cold in their own syrup as a side dish for meats, as you would cranberry sauce.

THE EARLIEST POTATO RECIPES appeared in a very elaborate and complete German cookbook first printed in 1581. It was called *Ein New Kochbuch,* and it was by master-chef Marx Rumpolt with handsome woodcut illustrations by Jost Amman. German table manners are depicted with considerable realism. Diners hover, knives in hand, alert to snatch a portion. Often they are muffled to the ear lobes against the chilling drafts. The German taste for robust fare was surely conditioned by the cold climate. Along with the prevailing stews and minces of general European cookery, the German books offered sauerkraut, stuffed gooseneck, meat dumplings and crapfeln.

Here are liver dumplings from the sixteenth-century German cuisine that are substantial enough to be served by themselves. Or they will add a gemütlich touch to a tureen of clear soup.

Liver Dumplings

1 *cup finely ground or chopped calf's liver* (*approximately* 3 *slices*)
1 *egg, beaten*
· *Salt and pepper to taste*
Dash of onion juice
½ *cup soft bread crumbs*

Combine the ingredients and form into balls a bit smaller than a walnut. Drop into boiling water, cover tightly, and boil 8 to 10 minutes. Drain.

boccalle con   il bacile

A ewer. From Cooking Secrets of Pope Pius V, *by Bartolomeo Scappi. 1570.*

The Italians were unquestionably the best cooks of the Renaissance period, but the Germans were the greatest eaters. By the end of the sixteenth century, Italian cookbooks were still being produced in limited numbers for the princely class, but German cookbooks had a much wider scope, appealing to a fast-growing middle class eager to enjoy a gemütlich table. During the sixteenth century, Germany was one of the leading producers of cookbooks.

Let the nobility have their master-chefs. The role of family cook fell more naturally on the Hausfrau, and in 1598 one Swiss cook—Anna Weckerin—completed the first cookbook ever written by a woman. A recipe in it bore a close resemblance to Rösti, the delicious sautéed potatoes that are as Swiss as William Tell. For delighted cheers, serve them with your next steak or roast beef.

Rösti

To make these delicious potatoes (now a national favorite of the Swiss) an ordinary non-mealy boiling potato is best. The day before you plan to serve the dish, boil 4 *generous-size potatoes* in their skins until a fork pierces them easily. Peel while hot and leave in refrigerator overnight. The next day, shred potatoes on a julienne shredder that yields a strip about a half inch wide. Mince *a medium-size onion* finely and mingle it with the potatoes, taking care not to break them. Heat an iron skillet and pour in enough *vegetable oil* to cover the bottom generously. Add the potatoes; douse with *salt* and *pepper* to your taste; sprinkle 2 *tablespoons of milk* over all and let cook over a fairly brisk fire until potatoes are golden on the bottom. Turn them carefully, trying to keep the round shape intact. (I invert the potatoes on a plate, then carefully slide them back into the skillet to finish on the other side. A bit of trouble, but well worth it for the golden, crusty result.)

There is no better way to prepare duck than with the raw fruit stuffing called for in an early German cookbook.

Duck Stuffed with Raw Fruit

Duck cooked in the following manner is invariably moist, succulent and quite devoid of fattiness. I recommend this as the best method of preparing duck—and the easiest.

(*Continued on next page*)

41

Season *duck* to taste with *salt* and *pepper,* inside and out. Peel, core and quarter *tart apples.* Fill the cavity of the duck with the raw apples and *an equal quantity of uncooked prunes.* Do not pack the fruit down, just pile it in comfortably. Place the duck on a rack in a roasting pan, puncture the fatty places to encourage the fat to run out, and roast, uncovered, at 350°, allowing about 25 minutes per pound. From time to time, drain off the fat as it accumulates.

You'll find that the raw fruit absorbs the fat and imparts a delicious flavor to the duck itself. The apples should be discarded, but the prunes can be arranged around the duck as a garnish.

For a gemütlich dinner, serve red cabbage along with the duck, and thin pancakes rolled around a spicy apple-raisin filling. The same duck, served with wild rice and orange sauce and accompanied by plump asparagus hollandaise, becomes a dinner party dish. If you shred orange rind over the duck and pour a jigger or two of brandy on the platter and set the duck aflame, you're ready to entertain royalty.

3

Elizabethan England

TREASURES OF THE
GOOD HOUSEWIVES

ENGLAND'S FIRST PRINTED COOKBOOK, *The Boke of Cokery*, appeared in 1500 and, like all early cookbooks, it was intended for "A Pryncis Household or Any Other Estates." Actually, there was a long silence before any other cookbooks appeared. When they did, the authors gave no sign that male chefs were anywhere around but addressed themselves directly to the housewife, promising to serve her as *The Good Huswifes Jewell, The Good Hous-Wives Treasurie, The Good Huswives Closet,* or *The Good Huswives Handmaid.* It seems quite clear that the housewife ran the English home—but the books that told her how were written by men.

43

In these little manuals, each slightly thicker than a soda cracker, the housewife's obligations were detailed as precisely as a needle-work pattern, and she was busy from morning to night carrying them out. She ordered the scullions about their tasks, saw that the buffet was heaped with surloynes of beef, with whole wilde boares resting placidly on beds of parsley, with peacocks and swans in their plumage and whole coveys of strange-sounding birds such as bittern, hearn, soveler and puets. She mixed plague cures, dried fox skins, carved joints of venison, directed that tea be steeped for as long as it took to say the Miserere slowly, and led family and servants in prayer. After the main meal at midday, she retired to the still-room to prepare a scented infusion of rose leaves or an elixir to ease a sore throat. She conferred with dairymaids about butter, and received accountings from serfs about the crops and cattle—estate as well as household matters were often left in her hands, for her husband might be off on a voyage, or fighting a war.

The cookbook writers considered nothing too demanding. They directed her to gild little meringues with pure gold, or bake biscuits in walnut shells and then artfully conceal a poem inside. How she found time for all this, in addition to spinning and performing all the other duties they outlined for her, is a marvel. However, Queen Elizabeth I was on the throne, setting an example of feminine efficiency. And in her own way, the housewife was queen in the home.

In *The Good Hous-Wives Treasurie,* which appeared in 1588, medieval and early Roman overtones still persisted in some of the recipes, such as the black puddings (blood sausage) and the haggis (which Robert Burns later called "Mighty chieftain of the Scottish race"). Meats were still cut up to be eaten with a spoon and combined with fruits and heavy spices. Typical was Minst Pye, and here is the original recipe from my own copy of *The Good Hous-Wives Treasurie,* using practically the same ingredients that go into a modern mince pie.

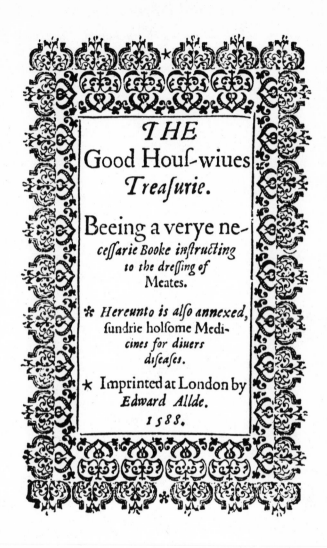

Title page of The Good Hous-Wiues Treasurie. *1588.*

To Make Minst Pyes

Take your *veale* and perboyle it a little, or mutton, then set it a cooling: and when it is colde, take three pound of *suit* to a legge of mutton, or fower pound to a fillet of veale, and then mince them small by them selves, or together whether you will, then take to season them *halfe an once of Nutmegs, half an once of cloves and Mace, half an once of Sinamon, a little Pepper*, as much *Salt* as you think will season them, either to the mutton or to the Veale. Take *big yolkes of Eggs* when they be hard, *half a pinte of rosewater* full measure, *halfe a pound of Sugar*, then Straine the Yolkes with the Rosewater and the Sugar and mingle it with your meate. If ye have any *Orenges or Lemmans* you must take two of them, and take the pilles very thin and mince them very smalle, and put them in *a pound of currans, or dates, half a pound of prunes*, laye Currans and Dates upon the top of your meate, you must take *two or three Pomewaters or Wardens* and mince with your meate, you may make them worse, if you will. If you will make good crust put in *three or foure yolkes of egges, a little rosewater, & a good deale of sugar.*

Meat balls also were easy to devour with a spoon or the hands, and one recipe for potted meat balls cooked with allspice is good enough to eat with a fork today. The *Treasurie* called these Balles of Italie. With potatoes added, they make an easy and appetizing casserole dinner.

Balles of Italie

Whole allspice, added to the stewed meat balls, is the important condiment here. I've substituted beef for the veal of the original recipe. Beef wasn't popular in those days.

Combine:
1½ *pounds ground beef*
2 *tablespoons cold water, dashed over the beef and mixed into it*
1 *medium onion, grated into the beef*

Now add:
1 *tablespoon catsup plus a dash of Worcestershire*
1 *tablespoon melted butter, margarine or any fat you choose*
½ *teaspoon celery salt*
Salt and pepper to taste
1 *beaten egg*

Blend well and add:
2 *tablespoons dried bread crumbs, or enough to bind mixture* (*commercial bread crumbs may be used for this*)

Butter the bottom of a Dutch oven or a kettle with a tight-fitting lid. Shape the meat into balls slightly larger than a walnut. Alternate them with chunky pieces of *raw potatoes*. Sprinkle paprika generously over all. Toss in *1 teaspoon whole allspice*. Add ¾ *cup bouillon* (even water will do), cover tightly and let simmer for an hour, or until potatoes are well cooked. (Do not stir.) A hearty dish for family dinner on a wintry night.

A salad of sliced pickled beets and onion rings topped with riced hard-cooked eggs goes nicely with this dish.

IN 1597 CAME *The Good Huswives Handmaid* with similar recipes, only more of them, and some bearing rather fanciful names. A dish of eggs, beef marrow, fruits and spices was called a Vaunt. Suet dumplings were named Fystes of Pottingale (perhaps inspired by a clenched fist). *Handmaid* recognized that mortals, even housewives, were only human after all, and offered a recipe for A Broth for a Weake Body. Another was A Tart to Provoke Courage Either in Man or Woman. Considering some of the ingredients, it must have taken courage to eat them. The following recipe is from my own copy of the book.

A Tart to Provoke Courage Either in Man or Woman

Take a *quart of good wine* and boile therein *two Burre rootes* scraped cleane, *two good quinces*, and a *potato roote* well pared, and an *ounce of Dates*, and when all these are boiled verie tender, let them be drawne through a strainer wine and al, and then be put in the *yolks of eight eggs*, and the *braines of three or fower cocke sparrowes*, and straine them into the other, and a *little rosewater*, and seeth them all with *sugar*, *cinamon* and *ginger*, and *cloves* and *mace*, and put in *a little sweet butter*, and set it upon a chafing dish of coales between two platters, & so let it boile til it be something big.

All recipes in Elizabethan books were not completely outlandish. A few were actually inspiring. The following tart of oranges and apples was adapted from a recipe in *The Good Huswives Handmaid*. It must have been a delicious dessert even in 1597:

Apple-Orange Tart

Pastry for a 9-inch pie shell
4 large navel oranges, peeled and segmented
5 or 6 large, juicy apples, cut like the orange segments and poached
for 2 minutes in boiling water, then drained thoroughly
½ cup sugar, combined with 1 tablespoon flour and ½ teaspoon
cinnamon
2 tablespoons orange marmalade or apple jelly

Make certain that all membrane is removed from the orange segments. Sprinkle a third of the sugar mixture over the bottom of pie shell, then arrange a layer of apples with a small quantity of orange segments scattered among them. (Reserve most of the orange segments for the top.) Sprinkle another third of sugar mixture on pie. Add another layer of apples and arrange balance of orange segments in an attractive pattern over top. Sprinkle with remaining sugar mixture, dot with the jelly. Bake in a preheated oven (375°) for 45 minutes to an hour.

Note: This may also be baked as a 2-crust pie, in which case distribute the oranges equally in the apple layers and do not poach the apples.

A recipe for Capons with Oranges or Lemmons evidently was so popular that the *Handmaid* gives it in two versions. Here it is, a piquant, mouth-watering dish, only slightly altered from the original recipe.

Capon With Lemon Sauce

Season the *capon* inside and out with *salt* and *pepper* to taste. (A plump roasting chicken may be substituted with good results.) Roast it uncovered in a moderate oven (350°) for about an hour, basting as needed. By this time, fat will have collected in the bottom of the pan; remove as much of it as you can spoon out. Now add: *1 whole lemon, cut into small dice; ¼ cup dry white wine; 2 tablespoons currant jelly, and a pinch of powdered thyme.*

Continue to roast the fowl until it is tender and nicely browned, basting several times with the sauce. If more liquid is needed (unlikely with a capon), add a bit more white wine.

Send the bird to the table garnished with *canned unpeeled apricots,* the halves put together with a filling of *cream cheese* mixed with *horseradish.*

ONE OF THE RAREST of early English books on food is *Dyets Dry Dinner,* a slim little volume written by Henry Buttes in 1599. Buttes introduced himself as the servant of "Dyet, Health's kindest nurse," and he wrote with chuckling humor about the effects of various foods upon the body. The dry dinner of the title excluded all liquid from the meal. Tobacco, which had only recently been introduced into England, he called the "dry drink." As one of the earliest discourses on tobacco in the English language, these remarks have added greatly to the interest of this Elizabethan book.

Although the book was dedicated to the Lady Anne Bacon, Buttes used the lusty, often vulgar language of the period, which seems hardly suitable for ladies. He found sexual symbols in many foods, called chestnuts "instruments of lust," and said that asparagus and carrots were aphrodisiac and "provoketh Venus." Nonetheless, he was a learned scholar and a gourmet as well, who could toss off a classical reference or a suggestion for seasoning lamb with equal ease.

Buttes' Way of Seasoning Lamb

Cut a *clove of garlic* in half. Energetically rub the cut end over every inch of *lamb*. Sprinkle with *salt* and *pepper*. Place in a roasting pan with a *whole onion*. Liberally sprinkle with *whole rosemary* and *ground sage*. Roast as usual.

Buttes hailed spinach and sorrel as wholesome greens for any age or condition but especially for youth. And he said that the juice of spinach, if drunk, "cureth any wound received of a scorpion and is therefore of much request in Italy." He gave no recipes, but his random hints are almost recipes in themselves. His way of cooking spinach with dill would tempt even a non-vegetarian:

Buttes' Way with Spinach

Before cooking the *spinach* add *a good handful of chopped dill* (the feathery part). Use at least 3 tablespoons to a frozen package; more if spinach is fresh. Slice in *an entire scallion stalk,* both green top and white end. Cook as usual.

Buttes also doted on soup made of sorrel (spinach works equally well). This makes a delicious chilled soup for a hot summer night.

Spinach or Sorrel Soup

> 2 *pounds raw spinach or sorrel*
> 1½ *quarts cold water*
> 6 *tablespoons lemon juice*
> 1 *beaten egg, with 1 teaspoon salt added*
> *Sour cream*

Put the raw spinach or sorrel through a food chopper, using the coarse blade. Then put it into a saucepan with the cold water. Bring the water to a boil and cook the spinach for 10 minutes. Cool slightly, then add the lemon juice. While the spinach is still quite warm, add the beaten egg, thinning it first with some of the spinach broth. That's all there is to it—until time to serve. The soup should then be ice cold. For each portion allow 1 tablespoon sour cream. Thin the sour cream with some of the soup, added gradually so that the cream will be well homogenized. When this is accomplished, pour the cream into the quantity of soup to be served.

An additional dab of sour cream may be used to garnish each portion. Or garnish with slices of hard-cooked eggs.

Buttes happily acknowledged the supremacy of Italian cooking. "The Italian," he said, "as all the world knows, is most exquisite in the composition of all sortes of condiments." An Italian Green Sauce drew his special praise. Apparently, this was the basil sauce known as Pesto that is still one of the delights of Genoese cooking. This recipe will enable you to make up a batch to serve over spaghetti or macaroni.

Italian Green Sauce (Pesto)

This ancient sauce should be made with fresh basil. (In season, basil is obtainable in Italian markets.) The ingredients should be combined in a mortar.

> 4 *tablespoons chopped basil*
> 2 *tablespoons ground pine-nuts or walnuts*
> 3 *garlic cloves, crushed or pressed*
> 3 *tablespoons grated Locatelli or Parmesan cheese*
> 5 *tablespoons olive oil combined with 2 tablespoons melted butter*
> (*7 tablespoons in all*)

Pound the basil leaves, the nuts and the garlic in a mortar (add a dash of salt). When the basil is quite crushed, add the cheese and continue to mash and pound until a thick purée is formed. Slowly add the oil and butter mixture, stirring so that a smooth consistency results. This is a thick sauce, and when properly made, the basil is hardly distinguishable. It is delicious over any pasta.

Two cookbook writers now omitted Housewife from their titles and addressed themselves to Ladies and Gentlewomen. But they expected the gentlewoman to be just as industrious as the housewife had been. John Murrell's *A Daily Exercise for Ladies and Gentle-women* had her baking, preserving, candying all sorts of confections that plainly required hours of tedious labor. Later he amended the title to read *A Delightful Daily Exercise,* which perhaps was meant to take the sting out of her work. He still kept her busy from the minute she brushed aside the heavy hangings around her bed to the hour when she retired behind them again at night.

In 1608, a charming little book, *A Closet for Ladies and Gentle-women* by Sir Hugh Plat, offered biscuits, marzipans, cordials and conserves together with an apothecary's store of medical recipes as well. Among them is this reminder of an age when long-bows were still in use, and when a random skirmish might send the lord of the manor home with an arrow in his thigh:

To Drawe an Arrowhead or Other Yron Out of a Wound

Take the juice of valerian, in the which, wet a tent and put into the wound laying the said hearbe upon it stamped, then make your binder as best fitteth, and by this meanes you shall drawe forth the yron, and after heale the wound.

And here are his fanciful little biscuits baked in walnuts:

To Make a Walnut, That When You Cracke It, You Shall Find Biskets, and Carrawayes In It, Or a Prettie Posey Written

Take *a piece of your Past Royall white,* being beaten with *Gumtraga-cant,* and mixed with *a little fine searced cynnamon,* which will bring your past into a Walnut shell colour, then drive it thinne, and cut it into two pieces, and put the one piece into the one half of your mould, and the other into the other, then put what you please into the nut, and close the mould together, & so make *three or foure walnuts.*

The words Closet and Cabinet frequently appeared in early cook-book titles, and implied that the author's revelations were secrets

First page of an early 17th-century manuscript cookbook. Small folio.

A Booke of Cookerye

To make Past Royall

Take fine fflower, yolkes of Egges. Butter and hotte Creame
then putt thereto a little Sugarr, and soe, worke it orderly

To make Past for Tartes

Take yolkes of Egges, breake them in a dishe, and then take a
little water, Butter and Saffrone, boile them all together and
therewith temper the flower and soe driue it thinne

To make a dish called Precocke

Take a Quantitye of Creame, yolkes of Eggs and a dishe of
sweete butter then putt in a little Sugarr and Saffrone sette
them on the fire, and lett it boyle vntill it be thicke:

To make a Tarte of Creame

Take a Pottle of Creame and Twentith yolkes of Eggs and a
dishe of sweete butter boile alltogether then streame them
through a Strayner and season them with Sugarr and Saffrone
soe putt them in the paste, and bake them

To make a Cleere Jellye

Take a Cocke and fower Neates feete dresse them and seeth
them all to peeces then straine them from the bones, and when
it is cold pare it all about, and putt it in a potte, with a Pinte of
Bastard or Redde wine, or Aquavite of Ginger with Sugarr
Synamond, and Ginger of each a little Quantitye bruised with
Mace then Cleere it with the whites of two Eggs and a
little Salt then coullerr it with Turnesalle:

To make

beyond questioning. Some of the recipes do make strange reading, like Sir Kenelm Digby's Tea with Eggs, and Partridge's Rhubarb Scrapings steeped in wine to make hair Yellow as Gold.

IN 1615 THE MOST INFLUENTIAL of early English cookbooks appeared. This was *The English House-wife* by Gervase Markham, who was the most exacting of all the writers of his time. He added no frills or promises to title or text, and his no-nonsense attitude was highly successful: *The English House-wife* continued to be reprinted until 1683.

His composite portrait of the early English housewife gives an idea of what he, and doubtless all Englishmen, expected of this remarkable woman: "Our English housewife," he wrote, "must be of chaste thoughts, stout courage, patient, untyred, watchfull, diligent, witty, pleasant, constant in friendship, full of good Neighbor-Hood, wise in discourse but not frequent therein—sharp and quick of speech but not bitter or talkative, secret in her affaires, comfortable in her counsels, and generally skilfull in the worthy knowledges which do belong to her vocation."

Above all, Markham expected the housewife to know her business in the kitchen. "To speak then of the outward and active knowledges which belong unto our English House-wife, I hold the first and most principal to be, a perfect knowledge and skill in cookery," he proclaimed.

And when it came to cookery, Markham was a stickler for quality in everything. He made a great point of presenting dishes enticingly, and he commanded the housewife to "invite the appetite with variety!" which was, and is, sound advice. And his recipes were more than passing good.

Before the fork was in use, the problem was to devise dishes that could be eaten easily. Roasted meat could be sliced and handed round on slabs of bread to be eaten by hand. Or a slice would be cut into fringes to be eaten off one by one. Stew could be eaten with a spoon. However, the English wanted other ways of making meats into tasty tidbits that could be eaten by hand, and Olaves were devised. They were usually made of veal and were similar to veal birds. Their popularity was so great that they persisted in cookbooks for centuries. Here is Markham's recipe, one of the simplest and best, given almost exactly as it appears in *The English Housewife,* and still a tasty way to prepare veal:

Veal Olaves

1½ *pounds veal cutlet* (*have the butcher cut the slices as thin as possible and flatten them with his cleaver*)
Salt and pepper
1 *small onion, minced fine*
1½ *tablespoons chopped fresh basil* (*or 1 tablespoon dried*)
2 *mashed hard-cooked egg yolks*
2 *tablespoons wine vinegar*
2 *tablespoons lemon juice*
Stock

Cut the veal into pieces approximately 2 by 4 inches; season to taste with salt and pepper. Combine the basil, onion and egg yolks into a paste and spread ½ teaspoon of the mixture on each piece of meat, nearly to the edges. Roll up and secure with a toothpick. Brown quickly in hot fat, then transfer to a covered casserole. Add the vinegar and lemon juice. Roast, covered, at 375° for an hour or until the Olaves are quite tender. Baste several times.

When Olaves are removed from roasting pan, add ½ cup of any stock that is not too strongly flavored. The basil- and onion-flavored drippings make a tangy sauce to pour over whatever accompanies the Olaves.

Markham also gave a number of recipes for apple pie, a dessert so much in favor with Elizabethans that Robert Greene could think of no greater compliment in praise of a lovely lady than to write, "Thy breathe is like the steame of apple pyes." As one might expect, Markham's recipes are some of the best. An adaptation of his delicious pie made with whole apples appears on the next page.

A Pippin Pie with Whole Apples

Golden yellow apples are best, but winesaps will do nicely. First, arrange the *uncooked whole apples* in a pie plate to determine the size plate needed. Allow a whole apple for each serving. Prepare enough *pastry* for a double-crust pie, and line the plate with half of it. Peel and core the apples and arrange on the pastry. Put a few *raisins* inside each core. Then to each apple add ⅛ *cup sugar* mixed with ¼ *teaspoon cinnamon, a pinch of cloves, ½ tablespoon butter or margarine* and ⅛ *teaspoon grated lemon rind* (optional).

Sprinkle raisins in the spaces between the apples. Roll out the remaining pastry in thin strips, a half inch wide and long enough to twist around each apple. These strips will prevent the apples from wandering into each other as they bake, and they create a handsome effect. Bake at 375° in a preheated oven for 1 hour.

Elizabethan pies served the double purpose of meal and platter, and they contained anything that could be swallowed. Often they reached staggering size—the crust might conceal an assortment of fish and eels, venison, a half dozen rabbits, a variety of fowl, or even a flock of live birds as in *Epulario*. One of Markham's pies, requiring several chickens, is an excellent entree *without* the pie-crust. Cooked according to his directions, the chickens alone make a delicious dish. This is one of my favorite methods of preparing chickens quickly.

Prune-Stuffed Chicken

2 *young fryers or broilers, left whole*
Salt and pepper
Pinch of ginger
20 *uncooked prunes*
3 *tablespoons butter or margarine*
1 *whole medium onion*
Sweet sherry or Madeira
Orange rind

Season the insides of the chickens with salt, pepper and a pinch of ginger. In each cavity place 10 prunes and 1 tablespoon butter. Spread remaining butter over the breasts and drumsticks, and sprinkle the birds lightly with salt and pepper to taste. Place them in a roasting pan with the onion. Roast uncovered in a medium-hot oven (375°) until tender. This should take about 1½ hours. Baste several times with the juice that collects in the pan.

When chickens are tender and brown, remove from the roaster and add ¼ cup wine to the gravy. Divide the chickens into halves or quarters and arrange on a serving platter, using the prunes as garnish. Tiny shreds of orange rind scattered over the prunes add zest and style to this dish.

SALLETS were on Richard II's table in the fourteenth century, as we have seen. By the sixteenth century, they were well established in English menus, and Markham made a great point of them in his book. Apparently, they often doubled as decorative centerpieces. Few housewives today would go to the effort of preparing the tremendous affair of fruits, nuts, and meadow and garden greens that Markham called Compound Sallet.

Of Compound Sallets

Your compound Sallets, are first the young Buds and Knots of all manner of wholsome Herbs at their first springing; as red Sage, Mint, Lettuce, Violets, Marigolds, Spinage, and many other mixed together, and then served up to the Table with Vinegar, Sallet-Oyl, and Sugar.

To compound an Excellent Sallet, and which indeed is usual at great Feasts, and upon Princes Tables: Take a good quantity of *blancht Almonds,* and with your shredding knife cut them grosly; then take as many *Raisins* of the Sun clean washt, and the stones pickt out, as many *Figs* shred like the Almonds, as many *Capers,* twice so many *Olives,* and as many *Currants* as of all the rest, clean washt, a good handful of the small tender leaves of *red Sage* and *Spinage:* mixe all these well together with good store of *Sugar,* and lay them in the bottome of a great dish; then put unto them *Vinegar* and *Oyl,* and scrape more Sugar over all: then take *Oranges* and *Lemmons,* and paring away the outward pills, cut them into thin slices, then with those slices cover the Sallet all over; which done, take the fine thin leaf of the red *Coleflower,* and with them cover the Oranges and Lemmons all over; then over those Red leaves lay another course of old Olives, and the slices of well pickled *Cucumers,* together with the very inward heart of *Cabbage-lettuce* cut into slices; then adorn the sides of the dish, and the top of the Sallet, with more slices of Lemons and Oranges, and so serve it up.

Flowers were used extensively in early cookery. They filled tart shells, decorated salads and were preserved and candied as sweet-meats. Candied violets are still used today to make superlative desserts. Here is a recipe (nearly identical to the 1608 version in *A Closet for Ladies and Gentlewomen*) for candying your own violets or rose petals:

Candied Blossoms

Rose petals or whole violets may be prepared in this manner: Select *choice petals or blossoms;* wash them; spread them out on flat plates to dry. Make a syrup of *1 cup sugar* and *¾ cup water.* Boil until it spins a thread. Pour the syrup into a bowl and place bowl on a bed of *cracked ice.* Have handy a pair of tweezers. When the syrup begins to crystallize, dip the blossoms, one at a time, and coat with syrup. Shake off any surplus and place them on waxed paper to dry. As they begin to harden, dust them with *powdered sugar.*

The following preserving method is easier, although it is not really candying: Beat the *white of an egg* to a froth. Using a small pastry brush, coat the *blossoms* with the egg white. Remove *all* surplus. Shake *granulated sugar* over the blossoms and set them in a cool place to dry.

A Floral Dessert

For an attractive floral dessert, arrange alternating scoops of *vanilla ice cream* and *lemon sherbet* in a handsome glass bowl. Mix equal parts of *violet liqueur* and *Cointreau,* and pour over the ice cream. Decorate with *candied violets.* (You may buy violets already candied in fine confectionery stores.)

FLORAL TOUCHES contrived by the housewife's hands were very English. But the occasional foreign recipes in these early cookbooks,

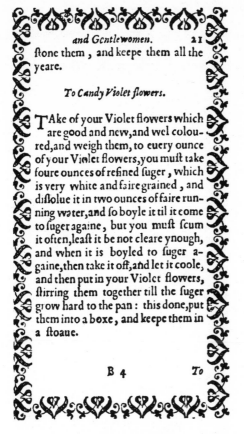

ftone them , and keepe them all the yeare.

To Candy Violet flowers.

TAke of your Violet flowers which are good and new,and wel coloured,and weigh them, to euery ounce of your Violet flowers,you muft take foure ounces of refined fuger , which is very white and faire grained , and diffolue it in two ounces of faire running water,and fo boyle it til it come to fuger againe, but you muft fcum it often,leaft it be not cleare ynough, and when it is boyled to fuger againe,then take it off,and let it coole, and then put in your Violet flowers, ftirring them together till the fuger grow hard to the pan : this done,put them into a boxe, and keepe them in a ftoaue.

B 4   To

A recipe from A Closet for Ladies and Gentlewomen, *attributed to Sir Hugh Plat. 1608.*

such as the Spanish Ollapodrida and Buttes' Italian green sauce, were to the taste of the daring travelers of the age. Thomas Coryat wrote somewhat wistfully in 1608 about the tasty food he had eaten in Italy and in Germany and was the first to bring back stories of "that Italian neatness, the fork." Most Englishmen wanted no part of the fork and little to do with foreign dishes. Gervase Markham said to his English housewife, "Let the provision of her meals be esteemed for the familiar acquaintance she hath with it, than for the strangeness and rarity it bringeth from other countries." His prophetic words soon developed into kitchen battle cries in England.

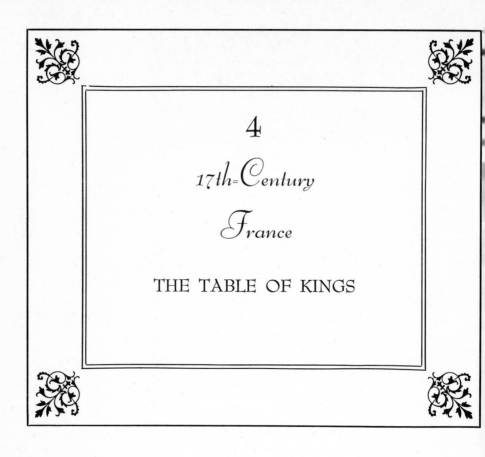

4
17th-Century
France

THE TABLE OF KINGS

WHEN LOUIS XIV came to the throne in 1643, French cooking was as young and unformed as the child king himself. When Louis died in 1715, French cuisine was one of the glories of his dazzling court. The foundations for this change were laid by a single cookbook: *Le Cuisinier François* by François Pierre de La Varenne, which first appeared in 1651.

Seemingly at a stroke, it altered the cookery standards which had prevailed in France, and the rest of Europe as well, since medieval days. Heavy spices were set aside; mushrooms and truffles provided subtle accents; mortar and pestle no longer ground almonds into a paste to mix with meats; roasts were finished off with simple sauces based on the meat drippings; butter replaced oil in the pastries; and for the first time, recipes were listed in an orderly alphabetical index. The incomparable Gallic touch was everywhere—in the ingredients and combinations, and in the writing—for others to read and copy.

The cuisine that La Varenne suddenly unveiled must have been developing for some time in noble French kitchens. The French were lazy about writing cookbooks—or perhaps chefs lacked the interest or skill to write them. At any rate, until this time there had been no books other than printed versions of the medieval *Le Viandier*.

La Varenne supposedly had learned to cook in the kitchen of Louis XIV's grandfather, Henry IV. Henry's wife, Marie de' Medici, had brought her own Florentine chefs to France, following the example of her cousin Catherine de' Medici, and all this Italianate influence gave rise to the notion that the French first learned the art of cooking from the Florentine chefs of the two Medici Queens of France. The notion can be traced to Montaigne, who was a contemporary of Catherine's and whose admiring description of an Italian chef at the royal court has been quoted and paraphrased ever since. The cuisine revealed by La Varenne was much more delicate than that of the Italians. Added to this, La Varenne had the skill to present the lighter, more imaginative cooking in tempting words. The words made culinary music that all the world has been singing ever since.

To this day, the imaginative use of fowl is basic to French cuisine. La Varenne demonstrated this at once, with recipes that used marinades or pâtés to lend savor to the versatile meat. Two interesting recipes follow.

Poularde Grasse

First prepare this simple pâté to apply to the surface of the chicken before roasting it. Combine *a sautéed chicken liver* and *a hard-boiled egg* (forced through a coarse strainer). To this add: *1 medium onion, finely* chopped and sautéed in butter until soft and turning brown; ¼ teaspoon salt; dash of pepper, and 3 tablespoons melted butter. Blend thoroughly. If necessary, add more melted butter to obtain a creamy texture.

Season *a tender roasting chicken* inside and out, according to taste. Place in a roasting pan. Spread the pâté thinly over the breast and drumsticks. Place in preheated oven (350°) with *a clove-studded onion.* After 20 minutes or so, the bird should begin to draw its own juices. Add 8 *medium mushrooms which have been sliced and sautéed in butter until soft; then chopped fine.* Start to baste every 20 minutes (this will cause the pâté to run off into the pan). If a little liquid is needed to help it run, add *a small quantity of chicken broth,* or a dissolved chicken bouillon cube. Three bastings at 20-minute intervals, and the bird should be about ready for the table.

Before serving, disjoint it and arrange the pieces attractively on a serving platter. Garnish with *fluted mushroom caps.* Add additional broth to the pan juices to make sufficient gravy; the chopped mushrooms and liver pâté make this a gravy with considerable body.

Poulets Marinez

Place 2 *tender young frying chickens cut in quarters or halves,* flesh side down, in the following marinade: ½ *cup salad oil; ½ cup cider vinegar; 1 teaspoon salt; ¼ teaspoon pepper,* and *1 teaspoon chopped basil.* Let stand at least 1 hour. Turn once, so that both sides are marinated. To cook, have ready a heavy skillet with *hot oil* mixed with *butter.* Coat the chicken with *seasoned flour* and shake off any excess. Fry quickly in the hot fat. Heat the marinade and pour into a heatproof serving dish. Return the chicken to the marinade and set in a moderate oven for about 20 minutes, turning the pieces once. Marinated chicken is also good broiled, but in this case do not dredge it with flour.

Garnish with stuffed *tomatoes,* or with thick slices of tomatoes that have been breaded and fried.

La Varenne used mushrooms in many recipes, but none surpasses the stuffed mushroom he introduced to French cookery (Champignons Farcis). He also devised the famous sauce of onions and mushrooms which now goes by the name of Duxelles, but which La Varenne called simply Champignons à l'Olivier. The custom of honoring a man's name in a recipe had not yet begun; at some later point the sauce was renamed for La Varenne's employer, the Marquis d'Uxelles. Just who selected the Marquis for immortality instead of La Varenne is not clear; at any rate it was an injustice.

Engraved illustration in Le Livre de Cuisine, *by Jules Gouffé. 1867.*

Champignons Farcis
[STUFFED MUSHROOMS]

12 *large mushrooms*
1 *cup cooked ham, chicken or veal, or raw hamburger*
2 *tablespoons minced onion*
1 *slice stale bread, crumbed (crusts removed)*
1 *tablespoon chopped parsley*
Salt and pepper to taste (ham needs very little)
¼ *cup cream*

Select large mushrooms. Remove the stems. Peel mushroom caps if necessary; dip in melted butter and set aside to be stuffed.

Prepare a stuffing as follows: Chop meat together with mushroom stems. Combine meat-mushroom mixture with all remaining ingredients except the cream, and cook for a few minutes in butter until well blended. Cool, or transfer to a cool dish before adding cream. Mix thoroughly with cream.

Fill the mushroom caps with the mixture. Bake in a preheated oven (425°) for 20 to 25 minutes.

Champignons à l'Olivier

[DUXELLES SAUCE]

La Varenne's mushroom sauce—really a ragout—was made with mushrooms from which all the juice had been extracted. To accomplish this, place the *peeled, chopped mushrooms* on a plate, sprinkle lightly with *salt,* and cover with another plate, weighted to press down the mushrooms. Or put the mushrooms in a towel (no salt) and twist until all the juice has been extracted. (La Varenne used the plate method.) Melt 2 *tablespoons butter* in a skillet or heavy saucepan. For ¼ pound of mushrooms use *4 finely sliced shallots,* or the bulb end of scallions. Sauté mushrooms and onions in the butter slowly over a gentle fire, covering at first to get things started. Add more butter if necessary, as the mushrooms cook. Cooking time should be about 6 or 7 minutes, until the onions are mushy and the mushrooms soft.

Add *salt* and *pepper* to taste, and *1 teaspoon chopped parsley.* Mix thoroughly. La Varenne's way was to add cream to this mixture—*½ cup of warmed cream* is just right. Modern chefs add white wine. Some even add tomato paste (!) but then it is no longer Duxelles Sauce. La Varenne's version is wonderful with chicken, or with veal scallops. Add more cream if you want a runnier mixture.

In La Varenne's time, sauces were simple preparations, often only vinegar, verjus (a tart liquid made from sour grapes), or lemon juice added to the pan drippings. The roux of flour and butter was not in use: sauces were thickened with a handful of moistened and strained bread crumbs, or with egg yolks. La Varenne much favored two ancient sauces, Poivrade and Robert, which are still in use today. Robert Sauce is a good example of gastronomic mythology. Some say it was originated by an early seventeenth-century saucemaker, Robert Vinot, but the sauce was described earlier by Rabelais and Vinot's claim can be disregarded. A logical derivation would be from the English Roebuck Sauce of vinegar and onions which was served with venison in medieval times; the Normans probably learned it in England and brought it back to France. La Varenne recommended it particularly with pork. Here is an adaptation of his recipe, followed by his own version of Poivrade:

Longe de Porc à la Sauce Robert

Season a *pork loin* with a mixture of *salt, pepper* and *½ teaspoon ground sage.* Set this to roast uncovered, at 350°, allowing 35 minutes per pound. (Pork must always be well done.)

About 30 minutes before the roast is finished, drain off the pork drippings in the pan and discard. Add the sauce which has been prepared as follows: Sauté *a large, finely minced onion* in *butter* or *margarine* in a saucepan. When the onion is soft and golden, add *1 cup of vinegar* and the *juice of a lemon.* Simmer together for a few minutes, then add to the roasting pan. Allow the pork to finish cooking in this sauce for at least 30 minutes.

To serve, strain the sauce through a coarse sieve, pushing the onions through with a wooden spoon. Or, pour the sauce into a blender and blend briefly until the onion is reduced to a purée. (La Varenne directs that this sauce should be well blended to guard against separating.)

Sauce Robert is an Old World accompaniment to roast pork and a pleasant change from the standard applesauce. Crisp eggplant fritters make a nice accompaniment with the Sauce Robert.

Poivrade Sauce

This is a tangy, tart sauce for fish, fowl or braised beef. And it is as easy as saying François Pierre de La Varenne, when made his way:

½ *cup cider vinegar*
1½ *cups stock*
1 *finely minced medium onion*
1 *finely minced carrot*
Butter
6 *peppercorns, crushed*

Sauté onion and carrot in butter until slightly cooked. Add stock and vinegar, and simmer gently for 15 to 20 minutes. Add peppercorns at very end. Strain before serving.

An excellent sauce for venison, if you happen to have any. Or with a roast of veal, for that matter. This seventeenth-century Poivrade Sauce is a perfect choice whenever you wish to endow meat with a tart, peppery finish.

Makes about 1 cup of sauce.

La Varenne provided an excellent recipe for a whole roast calf's liver—Foie de Veau Piqué. It is a succulent way to prepare this popular variety meat.

Foie de Veau Piqué

[A LARDED WHOLE ROAST CALF'S LIVER]

Have the butcher lard the *calf's liver*. (Or you can place thin strips of salt pork or bacon on it before roasting. If salt pork is used, be sure to wash it thoroughly so that it is free of salt.)

Marinate the liver for several hours in equal parts of *oil* and *vinegar*. To this add: *1 bay leaf; a sprig of parsley; a sliced onion,* and *¼ teaspoon ground allspice.*

After removing liver from marinade, season it to taste with *salt* and *pepper*. Place in an open roasting pan, and lay the marinated onion slices on top of the liver. Bake at 350° for about an hour (for the average 1½- to 3-pound liver). Baste every 15 minutes with some of the marinade.

Serve surrounded by whole baked tomatoes stuffed with sausage meat and bread crumbs, topped with crisp bacon rings.

La Varenne's arrangement of his recipes tells much about the age. A large section on field cooking shows that warring was a way of life and also that a nobleman departed for battle accompanied by his chef, a mobile stove, pots and the best of table furnishings. A contemporary author wrote that if all were done properly to make the master comfortable in war, "God would lend His grace." La Varenne's recipes for fighting men were carefully thought out and danced with originality. They include this chicken in a bottle, which could hardly be recommended for today:

Poulet en Ragout dans une Boteille

[A RAGOUT OF CHICKEN IN A BOTTLE]

Debone a *chicken* and carefully remove its skin. Put the skin into a bottle that does not have wicker on the outside [as Italian wine bottles do today.] Some of the skin should extend outside the neck of the bottle.

Prepare a forcemeat of *mushrooms, truffles, sweetbreads, pigeons, egg yolks* and *good seasonings.* With this you will stuff the boned meat of the chicken and then bend and push it into the bottle. You must then seal the mouth of the bottle with *paste* [pastry]. You will cook this well-seasoned bottle of ragout in a marmite and remove it [the bottle] a little time before you plan to serve it, and let it remain simmering before the fire. And when you are ready to serve it, cut the bottle with a diamond in a way that you can remove the contents whole. [The diamond was probably the type that is used for commercial cutting purposes.]

La Varenne devised other delicacies of turkey and capon for fighting men which make delicious dinners at home today:

Turkey à la Varenne

[POULET D'INDE À LA FRAMBOISE FARCY]

Season a *10- to 12-pound turkey* and stuff it with any *stuffing* of your choice. Roast at 350°, allowing 20 minutes per pound. Spread *softened butter* over the breast and drumsticks and cover these parts with wet cheesecloth to prevent the bird from browning too soon. After it has roasted for 2 hours, pour over it the following mixture, which has been prepared beforehand and simmered for a few minutes in a small saucepan: *2 tablespoons melted raspberry jelly; 2 tablespoons lemon juice; ¼ cup of hot water,* and *rind of half a lemon.* Baste the turkey with this mixture at 20-minute intervals. You will find that this is similar to basting a ham, and the result is a surprising and delicious variation on roast turkey. If more basting liquid is needed, add *fruit juice,* or a little more of the raspberry jelly, thinned with hot water. To follow La Varenne all the way, add *grated lemon rind* and *¼ cup vinegar* to the pan juices for a gravy.

Capon with Oysters
[CHAPON AUX HUITRES]

This recipe should be equally good with a plump roasting chicken. Season the *fowl* inside and out, to taste. Place an *onion* in the pan for flavor during roasting. Roast the capon uncovered, at 350°, basting often. La Varenne instructed that the capon be covered with buttered paper during the roasting process. Covering the bird with a piece of cheesecloth dipped in *melted butter* will produce a crisp, brown bird.

When the capon has nearly finished cooking, prepare the stuffing, using the following ingredients: *18 oysters, rinsed with cold water and dried in a towel; 1 large onion, chopped fine; 4 tablespoons (more if necessary) of capon drippings from the roasting pan; 2 cups soft white bread crumbs that have been sautéed lightly in butter* (or 6 to 8 slices of bread, cubed). Heat the capon fat in a skillet and cook the chopped onion. When the onion begins to grow soft and to turn color, add the oysters and sauté quickly until the edges curl. (They will release liquid, but don't be dismayed.) Sauté them until they are done, which should take about 4 minutes. Remove from fire and add the sautéed bread crumbs to the oyster mixture. Mix thoroughly, and spoon into the cavity of the capon just before it goes to table.

The strong influence of the Church is seen in *Le Cuisinier François'* division of recipes into Maigres and Grasses—dishes for fast days and meat days. Cardinal Richelieu had already extended *his* influence into dining by introducing the first dinner knives with rounded ends for use at his table. The sight of pointed knives being used as toothpicks had revolted him.

La Varenne deferred to the Church's authority and devised many recipes to make days of abstinence more bearable. For the meatless table he used artichokes in many ways that are still popular: whole artichokes stuffed with another vegetable, quartered artichokes sautéed in butter, and artichoke bottoms covered with a dressing that resembles hollandaise sauce. Several of La Varenne's ideas have been combined for the following recipe:

Woodcut of an artichoke from L'Escole Parfaite
des Officiers de Bouche. *From the 1676 edition.*

La Varenne's Artichauts en Cus

[ARTICHOKE BOTTOMS]

Artichoke bottoms are available in cans, or they may be prepared from
fresh artichokes. If fresh artichoke bottoms are used, drop them into
strongly acidulated water the minute they are pared, as they discolor
readily. (*One tablespoon vinegar* to 1 *cup of water.*) To cook them, use
an enameled or stainless-steel pan. Never aluminum: this will discolor
the artichoke bottoms. Drop them into *boiling salted water,* add 2 *tablespoons lemon juice per quart of water,* and simmer gently until tender,
about 30 minutes. Drain (after cooling in their liquid). Fill centers with
finely chopped broccoli or mushrooms combined with peas, or almost
anything your fancy dictates. (*Broccoli* was a popular vegetable in
France in La Varenne's time.)

Cover with hollandaise sauce, or with the following easy sauce. Combine: *½ cup mayonnaise; 2 tablespoons lemon juice; 1 egg yolk,* and
2 tablespoons cream. Place the artichokes in a hot oven (425°) for 10
minutes, or until sauce begins to brown slightly.

La Varenne's second book, *Le Pastissier François,* appeared in 1653, and it introduced puff paste to French cookbooks (although the paste was not unfamiliar to French kitchens). There was a recipe for cake waffles, Gaufres (perhaps the forerunners of breakfast waffles), baked on a waffle-like iron, and a recipe for Darioles, which La Varenne said could be made with almond milk if ordinary cow's milk were not available. In a recipe for raised cake dough, La Varenne referred the cook who wished to bake only a small quantity to special small ovens, "Petits fours, lately come into use in some kitchens." Also he gave a sugar icing for small cakes called pièces de fours. These two phrases very probably account for the title of today's petits fours.

In *Le Pastissier François,* he provided more than sixty egg recipes, including this delicious apple omelette:

Aumelette aux Pommes

4 crunchy apples, peeled and sliced thin
Melted butter
4 eggs beaten with 4 tablespoons water (use a fork and don't over-beat)
Dash of salt
Sugar
Cinnamon

Cover the bottom of a skillet with melted butter and sauté the apple slices until they are tender but whole. Add more butter if necessary, and pour the beaten eggs into the skillet. Cook over a low fire, lifting and pushing the eggs away from the side of the pan to prevent sticking, at the same time allowing uncooked egg to run under. When firm on top, omelette is cooked. (Run it under broiler for a few seconds, if you wish.) Serve at once, sprinkled with sugar and cinnamon. It may be folded in conventional omelette shape. Marvelous with crisp pork sausages for a brunch or luncheon.

In 1655 *Le Pastissier François* was reprinted by the distinguished Elzevier press and eventually became the most sought-after of Elzevier books, commanding such high prices in auction rooms that it

Illustrated title page of Le Pastissier François *by* La Varenne.
The notable Elzevier edition. 1655.

earned the title of the most expensive cookbook in the world. But except for bibliophiles and gastronomes, few people today know the name of La Varenne, despite the debt French cuisine owes to him.

It seems strange that there was not an increase in the number of French cookbooks after La Varenne's success. There was certainly no lack of interest. The court set a dazzling pace for elaborate dining, with nobles competing wildly to capture the best cooks and to spread the finest table. Nobles and their servants literally risked death in their attempts to outdo each other. Fouquet, the finance minister, brought about his own downfall and almost lost his life when the King suspected that money for his resplendent banquets was coming from the royal coffers. And the suicide of Vatel, maître d'hôtel to the Prince de Condé, when the fish failed to arrive for a dinner planned for the King is a well-known example of the fanatic zeal that attended culinary rivalries at court.

Even children were swept up in the fever. A late seventeenth-century schoolbook called *Rôti-Cochon* (Roast Pig) was filled with aphorisms designed to guide the young toward a proper appreciation of gastronomy:

Drink wine when you eat ham.
Soup is for ordinary hunger; roasts make a meal festive.
Venison pâté is too good for disobedient children.

Eating well was certainly a preoccupation of all who could afford it, although the poor found even a subsistence diet hard to come by. (Everything was taxed, and a peasant who boiled his cabbage in seawater to escape the salt tax was thrown in jail for his economy.) Thrift did not concern the cooks of the nobility—even though La Varenne had suggested that butter be bought when it was cheap, to be clarified and stored for future use. Ceremony and protocol, however, were of the greatest concern because of the emphasis that Louis XIV himself now began to place on cuisine. The King gave his cooks and stewards the title of Officers of the Household and divided them into categories according to their functions. An Officer had the right to wear a special uniform, and if he commanded a large corps of aides, he even had the right to wear a sword.

It was not long before a guide appeared for Officers of other households. This was *L'Escole Parfaite des Officiers de Bouche,* published in 1662, which mingled the art of cooking with the art of serving it to a prince.

The Pantry Officer saw to the table linens and was expected to fold napkins in ornamental shapes rivaling sculptures—a hen with chicks, a frog, or the Cross of Lorraine if the Duke of Lorraine were coming to dinner. It was quite a breach of etiquette to disarrange such creations, but the real need for napkins had passed since forks had come into use. For those who could not give up an old habit, bowls of water and towels were placed at each end of the table.

For the Carving Officer, there were pages of designs for whittling fruits into fanciful garnishes and explicit diagrams for carving and for serving the food at table: "Give the best portions to the most esteemed guests," *L'Escole Parfaite* directed, "and if they are of *great* importance, give them an *extra* portion."

But a lesser guest would still eat well, even if the carver had given out the best portions that fell under his knife. Here is a typical menu suggested by *L'Escole Parfaite des Officiers de Bouche:*

ENTREE

Good bread and good wine; salad of oranges; stuffed eels; calf's head vinaigrette; beef tongues; talmouses of the white meat of capon [a kind of timbale]

POTAGES

Partridges with cabbage; vegetable marrow stew; venison with turnips; stuffed cucumbers; hot venison pies

FIRST SERVICE

Young rabbits; chickens prepared in several ways; various stuffed birds; quail pie; kid with sorrel sauce

SECOND SERVICE

Young chickens in rose vinegar; rabbits garnished with oranges; suckling pigs; a cold pie of sparrows

73

ISSUE DE TABLE

[*a dessert service*]

3 *kinds of jellies: white, clear and amber; 3 Pièces de Fours* [*large cakes*]; *almonds and other nuts; cream cheese; cakes of puff paste* [*Napoleons and the like, probably*]; *rosewater*

Most of the recipes in *L'Escole Parfaite* had a characteristic seventeenth-century simplicity, and occasionally they were named with unexpected candor. Here is one dish, popular at the time, that sounds like its name:

Sauce D'Enfer

[HELL SAUCE]

Actually, this is a dish of minced pig's and sheep's feet, served in a sour sauce. The recipe reads:

Cook your *pig's feet* in a *good bouillon* and when they are well cooked, put them to roast on the grill. When done, cut them up in large pieces, set them on a plate, and cover them with a *sour green sauce* [or, a sauce of sour greens]. Chop up some *onions* very fine and steam these in *verjus* [sour grape juice] and when they are steamed enough add *a little mustard*. Take *sheep's feet* and cut them into pieces and put them in a pan over the fire. Make them very hot, but the minute the charcoal is alive under the pan, toss your sour sauce and the pig's feet over the sheep's feet. Serve this as an entree.

Here are two very quick and simple egg dishes with tantalizing names:

Oeufs Marbrez

This dish requires at least 10 eggs to make an effective appearance and can be made with as many more as you desire. So—*10 hard-cooked eggs.* Rice 5 whole eggs. For the balance, separate the yolks from the whites and rice separately.

Combine the whole riced eggs with *salt, freshly ground black pepper,* a *dash of prepared mustard* and enough *mayonnaise* to bind.

Combine the egg whites with *finely chopped onion,* dash of salt, and enough mayonnaise to bind.

74

Before adding mayonnaise to the egg yolks, combine them with *mashed anchovies* (for 6 egg yolks, 6 small anchovy fillets). Then add mayonnaise to bind.

Butter a mold or bowl. Pack half the egg white mixture into the bottom. Tamp down firmly. Pack down all the egg yolk mixture. Again, tamp down firmly. Now pack in the whole egg mixture. Add the remaining half of the egg whites. Tamp down firmly after each addition. Place in refrigerator for several hours.

Unmold by running a sharp knife between the eggs and the bowl. A sharp shake should be enough to dislodge it. If not, turn the bowl over, poke knife up around edge until the mold comes loose. Garnish with *anchovy fillets* or caviar and serve with a dressing of *sour cream* and *caviar*.

Oeufs à l'Intrigue

Oeufs à l'Intrigue are also prepared in layers, much like Oeufs Marbrez, except that in this recipe the mixture is cooked. I added the crust.

> *Pastry for a 9-inch pie*
> *4 large eggs*
> *¾ cup cream*
> *1 2-ounce can anchovy fillets or ½ cup flaked crab meat*
> *¾ cup grated cheese (Cooper sharp and domestic Swiss combined,*
> *or a combination of any 2 cheeses you choose)*
> *1 tablespoon grated onion*
> *Salt and pepper to taste*

Line a 9-inch pie plate with pastry. Prick bottom of pastry with a fork and bake it at 400° for about 5 minutes. You may line it with aluminum foil and weight this down with dried beans to keep the pastry from puffing up, but in my kitchen I usually proceed without this extra step since the puffing is usually negligible.

Prepare the custard as follows: Beat the eggs with the cream until well blended, then add the grated onion. Pour a third of the mixture into the pie shell, place in a preheated oven (400°) for 5 minutes to allow the egg mixture to set partially. Remove from oven. Arrange anchovies or crab meat on top of egg mixture, carefully spoon on another third of eggs. Return to oven for 5 minutes, or until second layer

(*Continued on next page*)

An illustration from L'Art de la Cuisine Française, *the five-volume work by* Carême. 1833-35.

begins to set. Remove from oven, sprinkle cheese over top and spoon on last third of eggs. Return to oven and bake for another 20 minutes, or until nicely puffed and brown on top. A delicious luncheon dish. Or serve it as a first course.

Fruits and vegetables were served in many delightful ways that translate well today. Broccoli served cold as a salad will delight even those who say they don't like broccoli.

Sallade de Brocolis

Cook the *broccoli* until it is just tender and still a lively green. (If fresh broccoli is used, first trim away most of the coarse stalk; frozen broccoli is already trimmed.) Chill broccoli thoroughly. Arrange the stalks, heads in one direction, on a salad plate. Douse liberally with a *tart French dressing* made with lemon juice as well as vinegar.

This seventeenth-century way of serving celery is also delicious.

Sallade de Sellery Cuit
[SALAD OF COOKED CELERY]

Green pascal celery is preferred. Cut the stalks into pieces about 5 inches long, trim them neatly and remove all strings. Cook in *boiling salted water* until just tender. Do not overcook. Drain, blot between paper towels to remove all excess moisture, and chill thoroughly. Arrange the celery on a salad plate as you would asparagus. Garnish the celery with *paper-thin half slices of lemon, julienne strips of beets,* and (as *L'Escole*

76

Parfaite directed) scatter *a few pomegranate seeds* over the salad. Pour over all a *French dressing* sharpened with a hint of *Worcestershire sauce.*

A recipe for cooked oranges runs through French cookbooks like a recurring theme. (Oranges were already grown in southern France, but were probably the sour Seville type.) The recipe for Oranges Entières in *L'Escole Parfaite* instructs the cook to "test the boiling syrup with your finger before dropping the fruit." Even to-day there are chefs who use their fingers as thermometers and wouldn't dream of putting their hands into dishwater lest they soften their protective calluses! Today, however, with handsome navel oranges available, it is not necessary to boil the orange shells before filling them; the cook's finger is safe. Oranges Entières (whole oranges) is the most refreshing dessert imaginable and easy to prepare, though your guests will never believe it. When it was placed before my husband for his approval, he said, "Very attractive, but no one will ever go to all *this* trouble." I assure you, it's al-most as easy as scooping ice cream.

Woodcuts showing fanciful ways of carving oranges and pears. From L'Escole Parfaite des Officiers de Bouche. *1676 edition.*

Oranges Entières

Slice off the bud end of *large navel oranges,* leaving an opening 1½ to 2 inches in diameter. The stem end will be the bottom. With a sharp knife, loosen the pulp and remove it from the orange shell. The easiest implement for this is a pointed grapefruit spoon. The pulp of many oranges can be pulled loose with its white skin attached, and this is the best way to arrive at a smoothly scooped-out shell. If the white stem in the center proves stubborn, snip it off with a scissors. Keep the orange shells in *ice water* until ready to use. (They may even remain overnight.) Drain them thoroughly before filling.

FILLING:
Vanilla ice cream
Orange ice
Chopped pecans marinated in Cointreau or Curaçao (6 tablespoons liqueur to ½ cup nuts is ample for 6 oranges)

Have the ice cream soft enough to spoon easily. Press a ½-inch layer of vanilla ice cream into the bottom of the orange shell. Cover with some of the nut-liqueur mixture. Spoon in orange ice (this should occupy half of the orange interior). Conclude with vanilla ice cream and mound or peak it at the top of the shell to avoid a flat appearance. Do this with the back of a teaspoon.) Plaster some of the nut mixture over the top and sides of the protruding ice cream. Leave in freezing compartment until ready to serve.

If you have an ice cream freezer, a delicious homemade ice cream can be made from the strained orange pulp, and used as a filling for the orange shells.

Orange Ice Cream

2 *cups heavy cream*
1 *cup sugar*
1 *cup strained orange juice*
2 *tablespoons lemon juice*

Scald half the cream and dissolve the sugar in it; add the balance of the cream and freeze until the mixture is mushy. Add the orange and lemon juice and freeze until firm.

THE BOURGEOISIE was now emerging as a part of French life, and in 1691 a new cookbook, *Le Cuisinier Roïal et Bourgeois* by Massialot, was the first to throw a bridge between the kitchens of princes and those of the bourgeoisie. But it was a passing nod of recognition in title only; the recipes were still the standard repertoire of the nobleman's kitchen.

Another book by Massialot, *Nouvelle Instructions Pour Les Confitures*, appeared in 1697. (This is the book I described earlier in the Introduction, and that I suspect once belonged to Jérôme Bonaparte.) Massialot had some excellent fruit recipes, including one for pears with orange juice that he had adapted from *L'Escole Parfaite*. It appears below, along with an adaptation of his Pears Flambées.

Pears in Orange Juice

Use *firm Bartlett pears of uniform size*. Peel them and remove bud ends carefully, but leave stems on. Make a *thin syrup of sugar and water—* 1 cup sugar to 3 cups water is a good proportion. Cover the pears and stew gently in the syrup until tender but still firm; test after 15 minutes and then watch carefully. Remove from syrup and arrange pears in a serving dish, stem ends up. Pour over them *fresh orange juice* combined with a dash of *Curaçao or Cointreau* and the syrup which has been boiled down. Carefully remove the *rind from an orange*, taking care not to lift any of the white membrane. Cut the rind into tiny slivers and scatter over the pears.

Pears Flambé

This makes a stunning dessert and is as easy as boiling pears. In fact, that is all you need to do, following the same method as above. Drain the *pears* thoroughly and arrange them in a shallow silver (or heatproof) serving dish. Blanch some *almonds* and cut into slivers. Scatter the almonds over the pears. Combine and warm *¼ cup each of brandy and rum*. Just before serving, light the liquor and pour it over the pears. Send to the table flaming. The almonds that have adhered to the pears will crisp in the flame, and the effect is as handsome as the taste is good.

L, A

MAISON
REGLÉE,

E T

L'ART DE DIRIGER LA MAISON
d'un grand Seigneur & autres, tant à la
Ville qu'à la Campagne, & le devoir de
tous les Officiers, & autres Domestiques
en general.

A V E C

*LA VERITABLE METHODE
de faire toutes sortes d'Essences, d'Eaux &
de Liqueurs, sortes & rafraichissantes, à
la mode d'italie,*

OUVRAGE UTILE ET NECESSAIRE
à toutes sortes de personnes de qualité, Gentils-
hommes de Provinces, Etrangers, Bourgeois, Officiers de grandes Maisons, Limonadiers & autres
Marchands de Liqueurs.

A AMSTERDAM,

Chez **PAUL MARRET,**

dans le Beursstraat, à la Renommée.

M. DC. XCVII.

Frontispiece and title page of La Maison Réglée, by Audiger. 1697.

LATE IN THE SEVENTEENTH CENTURY another book of rules appeared: *La Maison Réglée et l'Art de Diriger la Maison d'un Grand
Seigneur, et Autres* (Rules for Directing the House of a Great Lord,
and Others) by Audiger. Audiger explained that the "Others" of
his title were the bourgeoisie, who would find information in his
chapters for "homes of less consequence." A century later, however,
these were to become homes of more consequence.

5

17th-Century

England

THE QUEEN'S PANTRY

FROM THE MOMENT that La Varenne introduced imagination and order into French cookbooks, the English began to assert their conviction that they were the better cooks. To prove it, they produced more cookbooks than any other nation. Earlier books had addressed themselves to the Housewife and to Ladies and Gentlewomen; now it was the word Queen in the title—especially in combination with Ladies and Gentlewomen—that sold cookbooks.

One of the most popular of seventeenth-century English cookbooks was *The Queens Closet Opened*, published in 1655. The closet was supposedly that of Queen Henrietta Maria, a Medici descendant, and wife of luckless Charles I. But the book was a typical housewifely hodgepodge of Household Hints, medicines (some of them particularly gruesome), sausages and pies. The recipes were for the most part standard English fare, such as Banbury Tarts, Quaking Pudding, Gooseberry Fool, meat pies and cakes that started off with a peck of flour and were thick with raisins. There were also recipes for collaring—that peculiarly English method of potting a cut of meat. Anything from a pig to a side of beef could be collared. Meat to be collared was first cut into long strips, then rolled up tightly, tied fast and cooked in a spicy broth. Rabbit, pork, beef, venison, even fish was treated in this way. Collared beef was invariably first placed in a pickling brine with saltpeter for a few days to give it a reddish color when cooked. Collared beef is a tasty idea from the past; pickling it beforehand is entirely optional. The recipe that follows is adapted from one in *The Queens Closet*.

Collared Beef
[UNPICKLED VERSION]

3- to 4-pound flank steak
Salt and pepper
½ teaspoon whole allspice
¼ teaspoon each: thyme, peppercorns, powdered sage
1 bay leaf
1 clove garlic (optional, and added only for last hour of cooking)

Cut away all gristle and unwanted fat from the flank steak, sprinkle with salt and pepper, roll up tightly and tie with twine at each end and in the middle. Then wrap in 1 thickness of cheesecloth (this will keep the outside of the meat moist). Place in a stewing pot, cover with cold water, bring to a boil and remove all scum. Add the spices and herbs and allow to simmer 3 to 4 hours. Add garlic and 1½ teaspoons salt for last hour of cooking.

Collared beef is delicious served cold. Hot or cold, it should always be sliced fairly thin. (It may be pressed for several hours with a heavy weight before being sliced.) Served hot, it may be surrounded with carrots sprinkled with dill, and accompanied by scalloped potatoes. Since it is not a "gravy meat," a dill or horseradish sauce goes nicely with it. A recipe for dill sauce is given on page 84.

THE
QUEENS
CLOSET
OPENED.

Incomparable Secrets in Phyfick, Chirurgery, Prefer-
ving and Candying, &c.

Which were prefented unto the
QUEEN:

By the moft Experienced Perfons of the
Times, many whereof were had in efteem,
when She p'eafed to defcend to private Recreations.

Corrected and Reviewed, with many New and large
Additions : toge her with three exa& Tables.

Vivit poft Funera Virtus.

LONDON,
Printed by *J.W.* for *Nath. Brooke*, at the
Angel in *Grefham*-College, near the Ex-
change in *Bifhops-Gate-Street.* 1668.

S. *by Nat: Brooke*

*The frontispiece (Faithorne portrait of Queen Henrietta Maria) and the
title page of* The Queens Closet Opened. *1668 edition.*

How to Pickle Beef

To pickle beef first before cooking it, allow the meat to rest in an earthenware or glass dish in brine for 5 to 7 days. Keep it refrigerated. For a 3- to 4-pound flank steak, use enough water to cover and add:

2 *tablespoons salt*
1 *tablespoon saltpeter*
1 *tablespoon sugar*
1 *teaspoon pickling spice (optional)*

If pickled first, do *not* add salt to cooking broth.

Dill Sauce

1½ *tablespoons butter*
1½ *tablespoons flour*
1½ *cups heated skimmed soup stock (from the beef)*
2 *tablespoons fresh chopped dill*
1½ *tablespoons vinegar*
½ *tablespoon sugar*
1 *egg yolk*
Salt to taste

Melt butter, blend in flour, add hot soup stock and whisk until smooth. Add all other ingredients except egg yolk. When mixture has cooled slightly and all danger of curdling is past, add the egg yolk.

The Queens Closet had a number of other cookery ideas worthy of notice. Flounder cooked with anchovies; a pumpkin pie with apples; and this attractive and unusual way of preparing a chicken salad. When I do it at home, I call it the Queen's Chicken Sallet.

The Queen's Chicken Sallet

Slice *cooked chicken* in thin but wide pieces. The meat should not be minced or diced but should look more like escalopes. Mince *1 can anchovy fillets* and add to the chicken. Season to taste with *pepper* and *salt,* but use less salt because of the anchovies. Toss lightly to blend anchovies with the chicken. Add *2 stalks of thinly sliced celery.* Add *3 tablespoons vinegar* to *½ cup mayonnaise,* blend well and then mix through the chicken and anchovies. Garnish with *capers* and *slices of hard-cooked egg.* If you can lay your hands on some *barberries,* scatter them in among the capers and you will be duplicating the Queen's Chicken Sallet to the last detail.

The pie-loving English called pumpkin "pompion" and baked it with apples. This adaptation, inspired by a recipe in *The Queens Closet,* demonstrates how happily the two combine—and how far back pumpkin pie goes.

Pumpkin-Apple Pie

9-*inch pie shell, unbaked*
¾ *cup canned pumpkin*
¾ *cup canned apple sauce*
½ *cup firmly packed light brown sugar*
¼ *cup granulated sugar*
Pinch of powdered cloves
1 *teaspoon ginger*
1½ *teaspoons cinnamon*
2 *eggs, slightly beaten*
1 *cup milk, scalded (pie will be extra delicious if you use part cream)*

Combine pumpkin with apple sauce, add the sugars and spices. Beat in the eggs and add the milk last. Pour into an unbaked 9-inch pie shell and bake at 375° for 1 hour or until a toothpick inserted into center comes out clean.

And this is a simple but excellent way to dress up flounder fillets:

Flounder with Mustard and Anchovies

4 *thick flounder fillets*
1 *2-ounce can anchovy fillets*
¼ *teaspoon dry mustard*
Combine:
1 *crushed garlic clove*
¼ *cup melted butter or margarine*
Juice of 1 *lemon*

Arrange the fish, skin side down, in a buttered baking dish from which it can be served. Score the flesh side; sprinkle it with dry mustard. Arrange several anchovy fillets on each piece of fish. Place under a preheated broiler and broil slowly, basting with the lemon-garlic-butter mixture until nicely done, 15 to 20 minutes, depending on thickness of fish. Garnish with lemon wedges and scoop up sauce from the baking dish as you serve each portion.

As DINING BECAME more and more exciting in France and echoes of it reached across the Channel, it became the fashion among the rich to send their chefs to France for instruction. As chefs returned home, many wrote cookbooks boasting of their French training. The author of *The Perfect Cook,* who incorporated some of La Varenne's *Pastissier François* in his book, went so far as to apologize for presenting it "To this nation where every young matron and young damsel are so well vers'd in the pastry art, so that they may out-vie the best Forreign pastry cooks in all the world besides."

Another author-cook, Robert May, whose *Accomplish'd Cook* appeared in 1660, proved his French training by giving nine recipes for snails, and a recipe for frogs. These were also concealed live in a pie. When the pie was opened the frogs would leap up, wrote May, "and Cause the ladies to squeak and hop about." Earlier, in 1598, when the English had translated the Italian *Epulario* with its pie of live birds, "four and twenty blackbirds" undoubtedly had been presented live at many English tables.

Cooks often were engaged on a temporary basis, very much as caterers are today. Freecooks, they were called. Samuel Pepys wrote of the man cook he hired to prepare a company dinner of stewed carps, roasted chickens, a Jowle of Salmon, neat's tongues, a tansy and cheese. "Merry all the afternoon, talking singing, and piping on the flageolet," wrote Pepys, describing their entertainment.

In 1661, William Rabisha, who described himself as a master-cook with training abroad and service in the kitchens of noblemen, gave his book an ambitious title: *The Whole Body of Cookery— Dissected, Taught, and Fully Manifested, Methodically, Artificially, and According to the Best Tradition of English, French, Italian, Dutch, etc.* The book featured a poem lauding Rabisha's recipes and calling on the reader to follow him as a sort of culinary prophet who was bringing a new comprehension of cookery.

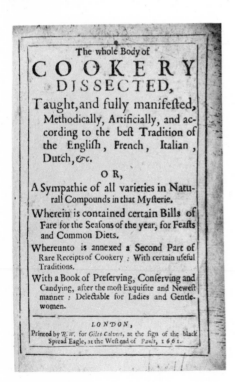

Title page of The Whole Body of Cookery Dissected, *by* Will Rabisha. 1661.

He did write in a clear and accurate style and some of his recipes are decidedly interesting. But most interesting of all is the picture Rabisha draws of the table customs of his day. He includes carving instructions from the early *Book of Kervynge* of 1508, which indicate that there had been little progress since that time—the English were still using bread trenchers for their meat, and eating with their fingers.

Rabisha had some interesting culinary ideas, particularly in the preparation of poultry.

Will Rabisha's Green Chicken

Chicken breasts
Salt and pepper
Minced fresh parsley (¼ cup for each piece of chicken)
Flour
Bread crumbs
Beaten egg (slightly diluted with milk)

Snap breast bone out of breast by bending the meat sharply back from the bone. Pull out cartilage and separate rib bones from the flesh with a sharp paring knife. Remove skin and divide breasts. Season with salt and pepper, dredge with flour and shake off every bit of excess flour. Dip into beaten egg slightly diluted with milk, then coat thoroughly with fine crumbs, and again shake off all excess.

Sauté over a medium fire until golden and cooked through. Remove from fire. Cool sufficiently to handle. Using a pastry brush, coat lightly with beaten egg, then with chopped parsley. Press down parsley to make sure it adheres. (I prefer to coat the chicken all around with the parsley, but the effect is achieved if only the top is coated.)

Place in a warm oven (325°) and bake for about 10 to 15 minutes. Remove chicken from oven promptly, or the parsley will lose its fine green color. (Quartered chicken may also be used, but be sure to remove all skin.)

To make the chopped parsley a beautiful green, collect it in the corner of a thin towel or dish cloth. Bunch the cloth around the parsley and wet it thoroughly under running water for a few seconds. Wring it dry as you can; open it; shake the parsley onto a flat plate. It will be as green as the Emerald Isle.

Rabisha's recipe for Forcing Birds according to the French Fashion was a lesson obviously learned in foreign kitchens, and requires a steady hand, a sharp knife and patience. Here is the recipe for those who would like to attempt it:

Forcing Birds According to the French Fashion

Use *tender, small chickens weighing about 1 pound each.* (Rabisha called them "Peepers.") Split them up the back and remove the breast and rib bones, leaving the breast meat, legs and wings intact. Season the chickens inside and fill them with a loosely packed *stuffing.* Sew them up the back and roast them as you would any young birds. Very handsome, I'm sure, and worth the extra effort they entail, but this is one recipe I haven't tried.

Some of Rabisha's French recipes were unrecognizable, like the omelette he presented as "A Fryed Meat Called an Amlet." But in any case, there were few egg recipes in his book, or in most English cookbooks; Protestant Englishmen, unbound to fast days, could eat meat whenever they pleased. Salads were more to the English taste than eggs, and Rabisha glorified the art of salad-making with his Grand Sallet:

To Make a Grand Sallet for Spring

Your gardiner, or those that serve you with herbs, must supply you with all manner of Spring-Sallets, as buds of *Cowslips, Violets, Strawberries, Primrose, Brooklime, Watercresses, young Lettice, Spinnage, Alexander-buds,* or what other things may be got. Then take *Sampier, Olives, Capers, Broom-buds, Cowcumbers, Raisons* and *Currans parboyled, blanched Almonds, Barberries,* or what other pickles you can obtain. Then prepare your standard for the middle of your dish; it may be *a wax tree or a castle made of paste,* washed in the *yolks of eggs* and all made green with *herbs* and stuck with *flowers,* with about twelve supporters fastened in holes in your Castle and bending out to the middle of your dish. Then having *four rings of paste, one bigger than another,* place them so they rise like so many steps. This done, place your Sallet, a round of one sort on the uppermost ring and so round the others till you come to the dish; then place all your pickles from that to the brim and place the colors white against white and green against the green.

Garnish your dish with all things suitable or afforded by the Spring. Your statues ought to have Cruitts placed in their hands, two with *Vinegar* and two with *Oyl*, sized over on the outside and strowed with flowers.

When this Sallet is made, let it be carried to the Table, and when the guests are all placed, unstop the Cruitts, that the Oyl and Vinegar may run on the Sallet.

After the same manner may you make your Sallet in Summer, Autumn or Winter; only take those Sallets that are then in season, and change your Standard: in Summer you ought to resemble a green tree; in Autumn a Castle carved out of Carrets and Turnips; in the Winter, a tree hanged with Snow. This is only for Great Feasts, and we may inform the Practitioner for the honour of his Master and benefit of himself: the Paste that you make your Castle or Standard with, must be made of Rye.

As befitted the salad-loving English, the first book on salads, *Acetaria,* was written in 1699 by a noted English diarist and horticulturist, John Evelyn. His green salad was as classic as any to be found in a fine French restaurant today. The greens and herbs were to be chosen carefully: "All should fall into their place like the notes in music, in which there should be nothing harsh or grating." They were to be washed, placed in a strainer and "Swinged and shaken gently." As for the dressing, Evelyn favored a simple one of oil and vinegar—and warned against using too much oil!

In 1710 Patrick Lamb's *Royal Cookery* was published. Lamb had served in the royal kitchens for almost fifty years as master-cook to Charles II, James II, William and Mary, and Queen Anne. In the introduction to his book, he lauds the plenty and the greatness of Britain in all matters including food; and visitors, he says, must "lament their own barrenness whenever they reflected on the Flesh-pots they left behind them. For the want of which substantial and wholesome plenty, the Quelque Chose of France, and the Vines of Italy make no better amends than the surfeits and fevers they usually bring on such as deal in them."

Perhaps as a mark of respect to William of Orange, Lamb introduced Dutch methods to English cookbooks along with such recipes as Dutch fish sauce (hollandaise) and Dutch beef (dried beef). He included some French recipes, but stayed mostly on the English side, delighting his readers with the "Surprises" that were still a feature of the English table. But now, instead of live birds and frogs, unexpected foods were concealed inside rabbits, chickens or almost anything that could be hollowed out for the purpose. Lamb's Chicken Surprise was a chicken hash concealed in a covering of chopped meat shaped to resemble a French bread roll. And his stuffed cabbage is a surprise in itself—an interesting variation for those who like stuffed cabbage today, and quite different from the Middle-European version.

Forc'd Cabbage

12 *cabbage leaves, blanched in boiling water 2 or 3 minutes*
1 *to 1½ cups stock*

FORCEMEAT:

1 *pound raw veal ground with ⅛ pound salt pork*
1 *medium onion chopped fine*
¾ *cup large dry bread crumbs*
½ *cup grated cheese (Swiss, Gouda or any mild cheese suitable for grating)*
¼ *teaspoon salt*
Pepper
Dash of nutmeg

Combine the forcemeat and divide among the cabbage leaves. Roll each leaf around its forcemeat, lap the ends securely, and fasten with a toothpick if necessary. Shred some of the cabbage that remains and make a bed of it in the bottom of an earthenware casserole. Place the cabbage rolls on the shredded cabbage. The rolls may be browned in a skillet first; a browner gravy will result. Pour on 1 to 1½ cups stock. There should be enough to keep the shredded cabbage completely moist and to bubble up around the cabbage rolls. Cover and bake for 1 hour at 350°. Uncover and continue to bake at 350° for another hour or longer. Long cooking improves this dish. You may sprinkle 1 teaspoon caraway seeds over the shredded cabbage in the casserole.

The ideal accompaniment for this dish is fluffy mashed potatoes, topped with crisp fried onion rings.

The Queen's Royal Cookery by T. Hall also appeared in 1710. It has a special place in my affections as the first cookbook I acquired.

The ancient Daryol recipe was included, but it was now called Cream Custards, as if to conceal its former Norman identity. Those recipes that Hall did call French were about as French as haggis pudding. In fact, the bread-and-suet pudding he labeled French Pudding closely resembled the Scottish horror. He included mutton broth in the batter for Fritters in the French Fashion (La Varenne would have exploded!); and in general, Hall's French touch was that of a blacksmith's smiting an anvil.

But when T. Hall entered the realm of pies, where the English were the acknowledged masters, he was very good indeed. The English were so fond of these pasties that an entire section of Cheapside market, called Pye Corner, was devoted to their sale. T. Hall's book was printed at Pye Corner and he was a Freecook who probably sold fried pies at his own stall there when he wasn't hiring out as a caterer for a private dinner. His fried pies are cousins to apple turnovers, and his Taffety Tart is a delicious variation of apple pie.

Apple Pie-Patties

[OVEN-FRIED PIES]

Pastry for 6 individual pie-patties
6 medium-size quick-cooking apples, peeled, cored and chopped

Mix together:
½ cup sugar
1 teaspoon cinnamon
1 teaspoon flour
A few gratings of nutmeg

Roll pie pastry thin. Using a saucer as guide, cut pastry into 12 rounds, 2 for each "pie." Combine the apples with the spice mixture. Place a mound on each of 6 pastry circles. Cover with remaining circles. Moisten edges and seal tightly. Pierce tops with a fork as you would any pie. Melt ⅛ pound of butter and pour onto a heavy cookie sheet or baking dish large enough to accommodate the 6 pies. Bake in a preheated oven

(400°) for about 30 minutes. This is ideal for those lovers of pie-crust who never seem to get enough from a conventional serving.

Taffety Tart

Pastry for an 8-inch pie
8 large pie apples, sliced thin
1 lemon: rind grated, lemon pulp cut into small pieces
¾ cup sugar, blended with the grated lemon rind
2 tablespoons butter
Simple confectioners' sugar icing

Line the pie plate with crust and arrange the apples in layers. Between each layer sprinkle the lemon-sugar mixture and some of the chopped lemon pulp. Dot with butter, cover with a top crust and puncture for escaping steam. Bake at 450° for 10 minutes; reduce to 370°, bake for another 35 minutes. While pie is still warm, frost top with a simple icing of confectioner's sugar, milk and a bit of lemon juice. Thin to a spreading consistency.

Hall's helter-skelter arrangement of recipes included random beauty hints for housewives, one of which, "A Beauty Mask used by the ladies of France," closely resembles today's cold cream.

But despite the continued reference to France, the French recipes in English cookbooks were becoming more and more English all the time. English housewives wanted less of French goings-on. Also, they wanted less advice from men on kitchen matters.

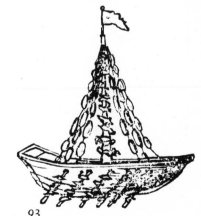

A little boat rigged with sausages (an early forerunner of cocktail sausages used decoratively). From Traité Historique et Pratique de la Cuisine, ou le Cuisinier Instruit. 1758.

93

6

18th-Century

France

GIFTS FROM THE PROVINCES

FRENCH ENCYCLOPEDIAS have surprisingly little information—and not even the first names—of Marin and Menon, who were the Manet and Monet of French cuisine. In the eighteenth century, these two led cooks into new and broader realms of the culinary art, and like the Impressionist painters, they reached out to the provinces and rural France for inspiration.

Marin's book, *Les Dons de Comus* (Gifts from the God of Joy), appeared in 1739. The gifts were intended to brighten the tables of the bourgeoisie. (This word did not appear, however, even in a subtitle.) Although the elaborate table of the nobility was not

LES DONS
DE COMUS,
O U
L'ART DE LA CUISINE,
REDUIT EN PRATIQUE,
NOUVELLE EDITION,
Revue , corrigée & augmentée par l'Auteur.
TOME PREMIER.
Le prix eft de fept livres dix fols relié.

A PARIS,
Chez la Veuve P i s s o t, Quai de Conti, à la
Croix d'Or, à la defcente du Pont-Neuf,
au coin de la rue de Nevers.

M. DCC L.
Avec Approbation & Privilége du Roi.

Title page and illustrated frontispiece depicting Comus, the god of joy, from
Les Dons de Comus, *by Marin. The 1750 edition.*

set for Parisian businessmen and lesser government officials who
lived in "Homes of Less consequence," this was a way of life these
gentlemen wanted to copy. Marin was ready with expert advice
on how a member of the bourgeoisie could eat like a prince, even
if his kitchen staff consisted of a single cook.

"I recognize that the cuisine of Comus is not practical for all,"
wrote Marin, "but with proper pots and pans, fresh food purchased
each morning and a good bouillon [which he termed the *soul* of
cooking], even third-class persons can dine with grace." He added,
"I cannot hope to please everyone, so I am selecting the recipes that
please *me*." The fact is that Marin wanted *everybody* to buy his

cookbook, and some of his hearty country dishes, like the following Carbonnade de Boeuf and the Côtelettes de Veau, were directed to the most provincial tastes:

Carbonnade de Boeuf à la Lyonnaise

For this, use *thin slices of beef* (2 pounds of meat) cut from the shoulder, chuck or round. Pound them as thin as you can and divide into pieces about 2 by 4 inches (as you would for escalopes, which is what they really are). Season with *salt* and *pepper*.

Brown quickly in hot fat and transfer to a casserole in layers. Between each layer of meat sprinkle some of the following mixture: 2 *tablespoons chopped fresh basil* (or 1 tablespoon dried); 2 *tablespoons chopped fresh watercress; 1 tablespoon dried tarragon* (or 2 tablespoons fresh); *¼ cup sliced shallots* (or white scallion ends), and 1 *tablespoon chopped fresh chervil* (optional). Now add *½ cup beef stock* (or bouillon cube dissolved) and 1 *cup red wine or beer.**

Cover and bake in a slow oven (325°) for 2½ hours, longer if necessary. If needed, add more liquid to maintain a suitable quantity of gravy. The gravy should be free of all fat before the Carbonnade is presented at the table. The easiest way to skim thoroughly is to strain the gravy into another dish and chill briefly until the fat rises to the top and can be removed easily. Excellent served with equally hearty broad noodles.

Côtelettes de Veau à la Provençale

Veal loin or rib chops, cut double-thick
Anchovy fillets
Salt and pepper
Flour
Butter and oil, for browning the meat
½ cup dry white wine
2 finely minced shallots or 2 minced scallion ends

MARINADE:
Equal parts oil and vinegar
1 *teaspoon orégano, added to marinade*
1 *clove garlic, crushed, added to marinade*

---

* Marin did not use beer, but most Carbonnades are now made Flemish style with beer. Whether the Carbonnade was conceived first by the Flemish or the French is not clear. At any rate, it is an ancient and hearty dish.

The ideal way is to "lard" the veal chops with the anchovy fillets by pulling the anchovy fillets through them, but if you lack a larding needle, or the expertise to use it, make gashes at the sides of the chops and insert slivers of anchovy. Place the veal chops thus prepared in the marinade and allow them to remain for at least 2 hours, turning once. Remove from marinade and blot dry with paper toweling. Season lightly with salt (remember the anchovies provide some salt) and pepper to taste. Heat a mixture of butter and oil in a heavy skillet, brown the chops and transfer to a casserole.

Add the wine, lemon juice, shallots and parsley to the casserole, cover tightly, and let chops bake in a moderate oven (350°) for 30 minutes, or longer if necessary. They are done when a fork pierces them easily. Three-quarters of a cup of cream may be substituted for the wine, with delicious results. Puréed lentils were much favored by Marin, and would make a hearty and suitable accompaniment for this dish.

MENON'S FIRST BOOK, *Nouveau Traité de la Cuisine* (A New Work of Cookery) also appeared in 1739, but Menon did not compete for popular attention until later when he saw how successful Marin's book had been. Menon wanted nothing to do with the "third class," and quickly made this clear. "I will not bother with Basse Boucherie (low meats) since this is only used by the lower classes," he said. "My dishes use only those parts and cuts that are known to the better classes—the Bourgeois—who keep a good table."

Marin, who catered happily to all classes, considered no meat too low in the scale for his book. Ears, cheeks, tails, feet, even the eyes, all were used by him. He demonstrated the versatility of the total animal in a series of menus, each based entirely on one beast and its by-products. "Most of these dishes are pure caprice," he wrote of them. But any chef who could devise a dinner ranging from soup to dessert—eighteen dishes—made of beef in some form had to be taken seriously as an inventive and pioneering spirit. (These menus were imitated and talked about right through the nineteenth century, but no one ever credited them to Marin.)

Both authors included many earlier recipes such as the ancient

Darioles, but more than a hint of the future was evident in Marin's book. He pioneered by introducing the first extensive list of sauces to French cookbooks. By actual count there are one hundred in his Sauces Particulières section. These start with Béchamel, evidently already well known in French kitchens, though this is the first description of it by name in cookbooks. It was clearly a culinary invention of Louis XIV's time and bears the name of his maître d'hôtel, the Marquis de Béchameil, an undistinguished man undeserving of such immortality.

I am not sure that Marin originated any of the hundred sauces he described, but his use of some as a "wardrobe" for a perfectly roasted bird was certainly an original idea. A perfectly roasted chicken could be transformed into any one of seven superlative dishes by means of a simple sauce. Menon admired this idea and copied it, though he did change a few sauces. The best suggestions of both authors follow. The technique is the same in each case: each sauce utilizes, in part, the pan juices of the bird.

An illustration from the frontispiece of Dictionarium Domesticum, *by Nathan Bailey. 1736.*

SEVEN SAUCES FOR A ROAST CHICKEN
The Perfectly Roasted Bird

Season a *tender roasting chicken* inside and out with *salt, pepper* and *a pinch of ginger*. Smooth *1½ tablespoons of softened butter* over the breast and legs of the bird, truss the wings and tie the legs. Place the bird in an open roasting pan with a *whole onion*. (The roasting pan should fit the bird and not be so large that the juices fail to collect properly. I find that a concave-bottom savory roaster does the best job.) Roast at 375° for about an hour and a half. (A large chicken will require longer.) Let it get underway for 30 minutes, then baste it with the pan juices at least four times during the remaining hour. Turn it as needed, to brown thoroughly on all sides. Test the upper drumstick with a fork for doneness, and when the chicken is tender, remove it and the onion from the pan. Scrape the sides of the roasting pan and loosen the brown residue left by the onion. To loosen further this collected goodness, swirl it with some of the liquid to be employed in the sauce.

1. Foie Gras Sauce

Butter
½ cup bouillon (or brown stock)
1 medium onion, chopped fine
The liver of the chicken
Salt and pepper

Melt 1 tablespoon butter in a small skillet. Sauté the liver until just tender; do not overcook. While still warm, force the liver through a coarse sieve with a wooden spoon. Set aside. Rinse out the skillet, melt fresh butter, and sauté the minced onion until transparent and beginning to turn color. (Stir it constantly to prevent heavy browning.) Add the liver purée to the onion. Blend well and add the bouillon and salt and pepper to taste. Combine this mixture and the strained pan juices of the chicken.

99

2. A Sauce of Grapes

1 *small can seedless grapes (or 1 cup fresh seedless grapes, parboiled for 1 minute)*
1 *tablespoon butter*
½ *tablespoon flour*
2 *whole cloves*
½ *cup dry white wine*
¼ *cup chicken stock or bouillon, heated*

Make a brown roux of the butter and flour, by cooking together for a minute or so until smooth and golden. Add the chicken stock and the cloves, stir again. Add the white wine, and when well combined, pour the entire mixture into the roasting pan. Bring to the boil and let simmer gently on top of the stove for a few minutes. Strain back into the saucepan; add the grapes. The sauce is now ready (and takes kindly to a sweet potato croquette along with the chicken).

3. Caper Cream Sauce

2 *tablespoons drained capers*
2-4 *tablespoons dry white wine*
¼ *cup sour cream, or ¼ cup Half and Half, soured*

After removing the chicken, add the wine to the pan juices and bring to a boil. Cool slightly, then slowly blend in the sour cream. Whisk until smooth, then strain through a fine mesh sieve to remove any little browned particles that may have loosened from the pan. Add the capers. Reheat if necessary, but don't allow sauce to come to a boil.

4. Pistachio Sauce

2 tablespoons brown sugar
1 tablespoon lemon juice
½ cup light red wine
¼ teaspoon ground nutmeg
¼ cup slivered pistachio nuts

In a saucepan combine the brown sugar, lemon juice, wine and nutmeg. Simmer together for 5 minutes. Pour into the roasting pan and blend with the pan juices. When thoroughly blended, strain back into the saucepan. Add the pistachio nuts and reheat only to serving temperature.

5. Sauce aux Petits Oeufs

[EGG SAUCE]

1 hard-cooked egg yolk, riced
2 tablespoons sautéed mushrooms, finely chopped (optional)
¾ cups chicken broth or chicken bouillon

Add the chicken broth to the pan juices. Bring sauce to the boiling point and let simmer for a few minutes. Taste for seasoning, and add salt and pepper if needed. If mushrooms are used, add them now and heat thoroughly. The egg yolk is to be stirred in just before the sauce is removed from the pan for serving.

6. Sultane Sauce

¼ cup red wine
2 slices lemon
2 whole cloves
1 bay leaf
1 scallion, top and bulb, finely minced
1 tablespoon currant jelly

Combine all the above ingredients in a saucepan and simmer for a few minutes. Strain into the roasting pan and blend thoroughly with the pan juices. Bring to the boiling point.

Cooked rice, lightly coated with rich chicken broth and mixed with chopped cashew nuts and raisins, is a receptive starch for this sauce.

7. Ravigote Sauce

½ cup bouillon (or brown stock)
1 tablespoon vinegar
1 tablespoon each (minced): tarragon, chervil, watercress and chives
1 clove garlic, crushed

This is the easiest sauce of all. Pour all the above into the roasting pan and bring the sauce to the boiling point. Taste, and add salt and pepper if necessary. The sauce may be served with the greens swimming in it (my preference), or it may be strained through a fine strainer.

This sauce takes kindly to macaroni or thin spaghetti which has been tossed with melted butter and grated cheese.

Marin dropped out of the competition after setting the pattern for eighteenth-century French cookbooks. Menon went on to become the foremost writer on cookery, and the most prolific of the century. In 1746 his *La Cuisinière Bourgeoise* appeared. Although the title was plain-spoken, Menon was still self-conscious about writing a popular cookbook. But his next book, *Les Soupers de la Cour* (Suppers of the Court), despite its haughty title, used all the parts of the animal he had disdained to touch in his earlier works. Today we would ignore his Stuffed Calf's Ears, but his Stuffed Onions— part of his recipe for A Matelote Fit for a General—are a delicious garnish or side dish.

Stuffed Onions

12 mild Spanish or Bermuda onions
Bread crumbs
Butter

FORCEMEAT:
½ cup of the removed center portion of onions, chopped
1 cup chopped cooked meat (poultry, veal or ham)
1 cup diced cooked potatoes
⅛ teaspoon each: thyme and sage
Salt and pepper

Parboil the onions 8 to 10 minutes in boiling salted water. Drain, then remove centers, leaving a thick onion "wall." Fill the onions with the forcemeat.

Brush onions with melted butter, and arrange in a buttered baking dish. Sprinkle white bread crumbs over tops, dot with butter, and bake at 350° for about 35 minutes. Brown the onions under broiler for the last 5 minutes of cooking, if you prefer a crisp exterior. Brush with additional melted butter before placing under broiler.

With the publication of *Soupers de la Cour,* Menon went all out to please bourgeois tastes for simple, country foods. His Terrine Paysanne is similar to Beef Bourguinon, and probably its forerunner. Menon included brandy in the stew; I do the same.

Terrine Paysanne
[THE PEASANT'S POT]

3 *pounds of cubed stewing beef*
¼ *pound slab bacon or salt pork, cubed*
Salt and pepper
10 *scallion bulbs*
1 *bay leaf*
¼ *teaspoon whole or ground thyme*
Several sprigs of fresh parsley, tied
2 *stalks celery*
¼ *cup brandy*
1 *cup red wine*
1 *cup beef stock or bouillon*

Render the bacon cubes until they are fairly crisp. Lift out with a per- forated spoon and drain on absorbent paper. Cook the scallions gently in the hot fat until they begin to take on color, but keep them whole. Drain them. Season beef with salt and pepper to taste and brown quickly in the same hot fat. Lift out and drain. Transfer meat, bacon cubes and scallions to a casserole, preferably of earthenware. Add the herbs, par- sley and celery. Cover with the liquid, place in a slow oven (300°) and simmer for 3 to 3½ hours, or until meat is quite tender. Skim off *all* fat. If necessary, strain off the gravy and chill to remove fat easily.

Menon's Veal Villageoise will add interest to an informal dinner and tempt city and country appetites alike. I have taken one liberty with this recipe and added cheese. Otherwise, it is exactly as Menon directed.

Veal Villageoise

[VEAL, COUNTRY FASHION]

Use *veal from the leg or loin,* cut as thin as possible and then flattened further with a mallet or the side of a cleaver. Cut into 3-by-4-inch pieces. (Torn parts will usually seal together in the cooking.)

Have ready an equal number of pieces of *boiled ham,* and an equal number of *½-inch sticks of Swiss-type cheese,* each stick 1½ inches long. Season the veal to taste with *salt* and *pepper.* Wrap each stick of cheese in a piece of ham, lapping ends securely. Now wrap each piece of ham in veal, again lapping ends. If necessary, tie veal or fasten with toothpick.

Brown the veal rolls in hot *fat.* Drain and transfer to an earthenware casserole. Mince 2 *or* 3 *shallots* and sauté lightly in *butter.* Add to the casserole. Cover, and bake in a moderate oven (350°) for 35 to 45 minutes, or until meat is tender when tested with a fork. If necessary as baking progresses, pour in enough liquid to keep the veal rolls moist and to provide a gravy. This liquid should be equal parts of *white wine* and *bouillon* (or stock).

The term "au gratin" began to appear in French cookbooks at this time. Apparently it was a new culinary term, and English translations of the French cookbooks carefully explained its meaning. A dish *au gratin* was sauced, then cooked in its own serving dish until the sauce had "caught" at the sides and bottom of the dish. Menon's Gratin of Tongue is as innocent of cheese as most Gratins. And delicious.

A Gratin of Tongue with Tarragon

Boiled smoked or pickled tongue, 3 to 3½ pounds, cut into thin
slices
2 tablespoons chopped fresh tarragon (or 1 tablespoon dry)
1 tablespoon capers
1 tablespoon cornstarch dissolved in 3 tablespoons water
½ cup bouillon or stock
½ cup red wine
1 teaspoon anise extract

Butter a shallow baking dish and arrange the sliced tongue in 2 or 3
layers, sprinkling capers and tarragon between the layers. Combine the
stock with the cornstarch and warm on top of the stove, stirring until
smooth. Taste for seasoning, and add salt and pepper if necessary. Add
the anise extract and red wine to the stock, and pour mixture over the
tongue. Place in a moderate oven (375°) and bake for 30 to 40 minutes,
or until the sauce "catches" at the side of the pan.

Menon's *Soupers de la Cour* was undoubtedly inspired by the
popularity the late-day meal had acquired at the court of Louis XV.
Sweets were important supper dishes. Menon offered many, including a recipe for Ices made as ice cream often is today, with a custard
base. The mixture was placed in a pewter container, buried in salt
and ice, and the cream beaten continuously with a spoon till it
began to freeze. We've improved on ice cream since the eighteenth
century, but Menon's whole apple baked in pastry ribbons is still
an attractive dessert. The recipe appears on page 106.

Apples Farbalant
[APPLES FESTOONED]

6 baking apples
1½ cups water
½ cup sugar
¼ teaspoon ground cinnamon
1 teaspoon lemon juice
1 teaspoon jam or jelly
3 teaspoons butter
6 teaspoons orange marmalade
Rich pastry for a large pie, made from any standard recipe

Core the apples almost through. Pare them. Combine the water, sugar, cinnamon, lemon juice and jam. Cook the apples in this syrup for 3 minutes. Fill the cavity of each apple with ½ teaspoon of butter and a teaspoon of orange marmalade. Chill.

Preheat oven to 450°. Roll out half the pastry into a large circle. Using an inverted teacup or biscuit cutter, cut out 6 pastry circles. Roll the remaining dough into long strips, and cut the strips into 6 ¾-inch widths.

Place 1 apple on each pastry circle, and gather the pastry around the sides of the apple, pinching the pastry to make it keep its shape. Loosely wind one of the long thin pastry strips around each apple but leave the top exposed.

Bake 20 minutes. Reduce the heat to 375° and bake 30 minutes longer or until the crust is golden. Sprinkle the apples with granulated sugar and place under the broiler for a minute or so until the sugar begins to melt.

Menon was so prolific that his books were often in competition with one another. He is even credited with books probably written by others. One of these is *Le Cuisinier Instruit* (The Well-Taught Cook) of 1758. It is doubtful that Menon wrote this, partly because it differs greatly from his books in organization and style. Also, the tone of humility is most unlike him. The author disclaims any knowledge of belles-lettres, apologizes for his grammatical errors, admits he owes a debt to the experienced chefs who taught him, and offers his book as an aid to amateurs.

Leaving aside the question of who wrote *Le Cuisinier Instruit,* this recipe from the book will still help an amateur cook turn out a handsome success:

Poulets à la Dom Phillipe

Split 2 *tender young broiling chickens* up the back; break and remove the breast-bone, cartilage, and as many of the ribs as will come away easily. Carefully loosen the outer skin of the breast meat, but do not remove it. Flatten the chickens and season them with *salt* and *pepper.*

Prepare a forcemeat using the following ingredients: *1 cup dried bread crumbs; ¼ teaspoon thyme; a pinch of nutmeg; 2 mashed hard-boiled egg yolks;* and *the livers of the chickens,* sautéed, then chopped. Mix the forcemeat with enough *melted butter* to bind it. Spread it on the chicken breasts, *underneath* the loosened skin.

Place the flattened chickens, skin side *up,* in a large baking or broiling pan. Roast uncovered at 375°, basting with melted butter until the skin is crisply browned and the chickens tender. (This dish gets a rave reception at my table.)

By THIS TIME, the French were borrowing a few ideas from the English, and "à l'Anglaise" was attached to many recipes, while "rostbif" was adopted as a general term for *any* joint of meat, with such results as "Rostbif of Lamb." In 1735 the French also translated an English cookbook, *The Modern Cook* by Vincent La Chapelle, who had been chief cook to the Prince of Orange and the Earl of Chesterfield.

The first restaurant came into being in Paris in 1765 when M. Boulanger, who sold a variety of hot soups as quick restoratives or "restaurantes," added a dish of sheep's feet to his soup menu (probably the Sauce d'Enfer of sheep's feet described in Chapter 4). The traiteurs—members of one of the many guilds, and dealers in ready-cooked meats—promptly brought suit. Boulanger won the case (and enough publicity to bring his sheep's feet to the attention of Louis XV). While the inns of the time provided only a fixed meal, at Boulanger's establishment one had a choice of *restaurantes.* The term later came to be applied to all establishments that offered a choice of foods. It was around 1782, however, that

the first real restaurant was introduced to Paris by Antoine Beauvilliers, a chef who had been in the service of the Count de Provence. Beauvillier's inspiration came not from Boulanger but from
the English, who had long been accustomed to dining out. He
acknowledged his debt by calling his establishment "La Grande
Taverne de Londres."

Meanwhile, there were no new French cookbooks, translated or
otherwise. The French suddenly stopped producing them late in
the reign of Louis XV, although life at Court was as lavish as ever,
and the continued success of Menon's *Les Soupers de la Cour*
proved that many were still interested in imitating a King's ways.
No new cookbooks appeared to share the inventions of Louis XVI's
table with the public: none were to come until after the Revolution.
When they did appear, they revealed that French cuisine had entered a new phase.

7

18th-Century
England

THE GOOD HOUSEWIVES
AS AUTHORS

W OMEN CAN SPIN very well, but they cannot write a good book of cookery," Samuel Johnson declared. If he hoped to stop the tidal wave of women cookbook authors, he failed utterly. Women finally seized the pen from men early in the eighteenth century and wrote most of the best-selling cookbooks that came thereafter.

Although there had been one or two women writers before, the century of the female cookbook author was really ushered in by Mary Kettilby in 1714, with *A Collection of Above Three Hundred Receipts in Cookery, Physick and Surgery*. In her Introduction she wrote: "I can assure you, that a number of very Curious and Deli-

A
COLLECTION
Of above Three Hundred
R E C E I P T S
I N
Cookery,
Phyfick *and* Surgery;
For the Ufe of all
Good Wives, Tender Mothers,
and Careful Nurfes.

By feveral Hands.

L O N D O N,
Printed for R I C H A R D W I L K I N, at the
King's Head in *St. Paul's Church-yard.*
M DCC XIV.

Title page of book by Mary Kettilby, one of the early female authors of English cookbooks. 1714.

cate House-wives Clubb'd to furnish out this Collection, for the Service of Young and Unexperienced Dames, who may from hence be Instructed in the Polite Management of their Kitchins, and the Art of Adorning their Tables with a Splendid Frugality." She says it may also "Teach Cookmaids at Country Inns to serve us up a very agreeable Meal, from such provisions as are Plainest."

As a pioneer in a man's world, Mary Kettilby was somewhat defensive about the simplicity of her recipes. "A poor woman must be laugh'd at for only sugaring a mess of beans . . ." she wrote meekly, then straightened up and threw a verbal skillet at her male competitors, ". . . whilst a great name must be had in admiration for contriving relishes a thousand times more distasteful to the palate." Apparently she pleased many palates with such simple recipes as this one for Thin Cream Pancakes Call'd a Quire of Paper. Her book was snapped up, and she quickly issued a paper-bound supplement; edition after edition appeared until 1757.

Thin Cream Pancakes Call'd a Quire of Paper

1 *pint light cream combined with ¼ pound melted butter*
8 *eggs*
3 *tablespoons flour*
3 *tablespoons sherry*
1 *tablespoon sugar*
¼ *teaspoon orange extract*
Dash of grated nutmeg

Combine all the ingredients except the flour. Add a little of the liquid to the flour, slowly, in order to keep it smooth. When the flour is well diluted and smooth, add it to the balance of the batter. Have ready a small heavy skillet, preferably one 6 inches in diameter. Heat, until a small dab of butter will foam in it. Use only enough of the batter to run thinly over the entire bottom of the skillet. Cook until golden. Turn and finish on the other side. Sprinkle each pancake with granulated sugar, piling them one on top of another as evenly as possible. Keep warm in the oven. A dab of orange marmalade or any jelly on top of the hot stack is a handsome finish and will melt and ooze down the sides.

Mrs. Kettilby's recipe makes 20 6-inch pancakes. These pancakes will wait patiently in a warm oven until you are ready to serve them.

Unlike most of her contemporaries, Mary Kettilby spoke favor-

One of many illustrations in The Whole Duty of a Woman. *1737.*

Wild Boar Pie

ably of French recipes, and offered an excellent one "To make French Cutlets Very Good."

French Cutlets, Very Good

6 *double-rib veal chops, with a pocket for stuffing*
¼ *cup sweet cream*
Butter and oil

STUFFING:

1 *cup toasted stale bread, diced*
½ *cup chopped mushrooms, sautéed*
2 *shallots, chopped fine and slightly sautéed*
1 *teaspoon parsley, chopped*
¼ *teaspoon thyme*
Pepper and salt to taste
1 *egg yolk to bind mixture*

Prepare a stuffing using the ingredients listed above. Insert stuffing in pockets of chops, fasten with a toothpick, and brown chops in a mixture of butter and oil. Transfer to a covered casserole and bake at 350° for 20 to 25 minutes. Warm the cream and stir into the juices collected in the casserole.

Lima beans, sprinkled with fresh parsley and combined with butter and a dash of cream, make an excellent starch with this dish.

In 1727 Eliza Smith's *The Compleat Housewife* appeared. "It has grown as unfashionable for a book to appear in public without a preface, as for a lady to appear without a hoop-skirt," wrote Eliza Smith. She boasted of her thirty years' experience as a cook, and then delivered a broadside against the French: "To our disgrace, we have admired the French tongue and French messes," she said, calling French chefs "upstarts who do such preposterous recipes as stuffing a roast leg of mutton with pickled herring." (Atrocities of this kind were all too common in English cookbooks, but the French could hardly have been blamed for them.)

She supplied a generous selection of medical recipes, including one for "A Distemper Got by an Ill Husband." From various comments in other cookbooks (most of them also supplied medical

Illustrated frontispiece of The Compleat Housewife, by Eliza Smith. The
1750 edition.

recipes), one suspects the condition was a hangover; Eliza treated it with a dose of nutmeg, sugar, cinnamon and gumdragon.

In the matter of recipes, Eliza was on solid ground. She stood over the housewife and told her how to garnish a dish. And she had a nice flair for compatible combinations. We serve pork with apple-sauce today, and she appears to have been the first English cook-book writer to suggest it. She garnished broiled steaks with minced shallots mixed with butter and vinegar—what could be simpler? Her pickled mushrooms and pickled beans later became standard. Eliza's way with shrimp or fresh tongue, is as good now as it was in 1727.

Buttered Shrimp

This is an attractive dish to prepare at the table in a chafing dish. Equally attractive prepared in the kitchen in a double-boiler, and brought to the table in a ring of curried rice.

> 1 *pound shrimp, cooked, shelled and deveined*
> ½ *cup Rhine wine or any dry white wine*
> 2 *tablespoons butter*
> 2 *egg yolks*
> *A grating of nutmeg*

Melt the butter, add the wine, and when the mixture is warm add the shrimp. Cook together for a few minutes until the shrimp are thoroughly heated and the wine and butter mixture is quite hot (but *not* so hot that it will curdle the egg yolks). Add 1 tablespoon of the hot liquid to the beaten egg yolks; repeat until egg yolks are sufficiently diluted and all danger of curdling is past. Then add the eggs to the shrimp and stir constantly and watchfully until mixture begins to thicken slightly. Remove from heat and stir in a grating of nutmeg.

Roasted Fresh Tongue

Cover a *fresh beef tongue* with cold water. Bring it to the boil and reduce heat to a gentle simmer. Add 2 *tablespoons vinegar* and 1 *bay leaf* to the water. Cover and cook for 2 hours. Skin the tongue while it is hot, and trim off all unwanted parts and excess fat. Stud tongue with *12 whole cloves* and place it in a roasting pan. Pour over it *¼ cup pickle juice* (from sweet pickles or pickled onions) mixed with 3 *tablespoons melted butter*. Baste with this mixture until tongue is tender to the touch of a fork. Roast, covered, at 350° for about 1½ hours, basting at least four times. Turn the tongue, if necessary, to keep the top from drying.

Lentils have a natural affinity for tongue and make a nice companion for this dish.

Eliza Smith offered her readers a choice of menus, and these menus were touched with bits of vivid description, all clues to the early-Georgian table of better-class families. For example, for the first course: Chicken and Bacon; Scotch Collops (this meant "scotch'd" or scored; collops were the English version of the French Escalope and the Italian Scallopini); Giblet Pie; A fine Boil'd Pudding; Roast Beef with Horseradish and Pickles Around. These dishes were removed, and the second course was then placed on the table: Three Woodcocks with Toasts (so few of the small birds indicated that Eliza's dinners were planned for a small family circle); A Tansey Garnish'd with Oranges; A Hare with Savoury Pudding (the pudding being a stuffing inside the hare); and A Buttered Apple Pie, Hot.

The men washed this repast down with wine. "Habit has made a pint of wine after dinner almost necessary to a man who eats freely," wrote an author of the period. After dinner, the ladies were excused from the dining room and the men lingered on to enjoy their cigars.

Another cookbook shows that the men were dallying in other quarters as well and were frequently the seducers of servant maids. The virtue of female domestics was evidently in great jeopardy at the time, and the subject was harangued from lecture platforms and pulpits as well as books. In 1743 *A Present for a Serving-Maid* appeared, and although it guided servants through simple recipes, it laid most emphasis on Deportment, with such chapter-headings as: "Chastity; Temptations from the Master," with a break-down by age and station of all male tempters ("If a Single Man; If a Married Man; If the Master's Son; If from the Gentlemen Lodgers").

THE MID-EIGHTEENTH CENTURY was a time of violent reaction against anything French, and the cookbooks clearly reflected this. Hannah Glasse, whose undeserved fame rests on a remark she never made—"First catch your hare"—raised the loudest voice of all in her *The Art of Cookery, Made Plain and Easy*, 1747. "If gentlemen will have French cooks," she said, "they must pay for French tricks." She ranted on against "the blind folly of this age, that would rather be imposed on by a French booby, than give encouragement to a good English cook!"

Despite her tone, Hannah included many French recipes in her book, as well she might: French cookery was far simpler than the involved "English" procedures Hannah presented in her book. She mangled French words ruthlessly and committed a few crimes against the English language as well, but, aware of her shortcomings, she asked the reader's indulgence "if I have not wrote in the high polite style." (Hannah was the target of Samuel Johnson's statement at the beginning of this chapter. Her book was believed by some to be the work of a Dr. Hill, but Dr. Johnson said it contained too many errors for that. For example, said Johnson, Hill would know that saltpeter and sal prunella were the same; Mrs. Glasse did not.)

She had evidently given diligent study to *The Whole Duty of a Woman*, published ten years earlier, which offered 514 pages of recipes in a section on The Art of Cookery, along with 175 pages on moral conduct. Here, French recipes were welcome—from Cutlets à la Maintenon to Sole in Champagne, it was vive la France all the way!

Veal Cutlets Maintenon

These cutlets baked in paper cases are supposed to be the invention of Mme de Maintenon, last companion of Louis XIV's twilight years. They are *veal rib chops,* baked in paper cases with a bit of bone protruding from the case.

To make them, prepare a topping for 6 chops as follows: Combine *½ pound mushrooms which have been sautéed in butter and chopped fine; 2 or 3 slices of boiled ham, minced fine;* and *3 shallots or 1 medium onion, chopped fine and slightly sautéed.*

Season the chops with salt, pepper and a dash of nutmeg. Sauté them gently in butter mixed with oil until they are nicely browned and about ready to eat.

An ordinary sheet of white paper (8½ by 11 inches), folded in half, will do for the case. Brush salad oil on the inside. Lay the sautéed chop on the paper, bone side against the fold, bone end protruding. Divide the topping into 6 portions and spread each chop with its share. Double over the edges of the paper securely at top and side, then pleat or fold paper around the chop to conform to its shape. Fasten with toothpicks or a paper clip, if necessary. Place on a baking sheet and bake at 350° for about 15 minutes, or until paper begins to brown. (Everything is precooked, and the object now is to mingle the flavors.)

The chops may be served in their paper cases (if attractive enough to pass muster), or they may be removed from the cases and arranged in a circle on a platter, bones pointing out like the spokes of a wheel. In the center of the platter, group stuffed tomatoes—an excellent accompaniment, and attractive with the mushroom-topped chops.

Fillets of Flounder in Champagne, with Shrimp Sauce

Champagne, in early eighteenth-century cookbooks, might have meant any white wine made in that province of France; however, if you have any leftover Champagne, use it for this dish by all means.

> 4 *large fillets of flounder or sole* (1 *per serving*)
> *Butter*
> ½ *cup white wine*
> ¼ *cup finely chopped boiled or canned shrimp*

The fillets should have all skin removed and be thoroughly rinsed. Blot them dry. Season to taste. Lay them in a serving-baking dish and dot liberally with butter. Broil for 8 to 10 minutes. Pour on the wine, sprinkle with the chopped shrimp, and transfer to a preheated oven (350°). Bake for 10 minutes, or until the fillets are tender. That's all there is to this simple, but superb, way of preparing flounder fillets.

Portrait of Mrs. Sarah Phillips. From her book, The Ladies Handmaid. *1758.*

The Ladies Handmaid by Sarah Phillips appeared in 1758. Mrs. Phillips' portrait, appropriately wreathed by the carcasses of a hare, a fish and several species of fowl, greets the reader from the frontispiece, and her energetic, highly personal style rings from every page. "It needs very few arguments to persuade people to prefer a good dinner to a bad one," she announced at the start. And her remarks on fish preparation were almost as bloodstained as those in the medieval *Forme of Cury:* "Rip open the belly. Gut it. Strip it and hack it with a knife." She was gentler with her recipes, however, though always direct. "Some people don't love any sage in the pig," she said, when writing of a sauce to serve with a porker.

At least two of her recipes seem quite original today, and both would enhance a summer menu:

Mutton (or Lamb) Kebob'd

Buy a *loin of mutton or lamb,* allowing 2 chops per serving if it is of young lamb. Cut down between the chops all the way to the bone, but do not sever. Season with *salt, pepper, ground thyme* and *crushed rosemary,* sprinkling down between each chop. Clap the chops together again (the verb is Mrs. Phillips'), and tie the loin securely to keep the chops close together while they cook. Fasten to a barbecue spit and roast over a quick fire.

Blend and heat the following mixture to use as a basting sauce: 2

118

tablespoons melted butter; 2 *tablespoons cooking oil;* ¼ *cup vinegar,* and 2 *tablespoons catsup.*

Along with this serve Mrs. Mann's Ohio Pudding or Mrs. Kellogg's Corn Puffs (see Index for both recipes), and combine the eighteenth and nineteenth centuries at your next barbecue dinner.

Beef Vinaigrette

This is a delicious way to serve potted beef in the summer.

Use *a first-cut brisket, a thick Swiss steak or any cut of beef that lends itself to pot-roasting* and can be sliced attractively. Rub it with *salt* and *pepper* to taste. Place in a heavy stewing pot with a tight cover. Add enough *water* to come up about ½ inch in the pot. To this add ½ *cup dry white wine.* Now add: *1 bay leaf;* 3 *sprigs parsley;* 1 *small onion;* ¼ *teaspoon whole allspice,* and ½ *teaspoon dried tarragon (or 1 teaspoon fresh).* Cover tightly and pot roast on top of the stove until the meat is tender. Turn it once to make sure meat cooks well on both sides.

Lift from the broth and chill thoroughly before slicing. Arrange the slices so that the meat presents its original, uncut appearance. Serve on a bed of *cubed meat aspic* (see below), sprinkle *capers* over top of meat and surround with *lemon slices.*

Cold, canned kidney beans (first rinsed in water) with dill and French dressing go well with this.

FOR ASPIC: Chill the *remaining broth* so that every vestige of fat can be removed. Reheat and season broth well; add *vinegar or tomato juice* or whatever your taste dictates to bring the quantity up to 1¼ cups liquid. Dissolve *1 tablespoon plain gelatin* in ½ *cup cold water* and promptly add to it the hot broth. The simple rule to remember: ½ cup cold water and 1¼ cups hot liquid to 1 tablespoon gelatin.

Mrs. Phillips' soundest advice concerned vegetables. Overcooked vegetables are popularly supposed to characterize English cuisine, and eighteenth-century cookbooks boiled them to death. Sarah Phillips was the one exception. Her instructions in *The Ladies Handmaid* read like the most modern directions one could find today.

For spinach, she directed: "Don't put any water in, but shake the pan often. As soon as you find the greens are shrunk and fallen to the bottom, and the liquor which comes out of them boils up, they are enough." And she advised serving them with butter. She dispatched cabbage, broccoli and string beans in the same way, repeatedly warning: "They will be quickly done; take care they don't lose their fine green."

It's too bad more women didn't read her advice. The book apparently had an extremely limited circulation, and is unknown today to most bibliographers (which makes it even more of a treasure in my collection).

Few men were daring enough to invade what had by now become a female realm. To make his voice heard above the din of women authors, a man had to be a noted chef, preferably in the employ of a nobleman. Lord Chesterfield's cook, Vincent La Chapelle, had succeeded in 1733 with *The Modern Cook*. Charles Carter, cook to the Duke of Argyle, wrote his *The Compleat City and Country Cook* at about the same time, but suffered the ignominy of seeing it reissued some years later with the notice that it had been "Revised and much improved by a Gentlewoman." In 1762, William Gelleroy, chief cook to the lord mayor of London, appropriately named his book *The London Cook,* and gave the women a few delicious recipes to follow.

Squab à la Soleil

Allow 1 *squab per person;* or use individual Cornish hens. Season the birds to taste, and roast uncovered at 350° for 45 minutes. Remove from oven and allow to cool.

Have ready a forcemeat made of *ground ham* mixed with enough *cream sauce* to bind. Smooth this mixture over the breast of each bird.

(At this point, I part company from the directions William Gelleroy provided. You may want to follow them, however, so here they are: Dip each bird in flour, then in beaten egg, and last in fine bread crumbs. Fry in deep fat until coating is nicely browned.)

I shake *flour* over the ham forcemeat, then brush it off. *Beaten egg* is then applied with a brush. Finally, *bread crumbs* are dredged over the breast and all surplus brushed off. Only the *breast* is breaded. I return the bird to the oven and roast it for another 30 to 40 minutes.

Chicken Livers Dressed with Mushrooms and Onions

1 *pound chicken livers, washed, blotted dry, and dredged with well seasoned flour*
½ *pound mushrooms, peeled and chopped coarsely*
1 *tablespoon catsup*
¼ *cup white wine*
1 *medium onion, chopped fine*
Butter

Cook the onion in butter until it grows soft. Add the mushrooms and more butter if necessary. Cook until mushrooms are done, stirring constantly. In another pan, cook the livers quickly in hot butter or margarine. When ready, combine them with the onions and mushrooms. Add the wine and the catsup to the pan. Mix all together.

John Middleton, cook to members of the English aristocracy, also was prominent enough to compete with the female authors. His *Five Hundred New Receipts in Cookery* included this one for fish, which he apparently had borrowed from Italy:

A Whole Fish, Broiled or Baked with Fennel

A small sea bass is ideal for this, but *any fish that can be baked or broiled whole* will do. Have the fish cleaned and scaled and delivered to you intact, with head and tail still in place. Marinate it in a mixture of *oil, vinegar* and chopped bits of *fennel* for at least 30 minutes.

Blanch several stalks of fennel in boiling water for 3 minutes, or until soft enough to bend. Wrap the blanched fennel stalks around the body of the fish and fasten with toothpicks. If stalks are not long enough for this, lay on top of fish. Baste with *butter* as the fish bakes (or broils). If possible, prepare fish in a serving dish that can come to the table; transferring a cooked fish to another serving dish is always precarious. The fish may be served in its fennel wrappers. Or, if you prefer a crisp exterior, remove the fennel carefully about 5 minutes before fish is finished cooking; then brush fish with melted butter and allow it to broil for a few minutes.

To enhance the flavor of the fennel and to emphasize the relationship, serve the fish garnished with *tiny boiled potato balls* doused with butter and sprinkled with *fennel seed*. *A tablespoon of Pernod* or *anise liqueur* dribbled over the fish itself, adds marvelous flavor.

DESPITE the contributions of a few men, female authors dominated the century. Elizabeth Raffald was undoubtedly the most amazing of these women, and the best qualified to write a cookbook. Her book, published in 1769, was called *The Experienced English Housekeeper,* and she describes it as "written purely from practise." It certainly was! Mrs. Raffald had been housekeeper to Lady Warburton, but this was only one of her qualifications. She operated, in succession, a confectionery store, two inns, a domestic agency, and a cooking school. At the same time, she bore sixteen daughters.

In the Warburton home, Mrs. Raffald became an expert in planning sumptuous Georgian meals for the most discriminating diners. Unlike Eliza Smith, who considered eight dishes a fair quantity to set upon the table for each course, Mrs. Raffald favored the round sum of twenty-five dishes for each of two courses—fifty specialties in all that would be produced under her supervision.

Fantasy was Mrs. Raffald's specialty. Desserts and side-dishes bore such names as A Transparent Pudding Cover'd with a Silver Web, and Globes of Gold with Mottoes in Them. A Rocky Island consisted of undulating crags of gilded flummery, meringues crested with myrtle, and molded lambs and ducks sporting near a calf's-foot jelly shore. A Thatched House Pye had a shaggy roof of macaroni baked onto the pastry covering of a meat pie.

Her Drunken Loaf is another dish that used macaroni. It might be served today for a family dinner.

Drunken Loaf

Make your favorite meat loaf recipe. Then, to make it a staggering success, follow Mrs. Raffald's directions for a Drunken Meat Loaf.

Boil *½ cup macaroni* in *salt water* until macaroni is tender. Drain well. Add to it *2 tablespoons soft butter or margarine* and as much *cream* as

Portrait of Elizabeth Raffald. From her book, The Experienced English Housekeeper. *The 1786 edition.*

will be absorbed without making the mixture too loose (approximately
¼ cup cream should do). Add *4 tablespoons grated Italian cheese.* Stir
and shake in a saucepan until the mixture is thoroughly blended and
thick enough to stick where it lands. Pour it over the meat loaf and
quickly brown under a hot broiler.

Mrs. Raffald did not overlook the simple basics of cooking. Hers
might well be called the best basic cookbook of the eighteenth cen-

tury. Among other things, it contains the earliest recipe I have seen for Yorkshire Pudding. A modern adaptation follows:

Perfect, Puffy Yorkshire Pudding

This recipe will fill an 8-by-12-inch shallow glass baking dish.

> 1 *cup flour*
> 1 *cup milk*
> ¼ *teaspoon salt*
> ¼ *teaspoon baking powder*
> 2 *eggs*
> 3 *or 4 tablespoons beef drippings*

Combine all the ingredients except the drippings in a mixing bowl and beat vigorously (1 minute at medium speed with an electric beater) until mixture is full of bubbles.

Pour the beef drippings into the baking dish and swirl around until bottom is thoroughly coated. Pour in the batter. Set on low rack in a preheated oven (425°) and bake for 35 minutes.

These unusual and delicious pastry-cloaked apples are really a combination of two of Mrs. Raffald's recipes. The meringue is *inside* the pastry.

Snowballs

> *Large baking apples, peeled and cored*
> *Pie pastry*
> *Meringue (2 tablespoons sugar per egg white)*
> *Sugar and cinnamon, mixed*
> *Drained, crushed pineapple, or preserved fruit*
> *Simple confectioners' sugar icing*

Prepare the meringue, allowing 2 egg whites for 5 or 6 apples.

Roll out a thin square of pie-crust for each apple, large enough to encase apple completely. (Since rolled pastry tends to dry out and is difficult to handle if it stands too long, I find it best to complete each apple before rolling out pastry for the next one.)

Sprinkle each apple liberally with cinnamon and sugar (I find a shaker does this job best), spread meringue on the bottom of the apple, and set it in the center of its square of pastry. Fill the core with crushed pineapple, orange marmalade, strawberry preserves, or whatever your fancy—or pantry shelf—dictates. Now cover the apple entirely with meringue about ¼ inch thick (and there's no harm in making it thicker if you wish). Bring the pastry up around the apple as you would for a dumpling; snip away excess pastry at the corners and pinch them tightly closed.

Bake in a preheated oven (450°) for 10 minutes. Reduce heat to 375°, and bake for another 40 minutes. While the apples are still warm, place a dab of icing at the top and allow it to dribble down over the sides. Snowballs are especially good served slightly warm.

By Mrs. Raffald's time, the English attitude toward French cooking had grown more temperate, and she wrote: "Though I have given some of my dishes French names as they are only known by those names, yet they will not be found very expensive, but as plain as the nature of the dish will admit of."

Translations of French cookbooks began to appear once again, after a lapse of nearly a hundred years. In 1767, Menon's *Les Soupers de la Cour* appeared under the English title of *The Art of Cookery Displayed,* and the English were able to read for themselves that a French sauce was neither so difficult nor so expensive to make as they had been led to believe. Later, Menon's *La Cuisinière Bourgeoise* was also translated into English as *The French Family Cook.*

French names cropped up on the menus that graced dinner tables; French chefs, many of them scattered like seeds in the wind by the French Revolution, now sputtered orders to English kitchen staffs. Some English cookbooks continued to grumble over this state of affairs, but upper-class kitchens rapidly adopted the new methods and recipes brought over by the French chefs, one of whom was Louis Eustache Ude, former chef to King Louis XVI himself. Their presence was responsible for the culinary renaissance that spread rapidly through England.

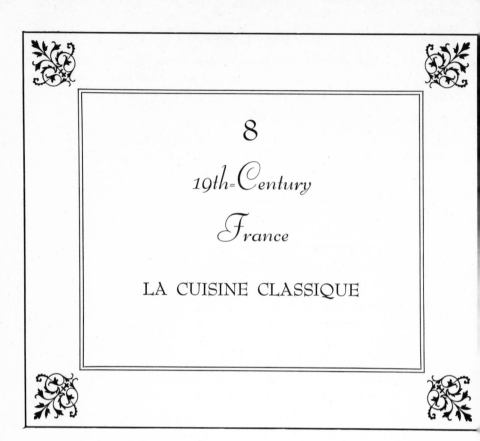

8

19th-Century France

LA CUISINE CLASSIQUE

WHEN THE FRENCH REVOLUTION resolved into the Napoleonic era, the forty-year cookbook drought ended, and a new, modernized French cuisine was unveiled. A good part of it was made possible by the experiments and inventions of an American— Benjamin Thompson of Massachusetts—who had gone to Europe to support the British during the American Revolution, and had remained to work his own revolution in the kitchen. Thompson was largely responsible for lifting cooking out of the fireplace and transferring it to ranges with built-in ovens. In 1789 he installed the forerunner of the modern kitchen range in a Bavarian nobleman's kitchen. A grateful Bavaria rewarded him with the title of Count

Rumford for the scientific researches he conducted in that country.

Heating stoves in various forms had been in use for centuries, but now stoves began to be used for cooking. They were attached to fireplaces to utilize the heat; and flues, dampers and removable plates on the stove-top permitted considerable regulation of temperature. French cooks quickly invented the Sautoir or sauté pan to use on the new stove, and they set soufflés to rise handsomely in ovens that Count Rumford had demonstrated could be heated externally by drafts (instead of by heated coals that were raked out before the food went in). They were able to invent memorable sauces based on a smooth blending of flour and butter, which was now possible because of the more readily controlled heat.

Rumford's experiments were just one part of the general scientific awakening. Cookbook authors filled their pages with jargon explaining what happened to beef as its gelatins and juices were released into bouillon. One writer was tempted to say of his science-minded rivals: "I'll wager they couldn't fricassee spinach if they had to!" But no one could dispute that the new cookbooks were a great change from the old. It was also clear that the readers had changed. Officers of the Mouth were no longer mentioned; instead there was a new word—amphitryon, or host. In the nineteenth century, there were many men cast in the mold of Napoleon himself—self-made men of humble beginnings, newly come to grandeur, who welcomed guidance in the social graces and in the deportment expected of a host. They were being advised and helped in this, even before the new cookbooks appeared, by Grimod de la Reynière.

La Reynière deserves much credit for the revival of interest in fine cuisine after the Revolution. He organized the Jury Degustateur, a group of gourmets determined to renew the glory of French cuisine, and from 1803 he edited the *Almanach des Gourmands,* a publication closely associated with members of the Jury. Later on, he published his own book, *Manuel des Amphitryons.* In his writings, La Reynière often described dishes in sufficient detail for a chef to follow; but he was not writing cookbooks, only manuals of advice.

For the householder new to managing help, La Reynière had a

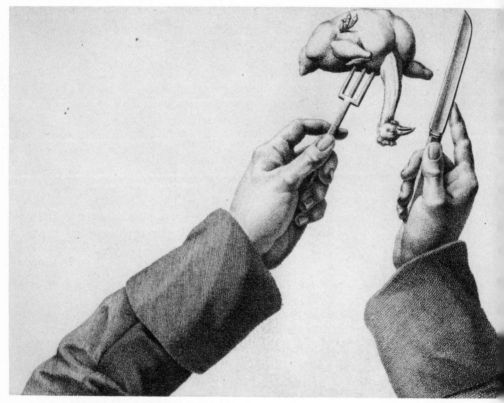

Frontispiece of Manuel des Amphitryons, *by Grimod de la Reynière. 1808.*

simple word: "Let them steal a little," he said; "it was ever thus." For the host at table, he laid down an inflexible rule: the host must give his undivided attention to refilling the plates of his guests before they emptied. "The host whose guest is obliged to ask for anything is a dishonored man," he decreed. The larger the company, the more extensive the menu; and pity the harassed host with the thirty-six Entrees and Roasts for sixty guests that La Reynière ordered placed on the table after the Soups and Relevés had been removed—and with the Desserts yet to come.

Here is a menu recommended by La Reynière for a party of fifteen. With such a small number to shepherd, the host might even find time to swallow a few mouthfuls himself.

Menu for Fifteen Guests

DEUX POTAGES
Un à la Condé
Un au Riz, au Blond de Veau

HUIT ENTRÉES
Des Grenadins aux Pointes d'Asperges
Une Épigramme d'Agneau
Un Vol-au-vent de Quenelles de Poisson
Un Filet de Boeuf Pique
Des Ris de Veau, Piques et Glacés, à la Financière
Des Côtelettes de Pigeon, Panées
Des Petits Pâtés à la Monglas
Une Poularde à la Poêle aux Tomates

DEUX RELEVÉS
La Pièce de Boeuf
Un Turbot

DEUX GROSSE PIÈCES
Un Jambon de Bayonne
Des Homardes

DEUX PLATS DE RÔT
Des Soles
Des Pigeons

HUIT ENTREMETS
Des Tartelettes
Un Gâteau au Riz
Des Épinards
Des Choux-fleurs
Des Petits Pots au Chocolat
Une Charlotte
Des Asperges en Petits Pois
Une Croûte aux Champignons

The Poularde à la Poêle aux Tomates (listed above under Entrées) shows another significant change in nineteenth-century eating. The tomato was first introduced to Parisians during the Revolution, by the men from Provence who formed the Marseillaise legion. The cooking of Provence was akin to that of neighboring Italy, where the tomato was already accepted. Parisian troops saw the Marseillaise legion eating the "love apple," overcame their fear of it and adopted it along with the legion's marching song, "La Marseillaise."

Poularde à la Poêle deserves to have the Marseillaise hummed whenever it is eaten! Prepare this delicious dish with fresh tomatoes, as they did in nineteenth-century Paris.

Poularde à la Poêle aux Tomates

For this dish, use *tender young chickens* weighing 2 to 2½ pounds each. *For each chicken, allow 1 firm, nearly ripe tomato.*

Cut chicken into quarters. Season with *salt* and *pepper*. Sauté gently, over a medium flame, in 3 parts *oil* to 1 part *butter*, until chicken is tender and slightly browned. As each piece of chicken is ready, remove it to an oven-proof serving dish.

Peel tomatoes (blanch for a few seconds in boiling water, or remove skin with a sharp paring knife), cut in quarters and remove all seeds. Dice tomatoes and sauté gently for a few minutes in fresh butter. Do not overcook them. Add a dash of salt and *white pepper* and pour tomatoes over the chicken along with ½ *cup dry white wine. One teaspoon grated onion* may be added to sharpen the taste, but should be kept strictly in the background; the fresh tomatoes are the theme of this dish.

Permit the dish to warm through in the oven for 10 to 15 minutes in order to "marry" all the flavors.

The "poêle" in which the dish was cooked was a deep skillet with a long handle that was used over the hearth fire. Interestingly enough, all the dishes on La Reynière's menu could have been prepared in a kitchen not yet equipped with the new ranges. This may have been his express intention, for he always tried to serve lesser households as well as great ones.

To him the greatest innovation in cookery was sautéing (derived from the verb sauter, to jump: when the fat jumped in the pan, sautéing could begin). Sauté de Volaille au Velouté Réduit he called "the ne plus ultra of the century." It was made somewhat along these lines:

Sauté de Volaille au Velouté Réduit
[SAUTÉED CHICKEN IN CREAM SAUCE]

For this dish, use *tender young fryers,* cut into quarters and flattened slightly with the side of a cleaver. Remove the wings and reserve for some other purpose. Season the chicken to taste and sauté gently in *butter* mixed with enough *oil* to keep the butter from burning. The object is to cook the chicken thoroughly, but not to brown or burn it. However, any such damage to its appearance can be remedied at the end, when all the skin should be stripped off. As each piece becomes ready, remove from the fire and transfer to a heat-proof serving dish.

Meanwhile, prepare *julienne strips of sautéed mushrooms* and set aside for garnish.

La Reynière's Velouté Réduit (cooked-down Velouté Sauce) was the result of long, slow cooking. However, a good Velouté Sauce can be quickly prepared as follows: Melt 2 *tablespoons butter,* add 2 *tablespoons flour* and blend thoroughly. Add 2 *cups hot chicken broth* all at once, and whisk thoroughly, preferably with the wire ballon whisk used by chefs (a most useful kitchen aid). Season sauce with *salt* and *white pepper.* If you like, swirl 1 *tablespoon sherry or white wine* in the mushroom pan and add this to the sauce. Finally add ½ *cup cream.*

Reheat sauce to serving temperature and pour over the sautéed chicken. Garnish with the julienne strips of mushrooms, and serve with a crisp accompaniment. Potato or rice croquettes are excellent with this.

Cream sauce was no longer the simple eighteenth-century preparation that could be dismissed in a paragraph. The original Béchamel had proliferated to include the Velouté (with chicken stock) and Allemande (a thicker version); and these in turn took other names depending on what was added to *them.* Brown sauces, pink sauces (lobster coral added), green sauces (spinach added)—the sauces that had formerly constituted the repertoire of the eighteenth century had exploded into a rainbow of colors. Stressing the importance of sauces, La Reynière wrote, "A well-made sauce will make even an elephant or a grandfather palatable." In his *Almanach,* La Reynière discussed the restaurants springing up all over Paris and the establishments where ready-cooked entrees and pastries could be bought. With kitchen staffs shrunk to one or two in many homes, a host might need to supplement the products of his own kitchen, especially if a large company had been invited. The patty shells and pâtés, all the dessert pastries, and even the decorated fish and the Bayonne hams of La Reynière's menus could be brought in from outside. The *Almanach* passed judgment on all of these places—reputations were made, destroyed and protected in its pages. One pastry-maker, indignant that an inferior pâté had been passed off as a product of his kitchens, had the matter publicly and satisfactorily adjusted there. The *Almanach's* pages sparkled with witty aphorisms, but La Reynière's humor in private life was sometimes macabre. Once he gave a dinner at which each guest was draped in a shroud before sitting down to table, and an open coffin was placed in back of each chair.

While La Reynière was giving his advice to amphitryons, the great cookbooks of the new Classic French cuisine were beginning to be written for their cooks. The first to appear was *Le Cuisinier Impérial* by A. Viard in 1806, appropriately named for the Emperor whose taste for classicism gave the new cuisine its name.

Le Cuisinier Impérial spanned the nineteenth century, its title changing like a moving reflection of every upheaval. After its Napoleonic start, it changed to *Le Cuisinier Royal* when Louis XVIII became King in 1814, became *Le Cuisinier National* when Louis Napoleon was elected President of the Republic and quickly reverted to *Le Cuisinier Impérial* when Louis Napoleon declared himself Emperor Napoleon III in 1852. Its fourth and last about-face was for the Third Republic in 1871 when it became (and remained) *Le Cuisinier National.*

From its first appearance as *Le Cuisinier Impérial,* this book presented most of the basic sauces of the new cuisine, along with soufflés, sautés, recipes using tomatoes, and the first recipes for curry to appear in any European cookbook. (With England and

France jockeying for power in India, both countries were interested in all things Indian, including Indian cuisine.) The potato was another newcomer to French kitchens. The English had been eating it for two centuries, but in France only the starving poor would touch it, despite the efforts of the scientist Antoine-Auguste Parmentier. (Parmentier planted fields of potatoes, and once served a meal in which everything, including a mock-fish course, was made of potatoes.) It was not until the Revolution, with its food scarcities, that the French were won over; then potatoes very quickly became a staple, judging from the number of potato recipes included in Le Cuisinier Impérial. One of the tastiest recipes, which also shows the continuing influence of Provençal cooking on Parisian tastes, is this one for Potatoes à la Provençale:

Potatoes à la Provençale

2 pounds boiling potatoes (not mealy)
1 medium onion, coarsely chopped
Grated rind and juice of 1 lemon
2 tablespoons flour
4 tablespoons butter, margarine or oil (true Provençale style requires oil)
2 tablespoons chopped parsley
¼ teaspoon ground nutmeg
Salt and pepper to taste

Peel the potatoes; cut into quarters or sixths. (The pieces should be large enough to provide 2 forkfuls for well-bred eaters.) Parboil in salted water for 3 minutes. Drain the potatoes, and toss with all the ingredients enumerated above, except lemon juice, until well blended. Place in a buttered casserole or oven-proof dish suitable also for serving. Dot top with butter and bake in a preheated oven (450°) for 20 to 25 minutes, or until nicely browned. Just before serving, pour lemon juice over the top and return to oven for a minute or two.

Le Cuisinier's recipe for buttered carrots inspired this puréed version.

Carrots au Beurre

Scrape and slice *tender young carrots* and cook in *salted water* until a fork will break them. They must be tender enough to go through a food mill. Reduce them to a purée and drain thoroughly. For each ½ cup of carrots add 1 tablespoon *melted butter* and 2 to 3 tablespoons *light cream,* plus a subtle grating of *nutmeg.*

Mound lightly in the center of a vegetable platter and surround with julienne string beans which have been cooked with savoury. Slivered almonds or chopped pecans may be dusted lightly over the top.

Le Cuisinier's author, Viard, sheds some light on how dishes were baptized: "Make your pastry," he said; "when it is ready and you have added whatever you please, give it whatever shape and name you consider suitable." He acknowledged La Reynière's influence on the revival of French cooking and modestly explained, "I don't pretend to cover all cuisine; this would require ten volumes. The student will find here, not the original style of La Reynière's *Almanach,* but simple explanations of all cooking operations." Nothing could be simpler than his approach to that haute-cuisine dish, Blanquette de Veau aux Champignons:

Blanquette de Veau aux Champignons

Season a *3-pound rump of veal.* Spread it with softened butter or margarine, wrap it in cheesecloth, and roast it, covered, at 350° until it is fully done. Cool sufficiently to slice. Cut into thin, 1-inch pieces.

While the veal is roasting, prepare *2½ cups of cream sauce* (follow the recipe for Velouté given with Sauté de Volaille on page 131, but substitute milk for the chicken stock).

Slice and sauté *1 pound of mushrooms* in *butter* and add them to the cut veal. Pour the cream sauce over the veal and mushrooms, and mix with a few deft spoon strokes. Reduce oven to 300°, and heat Blanquette for 10 minutes.

ONE OF THE PIONEERS of the new French cuisine was the same Antoine Beauvilliers whose "Grande Taverne de Londres" had been the first real Paris restaurant. After the Revolution, Beauvilliers

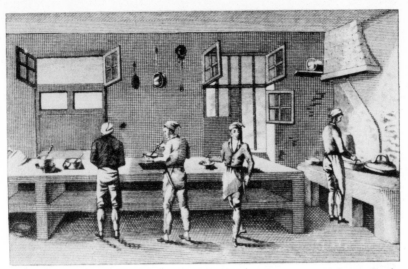

Illustration of a contemporary kitchen from the title page (Volume One) of L'Art du Cuisinier, *by Antoine Beauvilliers. 1814.*

reopened the Grande Taverne, and he also wrote a cookbook which reflected his admiration of English ways. This was the two-volume *L'Art du Cuisinier*, published in 1814. In it Beauvilliers offered "the best of English cooking which I have had the advantage of ·being the first to transplant to France."

He gave recipes for Wouelche Rabette (with the alternate title of Lapin Gallois), Plumbuting, and Mach-potetesse, plus one for Ket-Chop which was just becoming popular in England. (The early ketchups were made of mushrooms or walnuts and had only recently been adopted, along with soy sauce, from the Chinese.) Beauvilliers also went in for some of the fantasies the English favored: his Poulet en Lezard was a boned chicken shaped to resemble a lizard, with the stuffed neck making the tail.

He granted that English beef was superior to French, but said German beef was even tastier if it traveled to France on the hoof— by the time the animals ended their long journey, they were so fatigued that their fat had been incorporated into their flesh, thereby tenderizing it. While any roast was called a rostbif, a bifteck was strictly a beefsteak. Beauvilliers divided them into categories: the True Bifteck, the English style (rump steak), and the French style, which was the fillet. These fillet steaks later came to be called Tournedos (literally, "turn the back"). Beauvilliers' cooking in-

135

structions show how these delicious sautéed steaks came by their name; in France today they are still cooked as Beauvilliers describes.

Tournedos

Use *beef tenderloin steaks,* 1 inch thick and carefully trimmed of all gristle. Tie them with a string to keep them shapely. Heat a heavy-bottomed skillet to sizzling point (a copper or steel bottom is best). Add a small quantity of *oil* and *butter,* enough to keep the meat from sticking. As soon as steak is seared on one side, promptly turn it to the other side and sear. Cook for about 3 minutes on each side, turning as necessary to prevent scorching or drying out. (Can you see how the name developed?) Beauvilliers detached the meat juices in the pan by swirling *bouillon* in it; this he strained and poured over the steak. (Madeira is even better than bouillon.)

Properly cooked, this is a great dish, and invariably it is garnished handsomely. Serve Tournedos on a *toast round,* cut to fit the meat exactly, and spread with a *liver or ham pâté.* Top with *sautéed mushrooms*—or with a dab of butter creamed with parsley, or with Béarnaise sauce.

Surround with tomatoes filled with creamed peas, and crisp, browned potato balls.

One of the first recipes I have seen for a cheese soufflé appears in Beauvilliers' book. He used a combination of Parmesan and Gruyère; the result is a delicious, tangy soufflé.

Beauvilliers' Cheese Soufflé

FOR A 2-QUART SOUFFLÉ CASSEROLE:

    4 *tablespoons butter*
    ¼ *cup flour, sifted with* ⅛ *teaspoon salt*
    1½ *cups scalded milk*
    ½ *pound grated cheese* (¼ *pound each: Parmesan and Swiss*)
    ⅛ *teaspoon grated nutmeg*
    4 *eggs, separated*

Melt the butter in a saucepan, blend in the flour smoothly, then add the hot milk. Stir quickly with a wire whisk until thoroughly blended. Cool for a few minutes, then add the cheese, stirring to hasten the melting. Beat in the egg yolks, one at a time. Meanwhile, beat the egg whites to stiff (not dry) peaks. Turn the egg whites into the cheese mixture; cut and fold lightly, only enough to blend. Turn into a 2-quart ungreased soufflé casserole, place in a preheated oven (375°) and bake for 35 minutes. Serve immediately.

One of numerous illustrations in Les Classiques de la Table. *1844.*

AT ABOUT THE SAME TIME that Beauvilliers was introducing English dishes into French cuisine, Louis Eustache Ude was explaining "the principles of cookery as practised in the kitchens of the Royal Family at Versailles" to the English. Ude, who had been chef to Louis XVI, published *The French Cook* in 1813. He wrote in English, but when a phrase did not occur to him quickly he used French instead. The result sometimes reads like broken English; at all times it imparts Ude's Gallic personality.

Ude was reputed to be a great egotist. He dismissed all previously published cookbooks as "unintelligible and impractical," although he *did* allow that his English experience had expanded his knowledge of cooking principles. He revealed an undercurrent of affection for his adopted country throughout the book as well as many examples of economical methods he learned to practice there. For example, he placed his recipe for Meringues next to one for Gimblettes and explained: "I introduce the Gimblettes here because this paste is made with egg yolks only, whereas the whites only are used in making Meringues. It is by his adherence to these principles of economy that a good cook distinguishes himself." Ude's Gimblettes were the same as the sixteenth-century Ciambellette, the ring cookies that Scappi boiled (see Chapter 2). His filled Meringues are easy to make and handsome to serve.

Meringues à la Ude

6 egg whites
⅛ teaspoon salt, added to the egg whites
2 cups sugar
1 teaspoon lemon or orange extract

Beat the egg whites until very stiff. Now add 1½ cups sugar very slowly, a scant teaspoon at a time. Keep the beaters going constantly and when all the sugar is in, continue to beat for a few minutes. Add the flavoring and lightly fold in the remaining ½ cup of sugar.

Line a heavy cookie sheet with white paper. Drop the meringues by spoonfuls on the paper and, in Ude's words, "Give them the shape of an egg cut in halves." (This is easy to do if you trace outlines on the white paper; later you will put two halves together.) Place in a preheated slow oven (225°) and bake for an hour. Lift them off the paper while warm and scoop out the bottoms with a small sharp knife (or your finger) so that they will be hollow to receive a filling. (Handle carefully or they will break.)

Again I will quote Ude: "Remember not to use articles that are very sweet, the meringues being sweet by their nature." We suggest filling them with a tart lemon custard. A filling of lemon sherbet makes the meringues into a rhapsodic summer dessert. Or put the meringue halves together with whipped cream and serve with crushed strawberries or raspberries. This quantity makes about 30 halves.

Ude had his own way of making Velouté or white sauce. During one of his bouts with the English language, he described this sauce as "the fundamental stone, if I may use the expression." He used cream instead of butter to make the roux, and explained how he had discovered the method: "In summer time I was unable to procure butter fit to use. I was forced to do without, and found my sauce all the better for it."

What he did to hollandaise sauce when it didn't behave is obvious. "In case it has not curdled, you have no occasion to strain," he wrote. If I may borrow *his* expression, simplicity is the fundamental stone of his instructions and recipes. Simplest of all is his Chicken à l'Oignon, which requires only a roasting chicken, a large onion and seasonings to taste.

Chicken à l'Oignon

Select a *whole tender young chicken, 2½ to 3 pounds.* Season the inside of the chicken with *salt* and *pepper.* With your fingers, carefully loosen the skin over the breast meat, poking down toward the legs as far as you can go without tearing the skin. Cut 1 *medium yellow onion* into thin slices. Insert the onion slices under the loosened skin so that they form a layer between it and the flesh. Fasten down any loose ends of skin with toothpicks to keep the onion snugly lodged as the chicken roasts.

Before placing the chicken in a preheated oven (375°), spread *softened butter* over the skin that covers onions. Salt and pepper entire bird, to taste. Place it in a shallow earthenware dish or open roasting pan, and don't give it another thought for 45 minutes. Then baste it with the fat and juices that have collected in the pan. Repeat twice, and roast the bird for a total of 1½ hours. Serve it hot out of the oven, as soon as possible, to savor the crackling golden skin with the tender slices of onion oozing juice underneath. (Add a small quantity of chicken stock or bouillon if more sauce is wanted.)

For an accompaniment, parboil potato balls for 2 minutes. Sprinkle them with paprika and roast them along with the chicken, basting at the same time you attend to the chicken.

Marie-Antoine (Antonin) Carême is considered the boy-wonder of Classic French cuisine; he was also the first culinary spokesman of the nineteenth century. Most of the others—La Reynière, Beauvilliers, Ude—had been born in the mid-eighteenth century and could well remember the old days. Carême, who was not born until 1784, grew up with the nineteenth century and its reanimated cuisine.

He is supposed to have had an ancestor who was cook to Pope Leo X; this ancestor concocted an excellent Lenten soup, so the legend goes, and the Pope named him Jean de Carême (Lent), which became the family name. Whether or not the tale is true, it is clear that Carême had a gifted ancestor or two: he was a man of extraordinary talent—an artist, a writer, and one of the greatest chefs of all time. His own father was a poor workingman who sired twenty-five children—far more than he could feed. Carême was forced into a culinary career at an age when most children are leaving kindergarten. At seventeen he was already proficient enough to attract the attention of M. de Talleyrand, who was famed for his strategic use of the dinner table as an arena of diplomacy. In addition to Talleyrand, Carême was chef to the English Prince Regent, Czar Alexander I of Russia and Baron de Rothschild. Later, when the Prince Regent became King George IV, he sought to have Carême return to him; but Carême refused, saying that a Frenchman could only be happy living in France.

Carême's books are his enduring monument. They were the first really detailed works on Classic French cuisine, filled with precise drawings, many new recipes, and an egotism that could compete with anyone's. His first book was *Le Pâtissier Royal*, published in 1815. In it he wrote that he had found everything previously written on the subject "lacking in taste, full of witless remarks and wild promises that if instructions were followed, fame would quickly follow after." The only way to achieve success, he said, was through strenuous and dedicated effort, and he pointed to his own twenty-five years of experience as the proof.

He criticized others for their archaic recipes, but if an ancient recipe was worth preserving, it was there in his book, including one for Darioles.

Le Pâtissier Royal dealt primarily with pastries, but included many entremets (literally, "between foods"—though today the word stands for dessert). These were placed among the large platters on the laden table.

Carême's extremets included such farfetched dishes as Calf's Brains in Mayonnaise, but also some excellent croquettes. These Rice Croquettes come often to my table.

Title page of Volume One, L'Art de la Cuisine Française, the five-volume work by Carême and Plumerey. This volume, 1833.

Tailtevant — Menon — Liger — Bechamel

Elio — Larour

Kervau — Connet

Richand — Gaillan

Bardet — Morillon

L'ART
de la
CUISINE FRANÇAISE
AU XIX.ᵉ SIECLE

Traité Elémentaire et

Pratique

Suivi de dissertations Culinaires

et GASTRONOMIQUES

Utiles aux progrès de cet Art

par M. Antonin **CARÊME** de Paris

a Paris

CHEZ L'ÉDITEUR, RUE THÉRÈSE Nº 11.

Provence, Dauphiné, Périgord,
Bourgogne, Champagne, Normandie.

Rice Croquettes à l'Ancienne

Combine the following ingredients: *2 cups boiled rice; 1 teaspoon salt; ¼ teaspoon nutmeg; ½ cup thick cream sauce,* and *½ cup grated cheese* (Carême preferred Parmesan). Chill thoroughly.

Grind or chop some *cooked chicken or ham,* bind it with a little *mayonnaise* and season it as you like. Chill this and make it into small balls, using ½ teaspoon of the mixture for each.

When the rice is chilled, divide it into 12 or 14 equal portions. In the hollow of your left hand, make a cup of each portion, pressing it with the thumb of your right hand. Insert the forcemeat ball, close the cup, and shape it into a ball by rolling it between your palms. (Carême's directions exactly.)

Dip each croquette in *beaten egg,* then in *bread crumbs* mixed with *grated cheese* (same kind as you use in the rice), and fry in deep fat. Or you may bake in oven as directed for Chestnut Croquettes (see recipe next.) Makes about 10 croquettes.

Carême's Chestnut Croquettes are a tempting way to serve this delicious nut with meats.

Carême's Chestnut Croquettes

Allow *6 to 8 chestnuts per serving.* Roast or boil the chestnuts; peel them, and set aside 3 or 4 whole chestnuts per serving. Mash the remaining chestnuts.

Prepare a purée as follows: Combine *2 cups mashed chestnuts, loosely packed; 2 tablespoons melted butter; 2 tablespoons cream; 2 eggs,* and *salt* and *white pepper* to taste. Spread on a buttered plate and cover with waxed paper.

When purée is cool enough to mold, surround each whole chestnut with some of the mixture. Dip each wrapped chestnut in *beaten egg,* then in *fine dry bread crumbs.* Fry in *deep fat* as you would any croquette.

Carême's recipe for Croustades, delicious "edible dishes" made of bread, is much simpler than those given by Beauvilliers and Ude. These bread cases are another specialty of the Classic cuisine, easy to prepare and decorative to serve. Use them as containers for hot hors d'oeuvres, or for an entire luncheon dish of creamed chicken, crab meat, or Eggs Benedict. Here is the recipe adapted from Carême's book.

Croustades

Use *slightly stale bread*. Cut bread into thick slices, 2 inches thick if Croustades are to be used as an entree; 1 inch thick if used for an hors d'oeuvre. Trim off all crusts (round off the corners if you wish), and for hors d'oeuvres, divide slice into portions about 1½ inches square. Make a depression in the center with a cookie cutter, glass or cup. Brush top and sides with *melted butter,* place bread cases on a buttered baking sheet and bake in a hot oven (450°) until golden and well toasted. With a sharp knife, hollow out indented center previously marked. Brush the sides of this opening with *beaten egg yolk* or, if you have it, liver pâté (delicious when chicken is served in it). Return to oven to dry out. The bread case is now ready, and whatever is to be served can be heated right in it in the oven. With the egg or pâté protection, food will not soak through and make the Croustade soggy.

Other books followed, but Carême did not live to complete his most ambitious undertaking, the five-volume *L'Art de la Cuisine Française au Dix-neuvième Siècle,* which was published after his death in 1833, with the last two volumes completed by the great chef Plumerey. The work is filled with information about the Classic cuisine which Carême helped to bring to its highest glory, and the book reflects his deep interest in maintaining quality. "My book is not written solely for the great ones," he wrote; "on the contrary, I want it to be of service to all. It is an error for those of lesser station to try to pattern their tables after the rich, crowding them with badly prepared food, badly served because of inexperienced help. Better to serve a simple meal, well prepared; and not try to cover the bourgeois table with an imitation of les grands."

But Carême could uphold royal standards when necessary. With indignation that scorches the pages, he describes the humiliating treatment given Napoleon on the desolate island of Saint Helena, and his struggle to maintain a menage of sorts there. The food was uniformly dreadful, all except for bananas which grew plentifully on the island. Carême describes how Napoleon's cook marinated them in rum, then dipped them in batter to make delicious fritters. Carême's instructions were sparse, and I've taken the liberty of embellishing them slightly.

Napoleon's Rum-Banana Fritters

Slice 6 firm but ripe bananas in halves, and then into quarters, lengthwise. Marinate them for an hour in rum mixed with an equal quantity of orange or pineapple juice (optional).

Prepare the batter, using 2 *unbeaten egg whites, 2 tablespoons cornstarch,* and 2 *tablespoons flour.* Coat each piece of banana thoroughly with the batter, and fry in *deep fat* until light brown. Remove from oil and drain.

Now prepare the following mixture: 3 *tablespoons butter,* ½ *cup sugar, 1 tablespoon water,* and ¼ *cup rum.* Melt the butter, add the sugar and water, stir constantly until the sugar melts. Add the rum. Place the bananas in a buttered, oven-proof serving dish, and pour over them the rum syrup. Reheat for a few minutes in oven. Serve as a hot dessert.

Incidentally, the bananas are delicious just baked in the rum syrup, without frying or using any batter.

For the most part, Carême's recipes were for professional chefs; they required hours of preparation and embellishment and were much too involved to lend themselves to popular adaptation. Some of them required considerable time just to read—the recipe for Grosses Meringues à la Parisienne was seven pages long! Throughout his works, Carême emphasized pleasing effects, with instructions for Pièces Montées ranging from harps, lyres and terrestrial globes to such fantastic items as a grotto with moss, a cascade with palms, a Chinese summer house and a Venetian pavilion on a bridge, all constructed of spun sugar.

He also formulated many of the simpler garnitures that still grace a handsome platter today. For a fillet of beef, his favorite accompaniments were tomatoes and potatoes, which by then had become standard items on French tables.

STUFFED TOMATOES

HERE ARE THREE WAYS of preparing stuffed tomatoes, from *L'Art de la Cuisine Française*. For each method you will start with firm, nearly ripe tomatoes. Hollow out their centers and remove all seeds and watery pulp. Fill them with one of the following stuffings. (All three recipes provide filling for 6 tomatoes.) Sprinkle tops with fresh white bread crumbs, dot with butter, and bake at 375° for 20 to 30 minutes.

À la Sicilienne

1 *chopped onion, sautéed in butter till soft*
⅛ *teaspoon ground thyme*
1 *teaspoon dried basil (or 1 tablespoon fresh chopped basil)*
¾ *cup ground ham (boiled or baked)*
1 *tablespoon Madeira*

Bind the mixture with mayonnaise thinned with milk.

À la Provençale

¾ *cup chopped mushrooms, sautéed in butter*
½ *cup large white bread crumbs, sautéed in the mushroom butter*
1 *clove garlic, crushed*
Dash of grated nutmeg
Salt and pepper

Bind with mayonnaise thinned with milk.

À la Florentine

½ *cup minced cooked chicken*
½ *cup minced sautéed mushrooms*
1 *tablespoon chopped parsley or raw spinach*
Salt and pepper

Bind with mayonnaise thinned with milk. (Instead of bread crumbs, top tomatoes with grated Italian cheese.)

Despite his protestations that his works were for modest homes as well as grand, Carême shared the lofty attitude of other leaders of the Classic cuisine toward leftovers. They were unmentionable. Carême gossiped in print about Napoleon's arch-chancellor, Cambacérès, a leading amphitryon. Any man who salvaged the half-eaten foods at his table to be served again did not deserve this title, Carême declared. "A warmed over dinner is worthless," Grimod de la Reynière had thundered in 1807. The leading culinary architects of the Classic cuisine agreed.

Frontispiece portrait of Marie-Antoine (Antonin) Carême, from Volume One of L'Art de la Cuisine Française. *This volume, 1833.*

9

19th=Century

France

EVERY FRENCHMAN
DINES WELL

NOT ALL NINETEENTH-CENTURY French cookbooks were concerned with Classic cuisine or with the amphitryon and his problems. Many changes were taking place. The standard of living was rising; La Bonne Chère—the good table—was now the desire of every French family, and its joys were no longer limited to the upper classes. The working classes thronged Les Halles, the great market of Paris where fresh produce, fresh country butter, eggs and poultry were hawked along with French mutton and German beef in the crisp air of early morning. What had once been luxuries were fast becoming necessities. There was an improved table for all, and just as the amphitryon had needed guidance, so now did the housewife and the family cook.

A whole spate of cookbooks soon materialized for the housewife. For the first time, their authors were predominantly women: Madames with hyphenated names, and countless Mademoiselles—Françoise, Angélique, Léontine, Virginie—who all promised their readers Economy, Perfection, Easy Methods, Indispensable Information, Practical Secrets and La Grande Cuisine Simplified. The word "Bourgeoise," which had come to mean simple, home-style cooking, now appeared in many titles.

However, the cookbook most popular with French housewives was written by a man: Louis Eustache Audot's *La Cuisinière de la Campagne et de la Ville* (The Country and City Cook), published in 1818. The word country in the title had about the same meaning as Suburbia today, and it signified Audot's awareness that Classic cuisine belonged primarily in elegant Paris restaurants and households. He was content to serve the modest townsfolk in smaller cities, and to guide the mistresses of the numerous establishments dotting the French countryside where a meal was for family enjoyment and the fireplace was still the cooking center. A printed notice in the book listed the many cities and towns where it could be bought. From A (Alençon) to V (Versailles), it was everywhere.

Audot passed over sautés and soufflés that required modern equipment, concentrating instead on recipes with an eighteenth-century flavor, and on such housewifely matters as:

The best way to rescue meat with a bad taste: Drop the meat into boiling water. When a foam appears on the surface remove the pot from the fire and drop in two red hot coals. When the coals have ceased to hiss the meat is fit for use.

As time went on, Audot edited and published the cookbooks of other writers; under one title or another his name became as fixed in French kitchens as a wire whisk. His own book went through many revisions, and by 1890 it was three times its original thickness, although many of the original recipes had been dropped.

Among his early recipes are these two which demonstrate that Audot, like all French kitchen specialists, had a special skill with chicken and that he recognized its affinity for mustard and for shellfish.

Poularde à la Condé

Roasting chicken, 3 or 4 pounds
Salt and pepper
Butter
1 onion, studded with cloves

SAUCE:
2 tablespoons butter
2 green onions (tops and white bulb ends), minced
¼ cup Dijon mustard
2 tablespoons capers, strained
½ cup dry white wine

Season the chicken with salt and pepper to taste, coat it with 2 tablespoons softened butter, and place in an open roasting pan with the clove-studded onion. Roast at 375°, allowing about 1½ hours for a 3- to 4-pound chicken.

Prepare the sauce as follows: Melt the butter in a small saucepan. Cook the onion until soft, but do not brown. Thin the mustard gradually with the wine and add to the butter and onions. Last add the capers.

Shortly before the chicken has finished cooking, remove the whole onion and pour on the sauce. To serve, disjoint the chicken, arrange in a serving dish that will also accommodate the sauce.

In a little French restaurant some years ago, I was served a delicious preparation of chicken bathed in a subtle sauce that defied identification. When pressed for his secret, the proprietor answered, "It's seafood, Madame. My own invention." Well, why not? Oysters go well with fowl; Paella combines chicken with shrimp and mussels. But I never encountered a recipe in a conventional cookbook for a chicken sauced in this way. That is, not until I ran across Poularde à la Marquise, in the first edition of Audot's cookbook. (It did not appear in editions published later in the nineteenth century.) Here it is, for you to try. The secret is very simple; you must prepare a seafood butter. The directions follow, along with the recipe for the chicken.

Seafood Butter

For this, you may use the *shells of cooked lobster or shrimp; or you may use the seafood itself.* The traditional way is to pound, pound, pound the shells in a heavy mortar until they are ground to bits. Then they are strained and re-strained through a fine sieve until every morsel of shell is filtered out. Then measure what you have left, and combine it with *an equal quantity of butter*—combine by creaming the butter, then creaming the ground shell residue into it. It's really not as difficult as it may sound. An even easier way, however, is to use canned shrimp. (They're soft enough to work easily.) Grind or pound them small, then push through a fine sieve with a wooden spoon. (If you have a blender, the job can be accomplished with a few buzzes.) Combine the puréed shrimp with an equal quantity of butter as described above.

Poularde à la Marquise

You will need a 3- *to* 3½-*pound roasting chicken.* Audot buttered it with the *seafood butter* and I do the same. Don't slather it on, but use about 1 tablespoon and anoint the breast and legs. Then season the fowl to taste, inside and out. Roast it at 375° in an open roasting pan and put *1 tablespoon of water or chicken broth* in the pan to get things started. Baste as soon as some juice appears. And baste at 20-minute intervals until the fowl is ready to be removed from the oven. As the shellfish butter runs off, dribble a little more over the chest of the chicken. To serve, disjoint the chicken and arrange on a platter. Prepare a *rich cream sauce* and add to it 2 tablespoons of the shellfish butter and *1 or 2 tablespoons of Pernod or anise liqueur.*

Another book showed just how strongly the balance of power had shifted in the kitchen. The professional female cook was no longer the rarity she was in the days when Mme du Barry had employed a woman chef and Louis XV had bestowed the Order of the Cordon Bleu on her after a particularly delicious meal. In fact, Cordon

Bleu itself came to be an exclusively female cookery distinction. By 1827, when Mlle Marguerite wrote *Le Cordon Bleu*, there were enough female cooks at work to give the title selling appeal. Little girls were also encouraged in the direction of complicated sauces—there was even a cookbook for children called *Bébé Cordon Bleu*. The Bébé was expected to grow up to become a young housewife. Another book illustrated what she must expect from her Cordon Bleu cook. The frontispiece of *La Jeune Cuisinière* in 1842 pictured a young mistress in the kitchen trying to talk to her cook. The cook's sour face matches her reply: "Madame, as you see I am busy preparing dinner!"

By the mid-nineteenth century, the division between cookbooks for professional cooks and those for household use became more pronounced. Carême had not been above noticing the "average" kitchen in his books, but the highly professional works that now appeared—*La Cuisine Classique* by Urbain-Dubois and Bernard (1856), and the *Livre de Cuisine* by Jules Gouffé (1867)—were of use only to top professional chefs with expert assistants at their command. *La Cuisine Classique* eventually produced a profound change at upper-class dining tables, for Urbain-Dubois was a proponent of "Service à la Russe." This meant that hot foods were served directly from the kitchen and passed around to the seated guests. The customary "Service à la Française," which had begun in the days of Louis XIV, required all dishes, hot and cold, to be arrayed on the table at once. The table presented an impressive picture, but food grew cold during the hours required for consuming the vast display. For decades the controversy raged in cookbooks. Carême had held out for the old way, but eventually Urbain-Dubois won a large following for the more sensible Russian style.

By this time, the chief buyer of cookbooks was the thrifty French housewife, intent on making every morsel count. In the heyday of the amphitryon, La Reynière had damned *all* leftovers as unworthy of a discriminating host's table. But now, for the first time in cookbooks, leftovers were acknowledged to exist. (Indeed, they must have existed—considering that a company dinner for ten comprised at least sixteen main-course dishes.)

In 1856, Antoine Gogué's *Les Secrets de la Cuisine Française* managed to serve the requirements of wealthy and modest households alike, with such tact that it earned popularity with both. In it, Gogué gives some excellent recipes for leftovers. In sixteen imaginative recipes, he told the housewife how to dispose of leftover chicken. Here are four of them, all of which would lend themselves equally well to turkey:

Poulet à la Diable
[DEVILED CHICKEN]

Gogué's recipe needs no embellishment and is given exactly as he wrote it, along with his comments:

This dish, an English importation, is no ordinary dish. It is a tonic for blasé stomachs which need strong excitement. This receipt is especially good for *leftover roast chicken.* Cut the chicken into large pieces, the legs and wings are really best for this dish. Now "butter" them with *mustard;* season with *salt* and *pepper* and the tiniest dash of *cayenne.* Heat them over a gentle fire and serve.

Coquilles de Volaille

M. Gogué instructed that the chicken for this dish be cut in rounds or ovals about the thickness of a franc, and be baked in scallop shells. Do cut the previously cooked chicken in ample pieces, not too thick, and bake in shells or in a shallow baking dish. The shells make an attractive buffet service, and they keep the creamed food from roaming into salad on the same plate.

For a *4-pound stewed chicken,* make a cream sauce as follows: Combine 2 *tablespoons butter,* 2 *tablespoons flour,* and 1½ *cups scalded milk* (or ¾ *cup each, milk and chicken broth*). When the sauce is thoroughly blended, add: ½ *cup light cream,* 2 *tablespoons sharp mustard* (I use horseradish mustard), and *salt and white pepper to taste.* Pour over chicken and blend together carefully.

Arrange in individual shells or baking dish, and sprinkle top with *white bread crumbs* (see Bread Crumbs in Index). Knead *1 tablespoon butter* with *1 tablespoon sharp mustard* and when thoroughly mingled, dot the crumbs with this mixture. Place under a broiler until crumbs are nicely browned and the mustard-butter has dispersed over the top.

Marinade de Volaille

What Gogué called Marinade de Volaille results in chicken fritters, and a novel and tasty way to use up leftover chicken.

Cut *leftover chicken* into good-size pieces—the bottom quarter separated into the thigh and leg, etc. Make a marinade of equal parts *oil* and *vinegar.* Add to it a *bay leaf, thyme, parsley,* and some *sliced onion.* Allow the chicken to marinate for several hours.

Prepare a batter as follows: Sift together: *1¼ cups flour, ¼ teaspoon salt,* and *1½ teaspoons baking powder.* Add a well-beaten *egg* and *⅔ cup milk.* Batter should be thick enough to coat nicely. If too thin, add a bit more flour.

Dip each piece in batter and sauté until golden and crisp.

Oeufs Pochés à la Victoria

This makes an attractive luncheon dish, easily prepared with boiled or roast chicken.

Mince the *chicken* and combine it with a *rich cream sauce.* (Follow the directions on page 131 for Velouté Sauce.) Prepare *croustades* following the recipe on page 143. Now you need only to poach an egg for each serving. Fill the croustades with creamed chicken. Top with a *poached egg* and garnish with *julienne strips of mushrooms.* For a truly regal effect worthy of the name of Queen Victoria, garnish with julienne truffles.

It is interesting to note that Gogué expected the average French family to eat meat twice daily, except for Fridays when fish came twice to the table. He provided some menus to guide the housewife, and they followed the meat-twice-a-day rule without exception. A typical menu for a Monday follows.

LUNCHEON:

Mutton cutlets
Omelette aux fines herbes
Two desserts

DINNER:

Semolina soup
Boiled beef with various vegetables
Partridges with cabbage
Fried salsify
Three desserts

In Gogué's book, sauces were covered in a few pages of instruction on how to make the basic forms. After that, variations were up to the cook. And not too many variations, please, was his attitude. To him a sauce on a well-prepared dish was like a necklace on a beautiful throat: its purpose was to enhance what was there, not to conceal it. "Cooks of both sexes, remember this proverb," he said: "Much sauce, bad cook; little sauce, good cook."

Most cookbooks went into such housewifely matters as how to choose the best cuts of meat. Gogué's illustrations departed engagingly from the usual diagrams of carcasses showing the divisions into rumps, chops and sirloins. His animals were shown very much alive, grazing in a pastoral setting with dissecting lines drawn on their hides to show where their future beckoned. Even a porker about to drink from a brook wore guide lines to show how he would eventually become hams, bacon and spare ribs.

AFTER GOGUÉ, many cookbooks appeared which were devoted exclusively to the problem of leftovers. In 1864, there was the popular *L'Art de Utilizer les Restes.* Even so great a gourmet as Baron Léon Brisse did not hesitate to write about leftovers.

Brisse was the author of many culinary articles and the editor of a gastronomic journal; he was also an amphitryon of importance and appetite. He was so keenly interested in food that he abandoned an important post in the administration of Louis Philippe to devote himself to it.

Though he moved in a circle of gourmets that included Alexandre Dumas (himself the author of the monumental *Le Grand Dictionnaire de Cuisine*), Brisse's writings were for housewives. They followed him eagerly, finding inspiration and expert guidance in his book, *Les 366 Menus,* which gave one for each day of the year, with an extra for Leap Year. All of the menus were for family dinners, but as the following sample shows, even these seemed to require skill, time and loving cookery:

MENU
Clear soup with vermicelli
Red snapper with sauce tartare
Veal cutlets à la Milanaise
Roast duck with olives
Tiny peas
Meringues à la crème

The veal and the duck are both excellent recipes (see pages 156 and 157).

Engraved illustration from Le Livre de Cuisine, *by Jules Gouffé. 1867.*

Veal Cutlet à la Milanaise

Boned chicken breasts, pounded flat, can be prepared in this manner and are equally delicious.

1½ pounds veal cutlet, cut as thin as possible and pounded flat
¼ cup finely grated white bread crumbs (see recipe below)
¼ cup grated Romano or Parmesan cheese, mixed with the bread crumbs
1 egg, beaten with 1 teaspoon milk
Flour
Oil and butter

Be sure the cutlet is as thin as possible; it must cook through quickly. Divide meat into serving portions and trim away all fat and gristle. Dip each piece in flour and shake off excess. Dip into the beaten egg. Finally into the bread crumb-cheese mixture, coating the meat thoroughly. (This may be done in advance of cooking time and the meat set aside in the refrigerator.)

Heat a heavy skillet until fat will sputter in it (a mixture of oil and butter is best for this). Reduce heat to a medium flame, and sauté meat quickly until brown on one side. Turn and brown the other side.

This crisp dish should be served with something runny, but bland, so that the cheese taste of the meat prevails. I suggest noodles baked in cream sauce.

White Bread Crumbs

Dried white bread crumbs are easy to make, and I've never seen any available commercially.

Trim off all crust from stale white bread and set aside to dry for a day or so. When thoroughly dry and brittle, grind up or force through a coarse sieve. They will keep for weeks in a tightly closed jar.

Duck with Olives

Season a *duckling* inside and out. Truss wings, tie legs, and brown in *hot fat*, piercing the skin in a few places to encourage the fat to run out. Brown the bird on all sides.

When this is accomplished, transfer duck to an earthenware casserole or a covered roasting pan. Add *1 medium onion, 1 bay leaf,* and *¼ teaspoon each: peppercorns and ground thyme.*

Roast covered at 375° for about 30 minutes. Then, drain off all liquid that has accumulated in the pan. Add *½ cup white wine.* Continue to roast, uncovered, for perhaps an hour, or until duck is tender.

Shortly before duck is finished, strain sauce through a coarse sieve to remove peppercorns, onion and bay leaf. Add *⅓ to ½ cup of pitted green olives.* Return to oven for another 15 minutes. Carve the duck before bringing it to the table, and pour over it the olive sauce.

Red cabbage goes nicely with this duck. Another excellent accompaniment is ice-cold Horseradish-Apple Sauce. For this, add *1 teaspoon sharp horseradish to each ¼ cup of well-strained or canned applesauce.*

In 1868 Baron Brisse published a book which dealt exclusively with leftovers: *Manière de Servir à Nouveau Tous les Restes* (Ways of Using Leftovers Again). Though the following recipe is from his earlier book, a morsel of leftover ham goes a long way toward making the Baron's noodles a dish to applaud.

Ducks on a spit, from La Cuisine Classique, *Volume One, by Urbain-Dubois and Bernard. 1872 edition.*

Noodles Inspired by Baron Brisse

4½ cups (before cooking) fine noodles
4 tablespoons butter
2 cups scalded milk
1 small onion, chopped fine
1 slice boiled or baked ham, shredded (½ cup)
1½ tablespoons flour
1 teaspoon Worcestershire sauce
¼ teaspoon salt
2 slices packaged Swiss cheese, grated or cut up fine

Boil the noodles in salt water for 8 minutes. While they boil, scald the milk and set aside. Cook the chopped onion in 2 tablespoons butter (reserve remaining 2 tablespoons for later). When onion begins to turn golden and becomes glassy, sprinkle in the flour and mix with the onion. Add the scalded milk gradually, stirring constantly to keep sauce smooth. Add the salt and Worcestershire sauce.

Drain the noodles and toss quickly with the remaining 2 tablespoons butter. Pour on the sauce, sprinkle in the chopped ham and toss the noodles again to blend thoroughly. Pour mixture into a flat, buttered baking dish. (To guide you: a 12-inch pie plate is the right proportion for this quantity.) Sprinkle the cheese over the top, dot with bits of butter (optional) and place in a preheated oven (375°) until cheese melts, about 20 minutes. Transfer to broiler and watch carefully as cheese begins to form a golden crust. About 2 minutes is enough for this last operation.

This recipe provides 6 to 8 generous servings. And generous they had better be; guests love this dish.

La Cuisine des Restes (Leftover Cookery) was published in 1869. It was another popular book that dealt entirely with "remains"— although by now few cookbooks held themselves above disposing of a half-eaten chicken in some tempting manner.

In 1870, the ingenuity of Paris housewives was really put to the test. Paris was under siege during the Franco-Prussian War, and fresh meat was nonexistent. One enterprising butcher is said to have bought up all of the Zoological Gardens, including the elephants. Rats, cats and dogs were apparently common enough food to appear in cookbook recipes. *La Cuisine Pendant le Siège* (Cooking During the Siege) and *La Cuisinière Assiégée* (The Besieged Cook) were two of the books which appeared then, and they gave recipes for horse and donkey meat, as well as for rats and dogs. The versatility of the French housewife, plus a judicious sprinkling of herbs and wine, probably made these meats as palatable as even Grimod de la Reynière could have wished.

A fireplace in a contemporary French kitchen. From Les Secrets de la Cuisine Française, by A. Gogué. 1856.

10

19th-Century

England

THE UNCONQUERABLE
ENGLISH KITCHEN

IN NINETEENTH-CENTURY ENGLAND, the housewife continued to rule most upper-class kitchens with the authority of a traffic policeman. *Domestic Management* (1800) told her how to instruct the footman in the proper way to break the claws of a lobster at dinner: "He is not to crack it between the hinges of a dining room door, but take it into the kitchen," observed the author, providing some insight into dining room conduct at that time. The same footman could die of pneumonia for all this author cared. "When sent on a wet day for a hackney-coach, he is not to get into it and ride home. This will render it uncomfortably damp," she complained.

The author of *Domestic Management* concealed her identity, possibly to protect herself from the wrath of the footman.

Most cookbooks, however, bore their authors' names in bold type. Dr. A. Hunter's boldly displayed name was almost overshadowed by the imposing Latin title of his book, *Culina Famulatrix Medicinae*. It appeared in 1804, and combined recipes with a variety of philosophical observations and practical hints under the heading, "Men and Manners." Of his 267 comments, a good many were for the ladies. A sampling follows.

MEN AND MANNERS

An artful woman is a saint in the morning and a glow-worm at night.
Learn to dance well. If you have not a head, your heels may make your fortune.
A little spittle takes out grease spots from woolen cloth.
Remove the tax upon sugar by using only one lump to sweeten your tea instead of two.
When you take a journey in a stage coach, take with you a pillow. Put your head upon it in a corner of the coach at night and sit upon it in the daytime.
By overindulging a child, you will at last find him disposed to cry for the moon.
If you are disposed to grow fat, keep your eyes open and your mouth shut.
A bold deportment in a woman declares her to be half a man.
As beauty will fade, a handsome woman should lay in a stock of something to supply in its place.

Dr. Hunter's book included such strange-sounding recipes as Balnamoon Skink, Brado Fogado and Indian Burdwan. The first is a Scotch version of chicken-in-the-pot. The last two are Indian recipes, which engaged English interest at this time. Dr. Hunter was the first to introduce true curry to English cookbooks, though a few eighteenth-century authors had used turmeric in Indian dishes. His Brado Fogado is a novel way to serve shrimp.

Brado Fogado
[SHRIMP AND SPINACH]

½ *pound fresh spinach, all stems removed, coarsely chopped*
1 *medium onion, coarsely chopped, slightly browned in butter*
¾ *pound shrimp, cooked and shelled*
1 *teaspoon curry powder*
2 *to 3 tablespoons lemon juice*
1 *tablespoon coarsely chopped peanuts (optional, for garnish)*

Cook the spinach in a few tablespoons of water, only enough to prevent burning. Stir and watch until it is cooked (only a matter of a few minutes). Add the previously cooked onions and the lemon juice and curry powder. Last, add the shrimp and stir all together. Garnish with the chopped peanuts or thin slices of hard-cooked egg. An attractive dish for a buffet table or a first course. The quantity given will make approximately 4 portions.

Dr. Hunter's Indian Burdwan is a nice variation on the ever popular chicken stew.

Indian Burdwan
[A CHICKEN STEW]

1 *tender young chicken*
Salt
Celery sprigs
1 *large, sweet onion, sliced*
Butter

SAUCE:
1 *cup hot chicken broth*
1 *tablespoon cornstarch, mixed with 3 tablespoons cold water*
3 *tablespoons Madeira (or Sherry)*
Dash of cayenne pepper
1 *teaspoon curry powder (optional, not in Dr. Hunter's recipe)*

Season the chicken with salt and pepper, and steam it in a tightly covered pot with 3 cups of water, a few sprigs of celery and salt to taste.

Cook gently until tender but still firm. Cool; then disjoint the chicken. Remove all skin.

In a shallow pan or skillet, sauté the onion in butter until soft and slightly colored. To this, add ingredients for sauce as given above.

Return the cut-up chicken to the pot, and pour on the strained sauce. Cover tightly, and bake at 350° for 20 to 25 minutes. Before serving, add ⅓ cup sweet cream to the sauce.

Serve with rice and a variety of accompaniments, as you would curried chicken.

Dr. Hunter's recipe for Lobsters Dressed in the Shell shows a French influence; it is a variation on the dish that is better known as Lobster Thermidor supposed to have been invented for Napoleon. It may have been devised originally by some French cook displaced by the Revolution to an English kitchen. In any case, Dr. Hunter's is one of the earliest versions of stuffed or Thermidor lobster, and still is one of the best.

Dr. Hunter's Stuffed Lobster

2 or 3 lobsters, weighing approximately 1 pound each
Fresh white bread crumbs
Butter

CREAM SAUCE:
1 tablespoon butter
1 tablespoon flour
½ cup light cream and ½ cup milk, combined
½ teaspoon anise extract (or, if you have it on hand, 1 teaspoon
   Pernod)
Salt and white pepper to taste

Drop live lobsters into boiling water and boil for about 15 minutes. Cool in cold water. Split in half; remove the claws and extract the meat. Remove the meat from the body and discard stomach and intestinal tract. Cut the meat into ½-inch pieces.

Prepare the cream sauce using the ingredients listed above. Combine the sauce with the lobster meat (if the mixture is not loose enough, add a bit more cream) and refill the lobster shells. Sprinkle with fresh white bread crumbs, dot with butter and place under a preheated broiler until crumbs are delicately browned.

Because the lobster is in a shell and a runny dish in itself, it usually winds up with French fried or julienne potatoes for company. Try crisp corn oysters instead. And for accompaniment, whole peeled tomatoes filled with chopped, marinated cucumbers.

The title of Dr. Hunter's tasty potato cakes probably derived from the Westphalian ham used in them; Dr. Hunter doesn't say. Any ham will do for the loaves, but the smokier the better.

Westphalia Loaves

2 cups riced mealy potatoes (Idahos are best for this)
⅓ cup finely minced ham
½ teaspoon dried onion flakes or onion juice
Salt and pepper to taste
1 large egg (or 2 small ones), beaten
Butter and margarine

Combine the above ingredients and chill for about 30 minutes. Form into flat cakes, and sauté quickly in hot fat—a mixture of butter and margarine is best. Try to serve them as quickly as possible: they are best right off the fire. A truly delectable starch accompaniment for any meat, but best with something that has a thin natural or pan gravy.

ONE OF THE best-selling cookbooks of this period was Mrs. Maria Rundell's A New System of Domestic Cookery, first published in 1806. There was nothing especially new about Mrs. Rundell's recipes, and she was not at all receptive to the new ideas of the classic French cuisine. She expresses her disapproval of costly sauce bases thus: "I have avoided all excessive luxury such as essence of ham, and the wasteful expenditures of large quantities of meat for gravy which so greatly contribute to keeping up the price."

This must have been exactly what the English housewife wanted to read. How else can one explain the success of this undistinguished little book with its stodgy, unappetizing recipes? It was popular during most of the nineteenth century, in America as well as in England. It did strike a modern scientific note from time to time, and housewives may have enjoyed learning that stirring hastens the freezing and the boiling processes.

The Cook's Oracle (1817) by Dr. William Kitchiner was also well received in America. Its author's vivid prose style makes entertaining reading to this day, and his advice to "masticate, denticate, chump, grind, and swallow" has an Elizabethan directness. And his counsel to the young housewife is offered "to enable her to make the cage of matrimony as comfortable as the net of courtship was charming."

Dr. Kitchiner admired French cooking, but he had little respect for "those high-bred English epicures who cannot eat anything dressed by an English cook, and cannot endure the sight of the best bill of fare unless it is written in pretty good bad French." And the doctor says patriotically, "An Englishman's head may be as full of gravy as a Frenchman's."

Dr. Kitchiner has this to say about Mulaga-Tawny, a curried soup then new to England. Ascribing it to the East Indies, he writes: "This outlandish word is pasted on the windows of our Coffee Houses and often excites John Bull to walk in and taste. The more familiar word Curry Soup would perhaps not have sufficient charms or novelty to seduce him from his much loved Mock Turtle." The original recipe Dr. Kitchiner wrote for Mulaga-Tawny (Mulligatawny) soup differed considerably from the one eventually printed in his book. My collection includes Dr. Kitchiner's original manuscript; here is his original recipe for Mulaga-Tawny Soup followed by the adaptation, Mulligatawny Stew.

Mulaga-Tawny Soup

[DR. KITCHINER'S ORIGINAL RECIPE]

Take 2 *quarts of water* and a nice *fowl or chicken*. Then put in the following ingredients: *a large white onion; 1 large chili (the pods from which cayenne pepper is made); 2 teaspoons pounded ginger; the same of curry stuff; 1 teaspoon turmeric, and ½ dram black pepper.* Boil all these for half an hour and then fry some *small onions* and put them in. Season it with *salt,* and serve it in a tureen.

Mulligatawny Stew

When Dr. Kitchiner was writing his book, Mulligatawny soup was served as a stew, rather than a soup. It is really a curried chicken-in-the-pot, and there are as many ways to spice Mulligatawny soup as there are various recipes for it.

In a stewing kettle, cover a *young stewing chicken* with cold water, bring it to the boil, skim the broth, cover and let simmer slowly until tender, with the following spices added: *1 large onion, left whole; 1 bay leaf; ¼ teaspoon peppercorns; 1 teaspoon fresh ginger, pounded; 1 teaspoon coriander, and the rind of 1 lemon; salt to taste.*

When the chicken is tender, remove it from the pot, remove all skin and disjoint it into serving pieces. Place in a tureen. Mince an onion and cook this in *butter* until it is soft and transparent but not brown; add to the chicken in the tureen. Now combine *1 tablespoon curry powder* with *1 tablespoon flour.* Dilute this with sufficient broth to make a paste. Add it to 3 cups of the hot chicken broth and pour over the chicken. The Mulligatawny is now ready to serve.

Two tablespoons blanched, finely ground almonds may be added to the stew. And by all means serve it with *rice.*

Dr. Kitchiner specialized in sauces. Not the French kind, which he grandly ignored, but condiment sauces and catsups, forerunners of the bottled commercial sauces. He expanded the catsup repertoire beyond mushroom and walnut to include some made of cockles, oysters, and one of brandy and lemon shavings that he called Pudding Catsup. His Mushroom Catsup, boiled down to double strength, was good enough to be called Dogsup, he claimed. I haven't tried Dogsup, but here is one of his sauces that I have tested and liked:

Wow Wow Sauce

4 *tablespoons butter*
1 *tablespoon flour*
1 *cup bouillon or beef broth (heated)*
1 *tablespoon each: vinegar, catsup and prepared sharp mustard*
2 *tablespoons finely chopped parsley*
1 *tablespoon each: finely chopped pickles, finely chopped walnuts*

Two pages from the original manuscript of The Cook's Oracle, by Dr. William Kitchiner. c. 1816.

Brown the butter in a saucepan, add the flour, brown and blend well. Add the bouillon (or broth), and stir until smooth. Add the vinegar, mushroom catsup and mustard, and simmer gently until mixture thickens slightly. Last, add the parsley, pickles and walnuts.

Serve hot as sauce for ham or roast fresh pork.

THE SAUCES in *The Modern Cook* (1845) by Charles Elmé Francatelli were something else again. (Francatelli was maitre d'hotel and chief cook to Queen Victoria.) The very first recipe in his cookbook is a Common Stock for Sauces, based on Classic French cuisine. It calls for 120 pounds of stewing meat, plus ham, poultry and vegetable in similar Gargantuan quantities.

Francatelli also offers some original sauce inventions that were more British than French. They include the first sauce recipes I have seen that use melted jellies. A few are given here, and adaptations will probably suggest themselves to the imaginative cook.

FRANCATELLI'S JELLY SAUCES

Red Currant Jelly Sauce for Venison

This sauce is equally good with ham or duck.

1 stick cinnamon
12 cloves
¼ cup sugar
Pared rind of 1 lemon (be sure none of the white adheres to it)
¾ cup red wine
1 cup currant jelly

Crush the cinnamon and cloves in a small saucepan, then add the sugar, lemon rind and wine. Simmer gently for 10 minutes. Strain out the spices and add the jelly. Stir until jelly is melted. Allow to simmer for another 5 minutes.

Neapolitan Sauce

4 tablespoons horseradish (freshly grated, if available)
¼ cup unthickened brown gravy (leftover from a pot roast, or the like)
1 cup red wine
½ cup currant jelly

Melt the jelly. Combine all the ingredients, whirl in the blender for a few seconds, then simmer gently for a few minutes until white froth disappears. Excellent with braised beef or roast veal.

As a rule, Francatelli's instructions were concise, but even he could not compress the recipe for turtle soup. It ran to two pages, par for most cookbooks. "Procure a fine, lively turtle," Francatelli begins. Then he describes how the creature is to be slaughtered. Since he specifies a turtle weighing upwards of one hundred pounds as a desirable size, slaughtering that lively turtle should have posed a problem. Apparently not. Turtles were slain right and left in upper-class English kitchens: they were the first choice at elegant dining tables, with venison a close second. Francatelli cautioned his readers that if either or both of these favorites appeared at dinner, other dishes should be greatly reduced in size and number since they would not be eaten.

The Modern Cook includes many foods that seem odd to us to-day. Sheep's cheeks and jowls vied with ears and feet, and the latter formed some of Francatelli's favorite garnishes for elaborate entrees. Reindeer tongue seems strange and unappealing, but boiled smoked ox tongue is excellent teamed with sauerkraut, as Francatelli suggested.

Unexpected cookery hints are tucked away in his lengthy professional recipes. Cognac brandy added to a braised fowl is one example. Or swirl brandy in the pan juices of a roast capon or roast chicken, after the bird has been removed. Use this as a gravy; the result will delight you.

A calf's head, ready for serving, from Les Secrets de la Cuisine Française, *by A. Gogué. 1856.*

Francatelli's recipe for Goose à la Normande will work equally well with a duck or a chicken. It is a tempting way to use apples with a main dish.

Duckling à la Normande

5- to 6-pound duckling
1 medium onion, chopped fine, and sautéed in 2 tablespoons butter
2 cups plain mashed potatoes, combined with sautéed onions (above)
Salt and pepper
2 tablespoons crabapple jelly
½ cup apple brandy or cider
Juice of half a lemon

The potato and onion mixture is the stuffing. The cavity of the duck should be completely dry before this goes in. Season cavity to taste, with salt and pepper. Stuff; close the opening tightly with skewers. Pierce the duck in breast and thighs to allow fat to run out. Place on a rack in an open roasting pan in a preheated oven (375°). As fat drains out of bird, pour it off and pierce the skin again, if necessary, to draw off more fat. Roast for about 2 hours, turning the bird once or twice to make certain that it browns all over and that the fat is being drawn out.

For last half hour of roasting, remove every vestige of fat in the pan, and pour the apple brandy and lemon juice over the bird. Baste twice with this mixture during last half hour of roasting.

When duck is removed from pan, add the crabapple jelly to pan juices, and stir over a low heat until melted. (For a thicker sauce, add I teaspoon cornstarch dissolved in 1 tablespoon cold water.)

Serve the duckling garnished with *sautéed apple rings*. Better still, obtain small apples of uniform size. Peel and core them, and cook in a thin syrup until tender. Glaze them with melted crabapple jelly.

Like all haute cuisine recipes, Francatelli's emphasized garnish and eye appeal. He supplied many illustrations of fancy molds of rice, potatoes or macaroni that resembled embossed Wedgwood and required the hand of a sculptor. Francatelli actually suggested a chisel made of a raw carrot, evidently a common tool!

Too bad he didn't supply pictures of some of the puff pastries.

Some are easy to visualize from his descriptions. Love's Wells are obviously two pastry rounds, the top one smaller and hollow in the center to receive a dab of jelly. (This cookie can be made from any dough stiff enough to roll out and cut with a cookie cutter.)

But Harry the VIII's Shoestrings have nothing to do with shoes *or* strings; apparently they are turnovers filled with jelly.

Eliza Acton went far afield from classic haute cuisine in her *Modern Cookery for Private Families* (1845). She ranged the English countryside and the globe, figuratively speaking, to produce a collection of recipes with curious names and occasional strange combinations of food. Yorkshire Ploughman's Salad was a dressing of vinegar, molasses and salt. Burlington Whimsey was a jellied calf's head. Jelly of Siberian Crabs was a stopper, but a quick trip to the dictionary revealed that Siberian Crabs are wild crabapples, the ancestors of the domesticated variety.

Webster offers little help on Miss Acton's King of Oude's Omlet, or the strange measures used in the fiery original version.

The King of Oude's Omlet

Whisk up very lightly [says Miss Acton] after having cleared them in the usual way, 5 *fine fresh eggs;* add to them 2 *dessertspoonsful of milk or cream, a small teaspoonful of salt,* 1—or half that quantity for English eaters—*of cayenne pepper,* 3 *of minced mint,* and 2 *dessertspoonsful of young leeks, or of mild onions chopped small.* Dissolve *an ounce and a half of good butter* in a frying pan about the size of a plate, or should a larger one of necessity be used, raise the handle so as to throw the omlet entirely to the opposite side; pour in the eggs, and when the omlet, which should be kept as thick as possible, is well risen and quite firm, and of a fine light brown underneath, slide it on to a very hot dish, and fold it together "like a turnover," and brown side uppermost: 6 or 7 minutes will fry it.

This receipt is given above in a very modified form (the proportion of leeks or onions might still be much diminished with advantage). The original version, part of which we transcribe below [Miss Acton continues], is likely to find few admirers here, we apprehend.

Five eggs, two tolahs of milk, one masha of salt, two mashas of cayenne pepper, three of mint, and two tolahs of leeks.

Eliza Acton didn't say whether Veal Goose was from some English county, or perhaps of German origin. In any case, this rolled veal roast with sage dressing is excellent, especially served with hot applesauce, as Miss Acton recommended.

Veal Goose

An ideal way to prepare a flank or boned shoulder of veal.

Flank or boned shoulder of veal
Softened butter
Salt and pepper
1 *onion*

BREAD STUFFING:
2 *cups stale bread, cubed and slightly toasted*
¼ *cup butter, margarine or chicken fat, melted*
¼ *teaspoon salt*
¼ *teaspoon sage*
2 *tablespoons chopped onion*

I remove as much of the membrane-like covering on veal as possible. Arrange the meat in an oblong shape. Even if it is torn in many places it does not matter: the meat will seal together in the cooking. Heap the stuffing in the center. Wrap the meat around the stuffing and fasten any open places with toothpicks (pull these out before serving). Tie twine across the roast lengthwise to keep the ends from opening. Spread roast with softened butter or any fat, season lightly with salt and pepper (the stuffing will also impart seasoning) and place an onion in the roasting pan.

Roast, uncovered, at 350°. Allow 30 minutes to the pound. Baste frequently, and you will have a delicious, juicy roast. A little water or stock added to the juices that collect will make an excellent gravy.

Serve with red cabbage and applesauce, and choose a cold night for this filling dish. In its way, it is as rich as goose itself.

Modern Cookery for Private Families catered to all religions. It provided recipes for Fast days at Roman Catholic tables, and carefully noted those recipes that met the dietary requirements of Jewish households. (A year later, *The Jewish Manual* appeared, dealing exclusively with the Kosher table; apparently it was the first book of its kind in English.)

In her section on Home Brews, Miss Acton included the American mint julep, to be made with wine or brandy. "We apprehend," said she, "that this preparation is, like most other iced American beverages, to be imbibed through a reed."

Another bit of Americana is her recipe for Cold Dutch or American Sauce, which results in our familiar boiled salad dressing. (Perhaps further research will place this with the Pennsylvania Dutch.) Miss Acton also offered her own adaptation of the Rev. Sydney Smith's famous poem on salad-making. Both the poem and Miss Acton's adaptation are really salad dressings. Here is the original poem:

> To make this condiment, your poet begs
> The pounded yellow of two hard-boil'd eggs;
> Two boil'd potatoes, pass'd through kitchen sieve,
> Smoothness and softness to the salad give.
> Let onion atoms lurk within the bowl,
> And, half suspected, animate the whole.
> Of mordant mustard add a single spoon,
> Distrust the condiment that bites so soon;
> But deem it not, thou man of herbs, a fault,
> To add a double quantity of salt;
> Four times the spoon with oil from Lucca Brown,
> And twice with vinegar procured from town;
> And, lastly, o'er the flavor'd compound toss
> A magic soupçon of anchovy sauce.
> Oh, green and glorious! Oh, herbaceous treat!
> 'Twould tempt the dying anchorite to eat:
> Back to the world he'd turn his fleeting soul,
> And plunge his fingers in the salad-bowl!
> Serenely full, the epicure would say,
> Fate cannot harm me, I have dined to-day.

Here is Miss Acton's adaptation:

Eliza Acton's Salad Dressing

Two well-boiled potatoes, passed through a sieve; a teaspoonful of mustard; two teaspoonsful of salt; one of essence of anchovy; about a quarter of a teaspoonful of very finely chopped onions, well bruised into the mixture; three tablespoonsful of oil; one of vinegar; the yolks of two eggs, hard boiled. Stir up the salad immediately before dinner, and stir it up thoroughly.

N.B.: As this salad is the result of great experience and reflection, it is hoped young salad makers will not attempt to make any improvements upon it.

And here is the version I like at my house.

Poetic Potato Salad

Cook well-scrubbed new potatoes in their jackets until easily pierced by a fork. Pull off skins. Cool thoroughly, slice thin. Mince crisp green scallion ends and toss in with the potatoes. Add salt to taste and grind fresh pepper over all.

Make the dressing thus: Combine 7 tablespoons oil; 3 tablespoons vinegar; 2 riced egg yolks*; 2 teaspoons prepared yellow mustard, and 1 teaspoon anchovy paste. Mix in electric blender for a few seconds until thoroughly homogenized. Makes ⅔ cup dressing. Use as you would regular mayonnaise. With potatoes, this is much better than mayonnaise.

ALEXIS SOYER was the noted chef of London's exclusive Reform Club, and he, too, felt the urge to become a cookbook author. His first book, *The Gastronomic Regenerator* (1846), attempted to straddle all English kitchens from baronial manor to cottage; *The Modern Housewife* (1849) stayed more in the middle zone. But Soyer found his greatest audience with *A Shilling Cookery Book for the People* (1855). It sold 248,000 copies, and obviously inspired Francatelli, the Queen's cook, to do likewise with *A Plain Cookery Book for the Working Classes* (1862).

* Cook the egg yolks only and reserve the whites for some other purpose. Easy to do by separating the eggs, then sliding the yolks into boiling water.

Illustrated dedica-tion page from The Modern House-wife, *by Alexis Soyer. 1849.*

THE MODERN HOUSEWIFE

Soyer made no attempt to elevate public taste in any of his cookbooks. Typical of the dreary recipes he sponsored were Sheep's Head, Boiled Neck of Mutton, and Stewed Rump Steak.

But Soyer's knowledge of gastronomic history was impressive, and what he lacked in culinary inventiveness he balanced with a sense of humor or an interesting anecdote. He may even have grown inventive with his anecdotes. One concerns a delightful cheese tart. Upon closer examination, this turns out to be the medieval Daryol. As Cheese Tart or Custard Tart, it had been appearing in English cookbooks during the last two centuries, while the French had continued to use the name Dariole.

Soyer called the tarts Richmond Maids of Honor and said they came by their name at the Richmond palace of Queen Elizabeth I, where they were prepared by the Queen's maids of honor. But— and this is what makes for such interesting reading in old cookbooks —a philological detective writes that a variant of the word daryol apparently meant "maid of honor" in Chaucer's time.

The recipe had undergone minor changes during the past six centuries. Occasionally, it had been made of a soft cheese called dariole cheese; at other times it was a cream custard. It was unmistakably the same confection when it reappeared as Richmond tarts. I've borrowed from several old recipes and offer you one that combines the best of the fourteenth to nineteenth centuries—a creamy, custardy cheese tart to be topped with toasted almonds.

Darioles

[RICHMOND MAIDS OF HONOR]

Puff or pie pastry
¼ pound cream cheese⁻
5 tablespoons light cream
2 eggs
½ cup sugar
½ cup hot milk
1 teaspoon gelatin
½ teaspoon vanilla
½ cup heavy cream, whipped

Make sufficient puff or pie pastry for 12 fluted tart pans (or use muffin tins). Roll out to ⅛-inch thickness, and cut into rounds to fit the pans. Pierce with fork to prevent air bubbles, and bake at 450° for 15 minutes or until delicately browned.

Prepare Dariole filling as follows: Blend the cream cheese with the light cream to a fluffy consistency. Set aside. In the top of a double boiler over simmering water, beat the eggs and sugar together until creamy. Quickly add the hot milk, and stir until mixture begins to thicken. Remove from the fire. Dissolve the gelatin in 1 tablespoon cold water and add to the hot custard. Add vanilla. Stir well. When custard is cool, add it to the cream cheese mixture. Last, fold in the whipped cream.

Fill the baked tart shells. (No further baking is necessary.) Garnish with *toasted coconut* or *slivered toasted almonds*.

IN 1861, MRS. ISABELLA BEETON, the grand dame of Victorian cookbook authors, came on the scene with her three-pound, three-inch-thick cookbook, *The Book of Household Management.* Actually, Mrs. Beeton was a slim, pretty young woman, who wrote her book at the age of twenty-four and died at the untimely age of twenty-eight, greatly mourned by her young publisher husband, Samuel Beeton.

Her book was an extraordinary feat for a woman of any age. Even today, few cookbooks exceed its 1107 pages, and none exceeds the information thickly crowded into pages set with eye-straining type. Mrs. Beeton covered far more than household management. She went on for pages about manners, morals, discreet conversation, virtue and self-control, and she took the highest view of the role a woman must play.

As with the commander of an army, or the leader of any enterprise, so is it with the mistress of a house. Her spirit will be seen through the whole establishment; and just in proportion as she performs her duties intelligently and thoroughly, so will her domestics follow in her path. Of all those acquirements, which more particularly belong to the feminine character, there are none which take a higher rank, in our estimation, than such as enter into a knowledge of household duties; for on these are perpetually dependent the happiness, comfort, and well-being of a family.

Every head of a household should strive to be cheerful, and should never fail to show a deep interest in all that appertains to the well-being of those who claim the protection of her roof. Gentleness, not partial and temporary, but universal and regular, should pervade her conduct; for where such a spirit is habitually manifested, it not only delights her children, but makes her domestics attentive and respectful; her visitors are also pleased by it, and their happiness is increased.

In conversation, trifling occurrences, such as small disappointments, petty annoyances, and other every-day incidents, should never be mentioned to your friends. Greater events, whether of joy or sorrow, should be communicated; and, on such occasions, their sympathy gratifies and comforts. If the mistress be a wife, never let an account of her husband's failings pass her lips.

Despite husbandly failings, men had improved, Mrs. Beeton granted. "In former times, when the bottle circulated freely among the guests, it was necessary for the ladies to retire earlier than they do at present, for the gentlemen of the company soon became unfit to conduct themselves with that decorum which is essential in the presence of ladies. Thanks however to the improvements in modern society, temperance is, in these happy days, a striking feature in the character of a gentleman."

A gentleman might be tempted to fall from grace if he sampled too much of Mrs. Beeton's Tipsy Cake, also known in America as Tipsy Parson.

Tipsy Cake

A slightly stale sponge cake
Sufficient sweet wine or sherry to soak it
6 tablespoons brandy
Blanched almonds, slivered
2 cups soft custard
Whipped cream

Arrange the cake in a handsome shallow glass bowl or on a compote stand. It may be cut in 2 thick layers, or in separate squares for easier serving. In the bowl it should present a solid appearance. If in layers, smooth some of the custard between the layers. Pour the wine and brandy over the cake. When liquor has soaked through, pour on the remaining custard. Decorate with the blanched almonds and top with whipped cream.

Mrs. Beeton furnished the housewife with medical knowledge to deal with everything from toothache to drowning. "It is no longer considered good practise to hang the drowning victim by his heels," she cautioned. A warm bath and a massage was now the better way.

For a toothache Mrs. Beeton proposed a piece of zinc and a silver coin, these to be held in the mouth on either side of the tooth. "The zinc and silver, acting as a galvanic battery, will produce on the nerves of the tooth sufficient electricity to establish a current and consequently to relieve the pain," she stated, using the scientific language of the nineteenth century, but proposing a treatment that could only aggravate the pain! Questionable relief, but less harm, lay in the alternative: "Or smoke a pipe of tobacco and caraway seeds."

Mrs. Beeton's recipes were seasoned with sprightly anecdotes, but they were in themselves uninspired. Her Stew Soup of Salt Meat, with its turnips, cabbage, parsnips and oatmeal, is fairly typical of the dishes she provided for the English table.

Her book represents one notable advance. To Mrs. Beeton must go the credit for being the first to give exact measurements for all recipes, precise cooking times, and number of servings yielded. The approximate cost and the time of preparation were also noted. French Pancakes would require twenty minutes. Ginger Apples, on the other hand, demanded three days. Closer study of this otherwise brief recipe reveals that the three days were needed for soaking the ginger in brandy. Mrs. Beeton described it as "a pretty supper or dessert dish." So it is.

Ginger Apples

Whole ginger
½ cup brandy
3 pounds cooking apples
4 cups sugar
¾ cup lemon juice, strained
Candied orange peel

Heap a tablespoon with pieces of ginger. Bruise these with a mallet or pestle and place in a jar. Pour the brandy over the ginger and set aside for 3 days.

Peel and slice the apples, and put to simmer with the strained ginger mixture, sugar and lemon juice. Simmer gently about 10 minutes, until apples are transparent but firm. Serve cold. Ginger apples are excellent as a side dish with meats, but also delicious over vanilla ice cream.

Mrs. Beeton was aware that British cuisine was not enjoying happy days. With candor, and an underlying optimism that she could remedy all this, Mrs. Beeton wrote:

It has been asserted that English cookery is far from being the best in the world. We have been frequently told by brilliant foreign writers, half philosophers, half chefs, that we are the worst cooks on the face of the earth. . . . One great cause of many spoilt dishes and badly-cooked meats brought to our tables arises, we think, from a non-acquaintance with "common, every-day things."

With her 2751 entries, Mrs. Beeton meant to put an end to such "non-acquaintance," and perhaps she would have endowed English cooking with a new spirit had she lived longer and explored further. Her book continues to be a household bible in England, where it is still in print one hundred years after its original publication.

11

$\mathcal{A}$merican

$\mathcal{B}$eginnings

AN APPETIZING HERITAGE

THE TYPICAL AMERICAN cuisine grew out of memories brought over by English, French, Spanish and Dutch settlers, by African slaves, and by the Scotch-Irish and German colonists who followed the early settlers. The memories merged with the native American foods—with clams and corn, cranberries and potatoes, and later, tomatoes—until what was originally English or Dutch or French was barely distinguishable.

The English settlers found a way to supply the fruit for the dessert that was to become America's favorite, apple pie. In the early days, the English longed for apple pies but found no familiar apple trees here. They soon remedied this by bringing seedlings over from Europe.

French settlers gave America chowder (from the French chaudière—a kettle). New England's baked beans are more likely the contribution of English settlers who were familiar with the sturdy beans and bacon of the poorer classes in Britain. Puritan settlers in the New World, reluctant to cook on Sundays, developed the slow cooking process that makes Boston baked beans so delicious. Sweetening the beans with molasses was a cooking trick supposedly learned from the Indians, but we know how often sweetenings were added to vegetables and meats in early English cooking. The origin of dishes is fascinating to speculate about, but difficult to determine with any degree of certainty.

Creole cookery represented the blending of French and Spanish cuisines with those of native Indians in the West Indies and America. German settlers introduced such typical American favorites as waffles and cottage-fried potatoes.

The Dutch made their memorable purchase of Manhattan Island in 1626 and were soon baking koekjes. We adopted this name as cookies, rather than using the English "biscuit." Dutch kool (cabbage) and sla (salad) became our American coleslaw.

Dutch traders brought the first boatload of African slaves to Jamestown in 1619. As plantation life developed, Negroes became the expert cooks in the South. They were trained at first by their mistresses, who depended on memories and manuscript cookbooks. Soon the Negroes' appreciation of food and natural aptitude for cooking took over, and they were largely responsible for shaping America's distinctive Southern cuisine.

Undoubtedly the chief influence on early American life and cuisine, however, was English. By the mid-eighteenth century, Philadelphia, Boston, New York and Charleston had become urban centers of elegance that mirrored London life. The Virginia planters enjoyed the ease and luxury of European nobility. Whether they ate as well is a question.

The first American cookbook was printed in Williamsburg, Virginia, in 1742 and reprinted there in 1752. It was American by imprint only, for it was in fact Eliza Smith's *The Compleat Housewife,* at that time the most popular cookbook in England.

Years passed before *The Compleat Housewife* was reprinted in New York in 1764. A cookbook was published in Boston in 1772— Susannah Carter's *The Frugal Housewife,* a frugal 168 pages in length. Philadelphia, as befitted the capital of the new republic, produced the largest and most complete cookbook of all, *The New Art of Cookery* (1792) by Richard Briggs. It contained 557 pages of recipes and household hints, and was unequaled in size and content by any American cookbook until the middle of the nineteenth century.

These early books were really English cookbooks, although they were printed in America. None contained recipes using American foods, such as cranberries, clams, shad and terrapin, or recipes for the cornmeal puddings and corn cakes already basic to American cuisine. In all, there were only seven editions of these three cookbooks in fifty years. Cookbooks were not in demand in young America.

Apparently, they were not needed on colonial plantations, where the rivalry to set a well-provisioned table caused colonial dames to guard their recipes jealously, handing them down from mother to daughter as family treasures. Nor were they needed by rich city dwellers, content to follow the traditions they had brought with them from the Old World.

But there was an audience for truly American recipes, as was proved by the immediate success of a slim little book that appeared in Hartford, Connecticut, in 1796. *American Cookery* had modest recipes and a homespun touch. Its author, Amelia Simmons, introduced herself as "An American Orphan," and she introduced for the first time in a cookbook such strictly American dishes as Indian pudding, Indian slapjack (pancakes) and johnnycake or journey cake, as it was also called, because the flat corn cakes were so frequently carried on journeys.

American Cookery also included pickled watermelon rind (called

American citron), and these early American (and still delicious) cookies:

Amelia's Earliest American Cookies

Amelia's crisp cookies have the aroma of an old-fashioned kitchen. They are as simple and unpretentious as early America itself: quickly made and quickly baked, requiring neither rolling pins nor floured boards. Amelia used pearlash, a form of potash and an early leavening agent; I've substituted baking powder. The entire procedure may be done with an electric mixer.

> ½ cup butter or margarine
> 1½ cups sugar
> 2 cups bread flour (no need to sift before measuring)
> 1 teaspoon baking powder
> ¼ teaspoon salt
> ⅓ cup thick sour cream combined with 2 tablespoons milk
> 1 tablespoon ground or powdered coriander seed

Cream the butter until soft; add the sugar gradually and cream until fluffy. Sift the flour with the baking powder and salt, add the coriander. Add the dry mixture alternately with the sour cream and milk, beating after each addition. The dough will be quite firm and may be handled and baked at once.

Pinch off pieces the size of a hazelnut. Roll in balls, flatten out in circles on a greased cookie sheet. Bake in a preheated oven (375°) for 12 to 15 minutes, or until the edges begin to brown. Cookies may be sprinkled with colored sugar, cinnamon and sugar, or chopped nuts before baking. For variety, reduce the coriander to half, and add 1½ teaspoons anise flavoring. Makes about 75 2-inch cookies.

There were not enough purely American recipes to fill a cookbook, even as small a one as *American Cookery,* and in any case such a cookbook would not have met the demands of the average American table at the time. So Amelia included standard English recipes for meats, vegetables, boiled puddings, and that overwhelming English favorite, turtle. (Actually the turtle was another gift from the New World to the Old, imported to Europe from the West Indies.)

AMERICANCOOKERY:

OR, THE ART OF DRESSING

VIANDS, FISH, POULTRY, AND VEGETABLES.

AND THE BEST MODE OF MAKING

PUFF PASTES, PIES, TARTS, PUDDINGS,
CUSTARDS AND PRESERVES.

AND ALL KINDS OF

C A K E S,

FROM THE IMPERIAL PLUMB TO
PLAIN CAKE.

Adapted to this country and all grades of life.

BY AN AMERICAN ORPHAN.

WALPOLE, N. H.
PRINTED FOR ELIJAH BROOKS.
1812.

Title page of American Cookery, *by Amelia Simmons. 1812 edition.*

Amelia's cooking instructions were brief, to the point, and a few were surprisingly contemporary with today's methods. Of roast beef she wrote: "Rare done is the healthiest, and the taste of this age." Of green beans: "They will be soon done, make them boil up quick." In this method of cooking vegetables, Amelia was supported by a few English cookbooks, but the good advice soon went up in the steam of overcooking on both sides of the Atlantic.

Amelia urged all families to set out apple trees:

There is not a single family but might set a tree in some otherwise use-less spot, which might serve the two-fold use of shade and fruit. How many millions of fruit trees would spring into growth—and what a saving to the union. The net saving should in time extinguish the public debt, and enrich our cookery.

The Buttered Apple Pie in *American Cookery* is very like today's version, but try Amelia's Applesauce Pie for an interesting change.

Amelia Simmons' Applesauce Pie

Pastry for a 9-inch pie
3 pounds apples
½ cup sugar
Grated rind of 1 lemon
¼ teaspoon cinnamon
¼ teaspoon nutmeg

Peel and slice the apples. Combine with sugar, and stew in as little water as possible; cook until they begin to break apart. If too watery, strain off any excess liquid. Taste and add more sugar if not sweet enough. Add the spices and grated lemon rind. Pour into an unbaked pie shell. Cover the top with a lattice crust and bake in a preheated oven at 450° for 10 minutes. Reduce heat to 375° and bake for another 25 minutes or until crust is golden.

This pie is superb when topped with a dab of whipped cream, flecked with cinnamon.

The success of *American Cookery* soon earned it the distinction of being plagiarized. Lucy Emerson of Montpelier, Vermont, appro-priated even the "American Orphan" claim—as well as most of the recipes—in a book entitled *The New-England Cookery,* published in 1808. By then, *American Cookery* had been reprinted four times and expanded to include Fish Chowder and a number of recipes whose names reflected the young republic: Independence Cake, Federal Cake and Election Cake.

American cookery was shaping up, but it was still no match for a best-selling English cookbook. Maria Rundell's *A New System of Domestic Cookery* crossed the Atlantic to begin a fruitful American career in 1807. Editions were printed in Boston, Philadelphia, Charleston, and New York. By 1823, it was retitled *The Experienced American Housekeeper*, but its recipes remained typically English, except for terrapin and New England pancakes.

MEANWHILE a number of American ladies followed the lead of Amelia Simmons and her *American Cookery*. The most prolific of these was Eliza Leslie, who started out in 1828 with a small volume entitled *Seventy-five Receipts for Pastry, Cakes, and Sweetmeats*.

Miss Leslie's book was more general than the title implied. It included recipes for turkey, oysters, collared pork, beef à la mode, tomato ketchup (rather daring and advanced for American tastes at that time), and a delicious dressing for chicken salad that closely resembles the potato salad dressing in Chapter 10.

Miss Leslie's Dressing for Chicken Salad

Yolks of 4 hard-cooked eggs
½ cup salad oil
½ cup vinegar
¼ cup prepared mustard
Dash of cayenne pepper
¼ teaspoon salt

Mash the eggs into a smooth paste. Gradually stir the oil into them, then the vinegar. Last the seasonings and mustard. Stir until absolutely smooth. Beat if mixed in an electric blender.

Miss Leslie warned that this dressing should not be added to the salad until 5 minutes before it is to be served.

Miss Leslie used cornmeal in a Pound Cake, which was quite a change from the flapjacks, johnnycakes and hasty puddings that cornmeal usually produced. Her Indian Pound Cake has the flavor of early America, and a delicious grainy texture.

Indian Pound Cake

6 *tablespoons butter*
1 *cup sugar*
4 *eggs*
1¼ *cups sifted pastry flour*
¾ *teaspoon baking powder*
¼ *cup sifted white cornmeal*
⅛ *teaspoon freshly grated nutmeg (or ¼ teaspoon prepared)*
¼ *teaspoon cinnamon*
½ *teaspoon vanilla*
2 *teaspoons brandy, preferably apple brandy*

Thoroughly cream butter and sugar until fluffy. Beat in the eggs, one at a time. (An electric mixer may be used for these first two steps.) Sift together the flour, baking powder and cornmeal; combine spices with flour mixture. Blend the dry ingredients into the batter alternately with the brandy and vanilla (blend by hand). Pour into a greased, shallow cake pan, 8-inch square or 10 by 6 oblong (pan should be lined with wax paper). Bake at 325° for 1½ hours. Remove from oven. Allow to cool for 10 minutes. Invert on a cake rack, and strip off wax paper.

Miss Leslie's Sweet Potato Pudding is still outstanding among Southern recipes.

Sweet Potato Pudding

2 *cups cooked, mashed sweet potatoes*
3 *egg yolks, slightly beaten*
¼ *teaspoon each: nutmeg and cloves*
½ *teaspoon cinnamon*
½ *cup sugar*
¼ *pound butter, melted*
¼ *cup wine and brandy mixed*
½ *cup milk*
3 *egg whites, beaten stiff but not dry*

First, combine the potatoes with the spices and beaten egg yolks. Then add all the other ingredients, except the egg whites, and beat well.

(Miss Leslie's original recipe called for rosewater; I substitute the milk, to which I add ½ teaspoon of rose extract. Try it.) Last, fold the stiff (not dry) egg whites lightly into the potato mixture.

Heap in a buttered 2-quart casserole. Sprinkle top lightly with a mixture of sugar and cinnamon. Bake at 350° for about an hour. Serve with chicken, ham or pork.

Miss Leslie's second book, *Domestic French Cookery* (1832), indicated a growing American interest in French cooking. Louis Eustache Ude's *The French Cook* had already been reprinted here, and by the next decade Francatelli's *French Cookery* and Audot's *French Domestic Cookery* had made their American debuts.

Domestic French Cookery omitted much that was French. Miss Leslie scorned such dishes as sheep's tails and calf's ears, although they graced the most elegant Continental tables. "On this side of the Atlantic," she tartly explained, "all persons in respectable life can obtain better articles of food than these."

But her Veal à la Mode is typically French and a tempting way to prepare a roast of veal. I call it Miss Leslie's Bundled Veal.

Miss Leslie's Bundled Veal

Brush *a boned roast of veal—rump, leg or loin—*generously with *salad oil*. Season it, and sprinkle with a mixture of *chopped parsley, chopped scallions* and *a few chopped raw mushrooms*. Cover lightly with waxed paper and let stand overnight in the refrigerator.

When time to cook it, wrap the meat in buttered or oiled white paper, taking care not to brush off the seasonings. Place meat in an open roasting pan in a preheated oven (350°). Allow 30 to 35 minutes per pound.

When roast is done to your taste, remove paper and scrape off the seasonings into the natural gravy that has collected in the paper and pan. Add *1 tablespoon lemon juice* and *¼ cup stock*. Bring the sauce to a boil and serve with the roast.

Rice pilaf mingled with sautéed mushrooms goes nicely with this dish and echoes the subtle presence of the mushrooms cooked with the roast.

Miss Leslie wrote on and on, producing larger books each time. She never failed to include some French recipes, but as her books increased in size she leaned more heavily toward American cuisine and handed out laurels to Southern cooking and its Negro exponents. In *New Receipts for Cooking* (1854), she wrote, "A large number [of recipes] have been obtained from the South, and from ladies noted for their skill in housewifery. Many were dictated by colored cooks of high reputation in the art, for which nature seems to have gifted that race with a peculiar capability."

By the time the last of Miss Leslie's cookbooks appeared, her original 75 "Receipts" had expanded to a thousand in a book nearly two inches thick: *Miss Leslie's New Cookery Book* (c.1857). Along with the recipes, Miss Leslie now included large helpings of timely advice. To a recipe for Portable Soup, or what we could call bouillon cubes, she added a footnote:

If you have any friends going the overland journey to the Pacific, a box of portable soup may be a most useful present to them.

"Never send oranges whole to the table," Miss Leslie cautioned. "To ladies, they are unmanageable in company." She neatly solved the problem with Orange Coconut, the combination of sugared sliced oranges and grated coconut that we know today as Ambrosia.

Miss Leslie provided her readers with a long, laborious recipe for Maryland Beaten Biscuit, though this went against her better judgment. "This biscuit is most unwholesome even when made in the best manner. We do not recommend it, but there is no accounting for tastes."

I *do* recommend these recipes from *Miss Leslie's New Cookery Book*.

Veal Kebobbed

Of Veal Kebobbed, Miss Leslie wrote, "This is a Turkish Dish." I find it rather similar to Menon's Veal Villageoise, in Chapter 6. However, because it calls for curry, it is different enough to be included—even though the only thing Turkish about it is its name—if that. (Perhaps Miss Leslie could not think of an Indian name.) Sarah Phillips (Chap-

ter 7) provided a recipe with a similar name—Mutton Kebob'd—
but there is no similarity in the dish itself.

> *Thin slices of veal (1½ pounds), cut from the leg or loin*
> *Thin slices of onion*
> *Curry powder*
> *Salt and pepper*
> *Oil*
> *2 tablespoons lemon juice*
> *1 tablespoon water*
> *1 tablespoon catsup*
> *1 teaspoon Worcestershire sauce*
> *1 tablespoon vinegar*

Have the veal cut thin as possible to begin with, then flattened even
more with a wooden mallet. Cut it into pieces 3 by 4 inches. (If pieces
are torn, they will seal together in the cooking.) Lightly season each
piece of meat with salt, pepper and curry powder. (To season with
curry powder, we put the powder into a salt shaker or a discarded
garlic-salt container. Very handy, and the curry powder is distributed
as equally as salt.) Top with a half-slice of onion. Roll meat around
onion and fasten with a toothpick.

Lightly brown kebobs quickly in oil over medium heat. Transfer to a
covered casserole. Add the lemon juice and water.

Bake, covered, for 1 hour, or until tender. Fifteen minutes before
removing from casserole, add catsup, Worcestershire sauce and vinegar.
Stir this into the juices already collected in the casserole. If more sauce
will be wanted, add several tablespoons of stock at this time.

Serve these kebobs with rice; chutney belongs, too.

Disguised Ham

Miss Leslie recommended this as a breakfast dish, and it would be an attractive addition to a brunch menu. It is a distinguished way for baked or boiled ham to end its usefulness.

1 cup ground ham
4 eggs (3 of them separated)
Salt, pepper and mustard, to taste
Trimmed bread slices, toasted on one side

Combine the ground ham with the beaten whole egg and 3 egg yolks. All salt, pepper and mustard. If mixture is not sufficiently moist, add a bit of milk or mayonnaise.

Spread mixture on untoasted side of bread. Cover this smoothly with ½-inch thick coating of stiffly beaten egg white. Place in a preheated oven (350°), and bake until egg white is delicately browned.

Pumpkin Indian Cakes

Miss Leslie combined cornmeal with pumpkin in tasty griddle cakes that bake in a few minutes and have a tantalizing taste. Serve them for Sunday brunch, doused with maple syrup.

½ cup yellow cornmeal
1 cup boiling water
¼ cup canned pumpkin
⅞ cup milk, scalded
1 cup flour
2 teaspoons baking powder
¾ teaspoon salt
1½ teaspoons sugar
1 egg, beaten

Let the cornmeal stand in the boiling water until it swells, a matter of a minute or so. Then add the cold milk and stir smooth. Add the pumpkin, then the sifted dry ingredients. Last, add the beaten egg. Drop batter by scant tablespoons on a well oiled hot griddle or skillet. Flatten out with spoon. Bake until bubbles form all over; turn and bake crisp on other side. Serve with maple syrup.

SOUTHERN RECIPES were sprinkled through most American cookbooks, especially those printed in and around Philadelphia, but few cookbooks came from the pens of Southern writers. *The Virginia Housewife* by Mrs. Mary Randolph, printed in Washington, D. C., in 1824, and *The Carolina Housewife* (1847) by "A Lady of Charleston" were the most notable early examples of cookbooks that specialized in Southern foods (though both included Northern dishes as well).

The Virginia Housewife gave a few Spanish recipes, too. Here is a marvelous omelet called Ropa Vieja that combines fresh tomatoes with shredded leftover meat and beaten eggs.

Ropa Vieja

2 *large ripe tomatoes, peeled, with watery pulp and seeds removed*
Butter
½ *cup shredded leftover chicken, ham or veal*
4 *eggs, beaten only enough to blend whites with yolks*
1 *tablespoon chopped parsley*

Cut the tomatoes into sixths or eighths. Melt butter in a skillet large enough to accommodate a 4-egg omelet. Stir meat in butter until warmed through, shaking skillet back and forth. Add tomatoes to meat, and warm for a few seconds. Add more butter to skillet, if necessary to keep eggs from sticking, and pour beaten eggs over the meat and tomatoes. Quickly sprinkle the parsley over the top. Cover, and cook over a low flame until eggs are set on top, or cooked to your taste. Fold over as you would any omelet and serve at once.

The Philadelphia Housewife (1855) by "Aunt Mary" was a colorful volume bound in vivid orchid cloth, and it included such local favorites as scrapple, Philadelphia buns, Philadelphia milk biscuit and Journey Cake "baked on the center board of a flour barrel head." Aunt Mary also added a few fanciful desserts straight out of Classic French cuisine, such as this attractive apple dish:

Meringue aux Pommes
[APPLES WITH MERINGUE]

Peel and core *one large apple per pie serving* (use firm apples that do not cook too quickly). Sprinkle liberally with *cinnamon* and *sugar* and bake, covered, at 400° for 25 to 30 minutes or until tender. Cool. Arrange apples in *a baked pie shell,* and fill cored centers with *orange marmalade* mixed with *crushed macaroons.* Cover the entire top of the pie with a meringue made of 2 *or* 3 *egg whites,* allowing 2 *tablespoons of sugar per egg white.* (Two egg whites will be sufficient for an 8-inch pie. For a larger one, you'll need 3.) Make a swirled peak of meringue over each apple to guide you later when you serve the pie. Bake in a hot oven, 500°, until the meringue is delicately browned. *Slivered almonds* scattered over the top lend a festive look.

Baked Alaska Apple Pie

Do everything as directed in Meringue aux Pommes, but instead of filling the apple centers with marmalade, fill them with vanilla ice cream, and spoon ice cream in the spaces around the apples. Top with the meringue, bake and serve.

Another Philadelphia cookbook was *Cookery As It Should Be* (1855) by "A Practical Housekeeper." It offered information on marketing, medicines, soap-making, carving, and of course recipes. The recipes covered an interesting cross-section: East Indian curried and spiced dishes, German spiced beef, Carolina ginger cake, New Orleans gumbo, and most of the New England specialties as well. For okra soup, the author drew the Mason and Dixon Line and gave two recipes, one for the South and one for the North. Apparently Northerners had daintier appetites: their okra soup called for one pint each of okra and tomatoes to be cooked with chicken. Southern okra soup required two quarts each of okra and tomatoes and was to be cooked with beef.

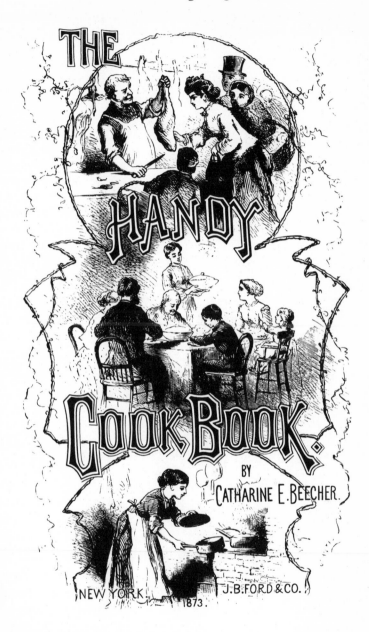

Part-title page from The New Housekeeper's Manual, *by Catharine Beecher and Harriet Beecher Stowe. 1873.*

Here are two excellent and typically American recipes from *Cookery As It Should Be.*

Clam Fritters

½ *cup water or* ¼ *cup water and* ¼ *cup clam juice*
2 *tablespoons butter*
⅛ *teaspoon salt*
½ *cup flour*
2 *eggs, well beaten*
A 7½ *ounce can or* 1 *cup thoroughly drained minced clams*
Cooking oil

In a saucepan bring the liquid and the butter to a boil. Dump in flour and salt and beat until mixture comes away from sides of pan. Remove from heat, cool for a minute or so, then add the beaten eggs. Beat with a rotary or electric beater until smooth. With a spoon, stir in the clams. Heat a heavy skillet. Cover bottom with cooking oil. Drop fritters by teaspoonfuls, and brown on each side. Drain on paper before serving.

Rhubarb Pie with Brown Sugar

Pastry for a 9-inch pie
3½ *to* 4 *cups sliced raw rhubarb (unpeeled)*
1 *lemon, peeled of all white membrane, sliced paper thin*
1¼ *cups light brown sugar*
2 *tablespoons flour, mixed with the sugar*

If frozen rhubarb is used:
2 *8-ounce packages rhubarb, well drained*
¾ *cup light brown sugar*
Flour and lemon, in amounts given above

Line 9-inch pie plate with pastry. Sprinkle a third of the flour-sugar mixture over the crust. Arrange a layer of rhubarb, scatter lemon slices over it, sprinkle with sugar. Repeat once or twice until all ingredients are used. Cover with a lattice crust (preferable, as this is a juicy pie) and bake in a preheated oven (375°) for 50 to 60 minutes.

ALONG WITH THE DEVELOPMENT of delicious and original American dishes came certain excesses of American cooking that were criticized at home and abroad.

Charles Dickens lampooned "the piles of indigestible matter" heaped on American dining tables, though he was hardly qualified to be a critic. His wife, writing under the pseudonym of Lady Maria Clutterbuck, had revealed the low state of the English table in her dismal little book, *What Shall We Have for Dinner?* (1856). What Dickens ate for dinner, judging from his wife's cookbook, was remarkably cheerless and uninspired. Her menus offered hot or cold mutton at almost every meal. The starch was inevitably mashed or browned potatoes. Batter pudding, suet dumplings and sole in brown gravy added to the dreary parade, digestible though it may have been.

Of digestive matters there were numerous critics and self-appointed guardians at home. As early as 1830, *The Cook Not Mad* took up the cause of American stomachs (after Dr. William Beaumont had observed one firsthand through the healed opening made by a gunshot wound in the stomach of a young soldier). The author of *The Cook Not Mad* disclaimed any intention of introducing to the American public "English, French and Italian methods of rendering things indigestible," and urged Rational Cookery on housewives.

Indigestible fried foods and hot breads were clearly irrational; liquor was another offender. These served as a springboard for the cookbook writers to project their views on thrift, morals, improved diet and the evils of drunkenness.

12

19th-Century

America

SANE, SOBER AND DELICIOUS

WHAT ARE AMERICAN WOMEN coming to! What is America coming to! From the beginning of the nineteenth century on, cookbook writers used their volumes as forums from which to view with alarm various shocking aspects of American life.

As early as 1807, the American editors of an English book, Mrs. Rundell's *New System of Domestic Cookery*, complained: "There was a time when ladies knew nothing *beyond* their own family concerns; but in the present day there are many who know nothing *about* them."

The prolific Miss Leslie, in her *House Book* (1840), added her voice to the clamor, and bewailed the great change that had come over American women "since, during the Presidency of her husband, Mrs. Washington, followed by a servant man with a basket, went daily to market in Philadelphia; and when the accomplished daughters of Mr. Jefferson made pastry and confectionery in a room fitted up for that purpose in their father's mansion at Monticello."

Frances McDougall, in *The Housekeeper's Book* (1837), was disturbed about American extravagance. "The rage for vieing with our neighbors shows itself in the bad taste by which houses are encumbered with unsuitable furniture. When I see showy furniture in the houses of people of small fortune I cannot help suspecting that it has been purchased without being paid for; the long upholsterer's bill rises like a phantom before the couches, ottomans and sofas crowded into small drawing rooms."

Mrs. Lydia Child in *The American Frugal Housewife* (1838) took a similarly stern view of extravagance. "Nothing should be thrown away so long as it is possible to make use of it, however trifling that use may be," she wrote, going on for breathless paragraphs about saving paper and twine. And in keeping with the prevailing philosophy that man must accept his fate without complaint, Mrs. Child headed one section of her book: How to Endure Poverty.

Reform was in the air. The temperance movement was founded in the early years of the century, and by the 1830s it had attracted more than a million members. Nearly all cookbooks stumped for the cause, and a few devoted themselves to it entirely, with such titles as *Total Abstinence Cookery* (1841), *Temperance Cook Book* (1841), and *Temperance Housekeeper's Almanac.*

Some supporters of the temperance movement held out for temperance in *everything,* not only alcohol, but tea, coffee, and food in general. Catharine Beecher, the noted educator, was one of the most effective leaders of this group. Her concern about the quantities of indigestible foods Americans were eating followed today's anti-cholesterol theme, though Miss Beecher was not aware of it then. "The most injurious food of any in common use is the *animal* oils, and articles cooked with them," she wrote prophetically in *Miss Beecher's Domestic Receipt Book* (1846).

The perils of fried foods exposed, Miss Beecher was not one to swim upstream if the current flowed in the opposite direction. "No book of this kind will sell without receipts for the rich articles which custom requires," she observed philosophically, "and in furnishing them, the writer has aimed to follow the example of Providence, which scatters both profuse good and ill."

Accordingly, in *Miss Beecher's Domestic Receipt Book* veal cutlets, hominy cakes and mush were fried in lard, and wine was added to a few puddings (it was supposed to lose its intoxicating effect in cooking). But most of her book was a compendium of wholesome cooking with great emphasis on fruit. Here are a few of her recipes that merit attention today.

An Ornamental Dish

[AN APPLE DESSERT]

This recipe for a whole apple in apple jelly is typical of Miss Beecher's imaginative use of fruits for dessert, and was suitably named.

Select the type of *apples* you would use for baking: Rome Beauty, Winesap or a similar type. Peel and core them. Prepare *a simple syrup of equal parts of sugar and water,* enough syrup to almost cover the quantity of apples you intend to prepare. Add a few tablespoons of *maraschino juice.* Boil syrup for a few minutes. Gently lower apples into the boiling syrup, reduce flame and cover. Cook gently until apples are tender. Carefully remove apples from syrup when cool enough to handle.

Place *paper-thin slices of lemon* in the bottom of ordinary cups. Then fill the core of each apple with *crushed nuts* mingled with *yellow raisins,* and lay apples on top of lemon slices. Pour in *lemon or apple jelly* to the top of each cup (see recipe for apple jelly given below).

When jelly has set, unmold apples and arrange in a serving dish or in individual bowls.

Apple Jelly

A jelly may be made from the *apple syrup* left over from An Apple Dessert (see preceding recipe). Taste the syrup, then add sufficient lemon juice to give it the desired flavor. Extend with any *additional fruit juice* you have on hand until liquid measures 1¾ cups. Bring it to the boil. Soften *1 tablespoon plain gelatin* in ¼ *cup cold water*, then promptly add the hot liquid. Stir until gelatin is dissolved.

Apple Ice Cream

Miss Beecher grated apples, sweetened them with sugar, froze them, and called this Apple Ice. I suggest you do it this way:

Add *cinnamon* to *sugar*, then mix into *grated apples*. Swirl the apple mixture into *slightly softened vanilla ice cream*. Return the ice cream to the freezer and let it firm up again. It's like eating frozen apple pie.

Mrs. L. G. Abell, author of *The Skillful Housewife's Book* (1846), also believed in wholesome cooking and sobriety, and her book provided Moral Hints and Safe Remedies for Common Diseases. The index is an amusing jumble of Happy Home, Hiccups, and Hominy; Cherry Pie, Cheerfulness, Chilblains; and Reputation, Rheumatism, and Red Sugar Beet Pie. The beet pie cannot be recommended, but the cherry pie, made with molasses, can.

Cherry Molasses Pie

Pastry for a 9-inch pie
2 cans red pie cherries
½ cup sugar
1½ tablespoons flour (combined with the sugar)
2 tablespoons molasses
3 tablespoons cherry juice

Line the pie plate with pastry. Scatter a third of the flour-sugar mixture over the crust. Add the cherries, which have been well drained, and cover with the remaining sugar-flour mixture. Dribble molasses over all; add the cherry juice. Cover with a lattice crust. Bake in a preheated oven (375°) for 50 to 55 minutes.

Mrs. Horace Mann (Mary Peabody of the famous Peabody sisters of Massachusetts) produced what was probably the most highly principled cookbook of them all. *Christianity in the Kitchen* (1861) opened with a grim Biblical quotation: "There's death in the pot." And before death, there were other evils stirring in the pot.

"There is no more prolific cause of bad morals than abuses of diet," she wrote, condemning alike excessive drinking, excessive eating and unhealthful preparation of food. Here is a list of "material" proclaimed both indigestible and un-Christian by Mrs. Mann:

Pie-crust made with butter or lard.
Wedding cake.
Suet plum pudding.
Turtle soup.
Butter, generally, but melted in particular; it contains butyric acid.
Lard.
Suet.
Pork, because of unsanitary conditions in raising pigs.
Fruit picked green. Anything shipped from a distance, such as oranges and pineapple.
Wheat flour. Caution to be observed since it was often adulterated with plaster of Paris.
Bottled fruits and vegetables. To be bought with caution; often adulterated with salts of copper.
Confectionery. Contained plaster of Paris; often painted with pigments and oils containing prussic acid.
Vinegar. Here, too, be cautious; could contain oil of vitriol.
Cayenne pepper. Colored with poisonous red lead.
Pickles. Often adulterated with salts of copper.

As for bread, *Christianity in the Kitchen* advised the housewife to make her own, and not to trust the adulterated products of commercial bakers who might substitute saleratus and baking soda for yeast.

These leavening agents were also used in cake-making, but Mrs. Mann would have none of them. Her cake recipes used eggs for leavening, and a typical cake recipe started out, "Take twenty eggs . . ." and instructed the cook to "beat the mixture for three hours."

Illustrated frontispiece from The Cook's Own Book, *by Mrs. N. K. M. Lee.*
1865.

It's easier today, with baking powder, and has been since the 1880s, although Mrs. Mann probably would not approve.

Christianity in the Kitchen starts out with the statement, "The object of this little manual is to show how healthful, nutritious, and even luscious, food can be prepared without the admixture of injurious ingredients." Mrs. Mann was as good as her word and excluded all ingredients she considered harmful, including butter, lard, suet and "all fatty substances in combination with wheat and other farinaceous articles of food." (What a definition of pastry!) Cream, she contended, would serve all the purposes of the banished fats. Here is Mrs. Mann's recipe for Cream Pastry, for those who care to try it. Personally, I prefer a pastry made with shortening.

Mrs. Mann's Cream Pastry

Beat *a teacup full of cream* to a foam like the white of an egg. Add the *well-beaten yolk of an egg, a teaspoonful of fine white sugar, half a teaspoonful of salt* (even spoonfuls of both) and pour this upon *a pint of well-sifted flour* in a bowl. Stir it as little as possible, or rather mix it quickly without stirring, but do not touch it with the hand. Lay a small heap of flour on the board, flour the roller well, dip the mixture out with a spoon and roll it immediately. If the cream is rich and well beaten, it will make very delicious pastry—at any rate it will be tender and harmless.

Mrs. Mann calls this Ohio Pudding "delicious," and I agree. She probably learned to make it during her eight-year residence in Ohio, while her husband was president of Antioch College.

Ohio Pudding

½ *cup cooked carrots, well drained, then put through a food mill*
½ *cup sweet potatoes (prepared as the carrots were)*
½ *cup dry white bread crumbs, finely grated (see Index for suggested recipe)*
1¼ *cups milk*
1 *large egg, beaten*
¼ *teaspoon salt*
2 *tablespoons brown sugar*

Combine the carrots, sweet potatoes, salt and sugar. Add the bread crumbs. Last add the milk and beaten egg. Mix thoroughly, and pour into a buttered casserole or baking dish (1- to 1½-quart). Bake for 1 hour in a preheated oven (350°).

This delicious pudding has the appearance of yellow spoon bread, and is excellent with chicken, ham or turkey.

There is a small section of French recipes at the back of *Christianity in the Kitchen*. Mrs. Mann could not deny that the French were indeed a nation of cooks and "have had the good sense to observe that health, and therefore to a good degree happiness, is dependent on good cooking and have applied themselves to the task of improving the art." Even so, they used too much melted butter, lard and oil, she believed.

Mrs. Mann had a keen eye for color and effect. She supplied two rose-colored recipes using currant jelly, one fetchingly named Pink Cream. I have combined them for a tempting and attractive dessert.

Currant Jelly Mousse

½ cup currant jelly, melted
Juice of half a large lemon, added to the melted jelly
1 cup light cream
4 egg whites, beaten stiff but not dry

Cool the jelly and beat in the light cream. When thoroughly blended, fold in the stiffly beaten egg whites. Spoon into a refrigerator ice tray and freeze, stirring once or twice during freezing. For best results, let the mixture freeze solid without disturbing it. Then rebeat with an electric mixer until it is the consistency of whipped cream. This will produce a smooth, professional consistency. Do not let it become too soft.

This delicious, tart dessert is refreshing after a rich meal. For added effect, serve each portion in the hollow of a canned pear half; pour a small quantity of Cointreau over all.

IN 1873, CATHARINE BEECHER and her sister, Harriet Beecher Stowe, combined their talents and produced *The Housekeeper's Manual*. They dedicated it "to the women of America, in whose hands rest the real destinies of the Republic, as moulded by the early training and preserved amid the maturer influences of home."

It was clearly woman's destiny to reform her fellow man. The Woman's Christian Temperance Union, familiarly known as the WCTU, was founded in 1874, and resolved not only to correct the problem of drinking, but to do away with the double standard of morals.

A cookbook was dedicated to "The women of the WCTU, who with their noble leader, Miss Frances Willard, are working for the uplifting of humanity." It was one of the best cookbooks stressing wholesome cooking: *Fruits and How to Use Them* (1890).

Its author, Hester M. Poole, managed to combine fruit and feminism in an interesting manner. The fruit industry was an excellent place for those women who needed to earn their own living, said Mrs. Poole. She cited a former Nantucket schoolteacher who, in 1886, had produced six thousand boxes of raisins and forty-five tons of dried apricots by working a hundred acres in Fresno, California. And two young Illinois females had established a Women's Fruit Preserving Union in Pasadena, California.

These were incidental remarks. The book's purpose was to substitute fruit temptations for the more dangerous temptations found in bottles, and Mrs. Poole's recipes are excellent. Here is a selection of them.

Illustration from Favorite Dishes, *a Columbian Exposition souvenir cookbook. 1893.*

Deep-Dish Saltine Cherry Pie

Mrs. Poole used crackers as a thickening for this juicy deep-dish pie.

Pastry for a double-crust 8-inch pie
2 cans red pie cherries (1-pound cans)
8 single saltine crackers, finely crushed
½ cup sugar (thoroughly mixed with the crushed crackers)
4 tablespoons cherry juice, mixed with ¼ teaspoon almond extract
Butter for dotting top of pie

Roll the pastry in an oblong shape to fit a 10-by-6 glass baking dish, and line with a bottom crust. Over the bottom sprinkle a fourth of the sugar-cracker mixture. Now a layer of cherries. Repeat until all ingredients are used. Pour the juice over the top, dot with butter, and cover with top crust. Puncture with a fork to allow steam to escape. Bake in a preheated oven (375°) for 50 to 55 minutes. Delicious served slightly warm.

Recipe serves 6.

Illustration from Favorite Dishes, *a Columbian Exposition souvenir cookbook. 1893.*

Double Coconut Cake

Mrs. Poole put coconut in the batter, a noble idea that will appeal to all lovers of coconut cake.

FOR TWO 8-INCH LAYERS:
½ cup shortening
1 cup sugar
2 eggs, separated (whites beaten stiff), or 3 whites
1¾ cups sifted cake flour
2 teaspoons baking powder
¼ teaspoon salt
¾ cup coconut milk (make this by soaking canned or dried coconut in milk)
1 teaspoon vanilla
¼ cup grated coconut, pulverized in the blender

Cream the shortening slightly. Add the sugar, cream until fluffy. Add the egg yolks, beaten with a fork. Add the sifted dry ingredients (mix the coconut in with the flour) and the milk alternately, continuing to beat after each addition. Blend in the vanilla. Add the stiff (but not dry) egg whites. Pour into lightly greased layer tins lined with wax paper and bake in a moderate oven at 350° for 25 minutes, or until cake pulls away from edges of pan. Frost with boiled icing and sprinkle lavishly with shredded coconut.

Orange Cream Pie

Mrs. Poole used oranges in many ways; this attractive pie is especially effective.

Baked 9-inch pie shell
3 eggs, separated
1 cup orange juice
3 tablespoons lemon juice
¼ cup hot water
1 cup sugar
5 tablespoons cornstarch

Combine all ingredients except the eggs in the top of a double-boiler. Cook for 5 to 8 minutes, or until smooth. Beat the egg yolks slightly and dilute gradually with some of the hot mixture. When eggs are thoroughly diluted and all danger of curdling is past, add them to the double-boiler mixture, and cook and stir for about 5 minutes. Cool the custard, then pour into baked pie shell.

Top with *fresh or canned orange segments.* (If fresh, remove all membrane from segments.)

Cover with a meringue made of the beaten egg whites, *a pinch of salt* and *6 tablespoons sugar.* Bake in a preheated oven (375°) for 8 to 10 minutes until meringue is delicately browned.

Mrs. Poole even made a form of catsup out of fruit. Two of these delicious fruit condiments are given below, one of grapes and one of gooseberries.

Grape Catsup

3 quarts green or purple grapes
2 pounds brown sugar
1 pint vinegar
2 tablespoons each: ground cloves, ground allspice, cinnamon
1 teaspoon each: salt and cayenne pepper

Simmer the grapes until soft, then mash through a colander. Return to cooking pot and add the other ingredients. Boil gently until mixture thickens. Store in sealed sterilized bottles.

Gooseberry Catsup

6 *pounds gooseberries, stemmed and clipped*
4 *pounds brown sugar*
2 *teaspoons cinnamon*
1 *teaspoon each: ground cloves and allspice*
½ *teaspoon cayenne pepper*
2 *cups vinegar*

Cook gooseberries, sugar and spices together for 2 hours. Add the vinegar, and cook for another 15 minutes. Strain and bottle in sterilized bottles. Seal.

BATTLE CREEK, MICHIGAN became a notable health center with the establishment there of the Western Health Reform Institute. Its name was changed to the Battle Creek Sanatarium in 1876 when its leadership was taken over by an able young pioneer in dietetic treatment, Dr. John Harvey Kellogg.

Among the ailing patients was Charles William Post, suffering from a chronic stomach complaint. Both Post and Kellogg became familiar names at American tables through the health cereals they developed.

The Sanatarium's kitchen, under the supervision of the doctor's wife, Ella Eaton Kellogg, was the scene of constant experiments to find new ways of making healthful, wholesome foods more tempting.

Mrs. Kellogg published two cookbooks, *Science in the Kitchen* (1892) and *Every-Day Dishes* (1898). Like other spirited reformers and cookbook authors, she advocated temperate eating. In fact, her formula to bring digestive problems under control was simple: don't tempt the appetite. "A great variety of foods at one meal creates a love of eating as a source of pleasure merely, and likewise furnishes temptation to overeat," she observed sensibly. "Let us have well-cooked, nutritious, palatable food, and plenty of it, but not too great a variety at each meal."

Mrs. Kellogg was very much concerned with guiding the housewife past the shoals of butter and lard, and she agreed that Pastry's guilt was undeniable. "So much has been said and written about the dietetic evils of Pastries that the very name has become almost synonymous with indigestion and dyspepsia," she wrote.

Like Mrs. Horace Mann, Mrs. Kellogg substituted cream for shortening, and her recipes naturally featured some of the patented "health" grains her husband's company promoted.

Cereal Pie Crust

CEREALS are available already crushed today and make excellent crumb crusts. Mrs. Kellogg's recipe is more or less standard, quickly made, and this is one crust no one can spoil.

FOR A 9-INCH PIE PLATE:
1½ cups cereal crumbs (or finely crushed vanilla wafers)
6 tablespoons melted butter or margarine
1 to 3 tablespoons sugar (use 3 for cereal crumbs)

Blend the sugar into the crumbs, then add the melted butter. Mix thoroughly. Use your fingers if necessary. Turn out into a pie plate and press firmly against sides and bottom. Place in a warm oven (325°) and bake for 5 to 8 minutes. Cereal crumbs take less time than cookie crumbs.

(A favorite dessert in my household is Ice Cream Pie. I always make it in a cookie crumb crust. Nothing but ice cream softened sufficiently to press into the baked crumb pie shell. Then the pie is returned to the freezer to wait until wanted. Jellies, fruit sauces or even maple syrup marbled through the ice cream creates all kinds of interesting variations. This dessert is handsome enough to serve at a formal dinner, and as easy to make as a boiled egg.)

To bring the family's craving for pastries under control, Mrs. Kellogg suggested the number be strictly limited, and fruit desserts provided to fill in the empty corners of suddenly deprived stomachs. Mrs. Kellogg's recipe for bananas in syrup inspired the following versatile dish. It can conclude a meal, or accompany poultry.

Illustration from Favorite Dishes, *a Columbian Exposition souvenir cookbook. 1893.*

Bananas in Syrup

Firm yellow bananas
2 tablespoons melted currant jelly
2 tablespoons hot water or heated fruit juice
1 teaspoon lemon juice
1 tablespoon butter

Slice the bananas in half, lengthwise, and arrange in a buttered baking dish. Combine the other ingredients into a syrup and pour over the bananas. Bake for 20 to 25 minutes at 350°. Baste once or twice with the syrup. To finish off in great style: Just before serving sprinkle the bananas with light brown sugar and place under a preheated broiler until sugar begins to melt and form a glaze.

Mrs. Kellogg also recommended bananas lightly dredged with flour, then sautéed in hot fat or baked in their skins. Any way you prepare and serve them, bananas are a delicious substitute for potatoes and other starches.

Cornmeal, always popular in American cookbooks, was featured in many of Mrs. Kellogg's recipes. These corn popovers are unusual, and a treat for breakfast, brunch, or with the dinner roast. Bake them in well-buttered preheated muffin tins.

Corn Puffs
[POPOVERS]

½ cup flour
4 level tablespoons yellow cornmeal
¼ teaspoon salt
2 eggs, well beaten
⅞ cup milk
1 teaspoon melted butter

Add the milk and butter to the beaten eggs; then stir gradually into the flour, cornmeal and salt, which have been sifted together. Beat the batter with an egg-beater until full of bubbles. Fill well-buttered hot muffin pans two-thirds full. Bake 15 minutes at 450°; reduce heat to 375° and bake for another 15 to 20 minutes. This quantity will make 10 popovers in 2½-inch muffin tins. Be sure tins are preheated.

Most of the women cookbook authors of this era were not only advocates of piety and sobriety but of women's rights as well. Catharine Beecher was a notable exception. A staunch supporter of the temperance movement, she was an equally determined opponent of woman's suffrage. In her opinion, women's place was in the home—not out voting, or doing anything else. Teach them how to run a home, said she. And how to cook.

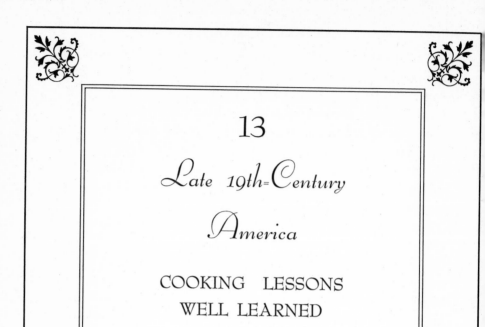

13

Late 19th-Century

America

COOKING LESSONS
WELL LEARNED

THANKS TO THE EFFORTS of Catharine Beecher, Domestic Science eventually became a part of American school studies; almost every public school now conducts classes in homemaking. No one could quarrel with the interest most women take in their homes today, or with the high standard of living they demand for their families. But it is interesting to look back and read in the cookbooks just how much times have changed.

In 1838 Lydia Child thundered in *The American Frugal Housewife*, "Our girls have no home education!" She accused American mothers of coaching their daughters in the art of catching a mate and overlooking the realities that would come later. Once a husband was caught, what then? "The bride is awakened from her delightful dream in which carpets, vases, sofas, white gloves, and pearl earrings are oddly jumbled up with her lover's looks and promises." (Some sociologists make similar charges against goals pictured in twentieth-century advertising.) "Perhaps some will think the evils of which I speak are confined principally to the rich, but I am convinced they extend to all classes of people," said Mrs. Child, sternly pointing her finger into every home.

She was only one of numerous critics. It seems that ladies drew away from cooking lest doubt arise that they *were* ladies. (It was different in England where well-bred young women were taught cooking along with other ladylike accomplishments, often in private schools. As early as 1678, a Mary Tillinghast had conducted a cooking school in London and published a cookbook for her scholars, *Rare and Excellent Receipts.*)

By the late 1870s, attitudes were changing. Prosperity followed the Civil War, but household help was reduced. ("Help" was preferred to "servant" in America where, in less affluent days, young people often hired out to neighboring families to help with the chores. And slavery undoubtedly helped to foster this fine point of semantics.) In a rising economy, the "help" were now prosperous enough to require help themselves.

A new supply was available in the waves of immigrants who arrived in America to share in its burgeoning prosperity, but if the mistress of a home expected the wheels to turn smoothly and meals to be cooked, she now had to be prepared to instruct the green newcomers. And in general, kitchens required more skill and knowledge. Coal stoves were far more versatile, and in some kitchens they were being replaced by gas ranges. A wider use of baking soda and cream of tartar, and the introduction of baking powder, gave a new dimension to baking and soon caused it to be ranked with china painting and needlework as an accomplishment. For those who wanted to excel as cooks, private cooking schools were the answer.

Juliet Corson opened one of the first cooking schools in New

York, in 1876. If some still looked upon ignorance in the kitchen as a status symbol, Miss Corson made it clear that such pretensions were as hollow as a popover. In her *Cooking Manual*, 1877, she wrote, "The day has passed for regarding cooking as menial and vulgar labour." She cried out against American waste: "In Europe provinces would live on what towns waste here." And she urged housewives to learn thrift from the French and other Europeans. It is not clear whether her recipe for Spanish Fried Chicken is from Spain or from Cuba, but it is a good one.

Spanish Fried Chicken

3½-pound frying chicken, cut up and disjointed
Fat for sautéing
1 medium onion, sliced thin
½ cup julienne strips of ham (cut from a ¼-inch thick slice)
2 fresh tomatoes, seeds removed, peeled and diced
Paprika
Salt and pepper
1 clove garlic
Bouquet garni: 3 sprigs parsley, 1 sprig thyme, 1 bay leaf, tied together
½ cup stock or wine

Sauté the onion in hot fat until soft. Lift out and set aside. Season each piece of chicken with salt and pepper, and sprinkle liberally with paprika; sauté in the same fat. As chicken browns, lift out each piece to join the onion in an ovenproof baking dish or shallow casserole. To this casserole, add the diced tomatoes, the bouquet garni of herbs, and the clove of garlic.

Add stock or wine, and place casserole in a preheated oven (350°). Bake uncovered for 20 minutes. Then scatter the strips of ham over the chicken, baste with the liquid in the casserole, and add more if necessary. Bake another 20 minutes.

Remove bouquet garni and garlic. Serve right in the casserole.

Unfortunately, most of Miss Corson's recipes were uninspired. She was more of a crusader than a cook, and followed Catharine

Beecher's lead to promote cooking instruction in schools. Most of her cookbooks—really trifling small pamphlets—were directed to the working classes, like those written earlier in England by Francatelli and Soyer. *Fifteen Cent Dinners for Workingmen's Families* was soon followed by *Twenty-Five Cent Dinners for Families of Six.* (Crisp copies of Miss Corson's drab little works are in my collection.) In her *Cooking Manual* under Sunday Dinners, Miss Corson began, "Sunday is the workingman's festival." How he could feast on chicken on Sunday and still stay within the twenty-five cent budget was simple her way: "The chicken need not be tender, but it ought to be fleshy enough to furnish the basis for two meals."

HAPPILY for the future of American cookery, most of the expert ladies who conducted cooking schools brought imagination and artistry to their work. One of the best was Maria Parloa. She taught cooking to housewives in Boston, and left behind her a number of cookbooks, though her partner Miss Johanna Sweeney seems to have vanished without leaving a trace of a recipe.

Miss Parloa's modest *Appledore Cook Book* (1872) offered "practical receipts for plain and rich cooking," but by 1880, when she wrote *Miss Parloa's New Cookbook and Marketing Guide,* she had doubled the size of her cookbooks and her reputation. Her recipes included one for Snow Pancakes (a cup of snow was one of the ingredients). The ancient Dariole recipe, last heard from in Soyer's *The Modern Housewife* as Richmond Maids of Honor, was also in her book, with the same anecdote Soyer had told. She was very strong on frozen desserts and ice creams, which included one made with brown bread. Her Strawberry Ice Cream Surprise is a refreshing dessert.

Strawberry Ice Cream Surprise

Soften sufficient *strawberry ice cream* to line a bombe mold thickly. In the center, pack *sugared strawberries, whole or cut up.* Pack bottom of mold firmly with strawberry ice cream, cover with wax paper, and place in freezer.

(*Continued on next page*)

Turn out on an ice-cold plate, and surround with handsome *whole strawberries.*

Serve with a sauce prepared in the following manner: Beat 2 *egg yolks,* add ½ *cup confectioners' sugar,* and beat until well blended. Whip ½ *pint of heavy cream.* Combine egg yolk-sugar mixture with the whipped cream. Last, add *1 tablespoon kirsch.* Chill well before serving.

Miss Parloa also gave a recipe for coconut ice cream, but an even easier way to create a frozen dessert is to roll balls of vanilla ice cream in grated coconut. It is a superlative dessert if the coconut is freshly shredded. The shreds should be at least an eighth of an inch wide. To *shred,* coconut must be pulled in one direction, not pushed back and forth in a grating motion. Once prepared, this dessert will wait patiently in the freezer until you are ready to serve it. The best of all sauces to serve with it is a fudgy chocolate sauce. I create some surprising innovations by melting a handful of chocolate creams and adding them to ordinary chocolate syrup.

If you have an ice cream freezer, you may want to try Miss Parloa's recipe for homemade coconut ice cream.

Miss Parloa's Coconut Ice Cream

1 *quart cream*
1 *pint milk*
3 *eggs*
1½ *cups sugar*
1 *cup grated coconut*
Rind and juice of 1 *lemon*

In the top of a double-boiler, beat the eggs and lemon rind. Add the milk and sugar. Cook and stir until the mixture thickens. Add the coconut and set aside to cool. When cool, add the lemon juice and cream. Freeze.

Miss Parloa was not a health food faddist and would even fry a parsnip. As it turned out, this was a pleasant way of serving a nutritious vegetable. Her parsnip balls are also worth trying.

Crisped Parsnips

Scrape *fresh parsnips*, or peel them thinly as you would carrots. Split in half lengthwise, and cook gently in boiling salted water until tender. Drain, cool, and cut them once again lengthwise. (Each parsnip has now been divided into fourths.) Roll in *melted butter or margarine;* set aside on a plate to chill. When chilled, dredge with *flour* and sauté gently in butter until crisp. A delicious vegetable; so good that my family forgets manners and eats this with their fingers, like candy.

Parsnip Balls

Scrape or peel the *parsnips,* and cook as for Crisped Parsnips until quite tender. Drain and force through a food mill or ricer. Measure, and for each 2 cups of riced parsnips, combine with the following: *1 teaspoon salt; pepper to taste; 2 tablespoons cream or milk, and 1 beaten egg.* Chill thoroughly in freezer section of refrigerator. (To hasten chilling, spread the mixture on a plate.) When cold, form into balls. Dip parsnip balls in *beaten egg,* then in *fine brown bread crumbs.* The mixture may be soft, but once it is rolled in bread crumbs it will handle easily. Fry in *deep fat* until brown and crisp. Excellent with any dish that will benefit by a crisp partner.

The social life of the nineteenth century could be reconstructed from some of Miss Parloa's recipes. For example, she offered a Bouillon for Germans and Other Parties. This was a puzzler until the dictionary explained that the German was a dance performed at cotillions. Of course! The whirling couples paused to enjoy a cup of Miss Parloa's strengthening bouillon between Germans. Later they supped more substantially on Miss Parloa's Chicken Livers and nibbled on her Sponge Drops (one of Miss Parloa's many recipes for pastries). Both recipes are given on the following pages.

Miss Parloa's Sponge Drops

3 *eggs, separated*
1 *cup sugar*
⅓ *cup water*
1 *cup pastry flour*
1¼ *teaspoons baking powder*
1 *teaspoon vanilla*
Pinch of salt

Beat yolks until they are light in color. Then add sugar, and beat another minute or so. Add water and vanilla, but continue beating all the while. All of the preceding steps may be done with the electric beater; however, the last steps must be done by hand. Lightly fold in the dry ingredients by hand. Last, fold in beaten egg whites (these should be beaten until peaked, but not dry).

Thoroughly butter muffin tins and fill them not more than half full. A candied whole cherry or a tiny ball of chopped dates and nuts may be dropped into the center of each cup. It will sink to the bottom, but will be there in the center, to bite into, once the Sponge Drops have been frosted. Anything that is not runny may be used in the center; jelly will not do as it will melt and disturb the batter.

Bake the Drops at 325° for 30 to 35 minutes, or until the edges begin to pull away from the pan. Allow to cool slightly. Loosen Drops with a knife, and invert muffin pans on cake racks.

This recipe will make 3 dozen 2-inch Drops, or 2 dozen 2½-inch Drops.

Frost with an icing made of: *1½ cups sifted confectioners' sugar; 1 slightly beaten egg white; 1 teaspoon flavoring* (almond, vanilla, rum, etc.). The icing may be tinted with a drop of vegetable coloring.

Top each Drop with a nutmeat, a cherry half or a chip of chocolate.

Miss Parloa's Chicken Livers

Miss Parloa directed that these be baked in paper cases, like Veal Cutlets Maintenon. This is unnecessary; we find that the livers turn out best in an ordinary gratin dish.

8 *chicken livers*
2 *tablespoons butter*
1 *tablespoon flour*
½ *cup bouillon or brown stock*
Half a small onion, grated
¼ *teaspoon soy sauce*
½ *cup julienne strips of boiled or baked ham*
1 *tablespoon Sherry (optional)*

Poach the livers in boiling water for 1 minute. Drain thoroughly, then divide each liver in half. Melt the butter, add the flour, and stir until quite brown. Add the stock, and stir until smooth. Add the onion, soy sauce, and sherry, if used. Pour this over the livers in a baking dish that can be used for serving. Garnish with the ham strips. Place in a preheated oven (350°) and bake for 15 to 20 minutes.

Serve on toast rounds as a filling first course, a luncheon dish, or an after-theater snack.

Most of Miss Parloa's cake recipes are not original by today's standards. Her recipe for chocolate cake was a pioneer effort in her day, however; it required baking soda, then widely regarded with suspicion by many. A noted chocolate company engaged Miss Parloa to prepare pamphlets of recipes using its product, and chocolate cakes were quickly sped on their way to popularity. I've taken a few liberties and added extra chocolate to Miss Parloa's recipe for Marble Cake. It can be baked in layers or in a loaf pan, but any way you bake it, it is one of the best cakes you will ever eat.

Rich Chocolate Marble Cake

¾ cup butter
1½ cups sugar ·
3 eggs
⅞ cup milk
2½ cups pastry flour (measured after sifting)
1 teaspoon salt
3 teaspoons baking powder
1½ teaspoons vanilla
4 squares bitter chocolate, melted

Use 2 9-inch layer pans or a loaf pan 9 by 13 by 2 inches. Grease pans generously and line with wax paper. Cream the butter and sugar until fluffy. Add the eggs, one at a time, beating only enough to blend after adding each one. Resift the flour with the baking powder and salt. Add to the creamed mixture alternately with the milk, blending quickly after each addition. Add the vanilla.

Have buttered pan or pans ready, lined with wax paper. Spoon off 6 heaping tablespoons of the batter, and to this add the melted chocolate. Pour balance of batter into wax-paper-lined pans. Drop spoonfuls of chocolate mixture at intervals in the white batter, then marble in broad streaks, allowing chocolate to remain as undiluted as possible. The rich streaks of chocolate add to the special quality of this cake.

Place in a preheated over (350°). Bake loaf cake 40 to 45 minutes or until cake tests done; layers 25 to 30 minutes.

Cool for a few minutes, then invert on a cake rack. When thoroughly cool, turn onto cake plate. The loaf cake needs nothing but melted chocolate dribbled over it generously in casual streams. Sprinkle chopped nuts over the chocolate. If made as a layer cake, frost with boiled white icing; when icing hardens, brush on melted chocolate, completely covering the white icing.

The *Boston Cookbook* (1887) by Mrs. D. A. Lincoln differed from the others; it tabulated the ingredients at the head of each recipe and offered a detailed table of weights and measures to guide the housewife who might be confused by the meaning of "butter the size of an egg." Mrs. Lincoln made it clear that this was 2 ounces or one-fourth cup. The standard measuring cup was already in use, and glass ones were advertised in her book.

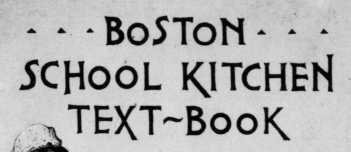

· · · BOSTON · · · SCHOOL KITCHEN TEXT~BOOK

LESSONS·IN·COOKING

For the Use of Classes in Public and Industrial Schools·

❈ BY ❈

MRS·D·A·LINCOLN·

ROBERTS-BROTHERS· PVBLISHERS· · · BOSTON · ·

Cover of the Boston School Kitchen Text-Book, by Mrs. D. A. (Mary J.) Lincoln. 1887.

Among the seafood categories, she included one for Reptiles, but only frogs were assigned this unpleasant connotation. (In defense of frogs, Webster does not call them reptiles.) Mrs. Lincoln's sniff of disapproval can almost be heard: "Frogs are considered a delicacy by those who have cultivated a taste for them."

She was equally forthright about baking powder, since many were suspicious of this new baking ingredient. "When your chemist is not to be relied on, use a Baking Powder that has been tested and proved true," said Mrs. Lincoln flatly. No baking powder was needed in a recipe for Almond Wafers, one of several "dainty desserts" from a pamphlet prepared by Mrs. Lincoln and Carrie Dearborn, also of the Boston Cooking School. It is indeed a dainty dessert, and attractive.

Almond Wafers

These cookies are easy to mix, but tricky to remove from the pan after baking. Try a few to get the feel of handling them, and do not try to do more than 8 or 10 at a time. With 3 cookie sheets going at staggered intervals, you can turn out quite a batch, once you get the hang of doing them.

½ *cup butter*
½ *cup granulated sugar*
½ *cup brown sugar, packed down*
½ *cup milk*
1 *cup bread flour*
½ *teaspoon almond extract*
½ *cup finely chopped almonds (do these in the blender, if you have one)*

Cream the butter with the sugar. Add the milk, then the flour, the extract and chopped almonds. Butter the outside of a cookie pan (or any large-surfaced pan), and drop the dough by teaspoons on it, leaving 2 inches between each cookie. Bake the cookies at 350° in a preheated oven for 8 to 10 minutes. Remove with a flexible spatula, and hang cookies over the handle of a wooden spoon or over a rolling pin. Work quickly, and keep the pan of unrolled cookies in a warm place as they become brittle quickly (a trip back to the oven will usually make them manageable again).

By 1887 Mrs. Lincoln's influence had extended into the Boston public schools where the students followed a textbook prepared by her. In it, she lectured, "It is as really a part of education to be able to blacken a stove, to scour a tin, or to prepare a tempting meal of wholesome food, as it is to be able to solve a problem of geometry." At least she approved of geometry, which is more than can be said for the foremost champion of cooking education, Catharine Beecher. (In Miss Beecher's dim view, a young woman was well rid of higher mathematics and better equipped to face life "if she knew about ballcocks, high and low pressure on water-pipes and boilers, and many other mysteries which make a woman the helpless victim of plumbers and other jobbers often as blundering and ignorant as herself.")

One of Mrs. Lincoln's recipes for schoolgirl-cooks was a Cracker Brewis, almost identical with the medieval bread and milk gruel called by the same name in the ancient English *Forme of Cury* described in Chapter 1 of this book. Mrs. Lincoln's Cracker Brewis, along with Miss Parloa's Darioles—Richmond Maids of Honor—had been traveling through cookbooks for more than five hundred years.

Some of Mrs. Lincoln's recipes did not fare as well as the ancient Brewis and were fated for quick oblivion, though her *Boston Cook-book* continued to be reissued. (In 1896 it was taken over by Fannie Farmer, whose name is now the only one associated with it.) Orange Cake and Gateau à la Princess Louise vanished from the later editions, but I've resurrected them for my kitchen. You may wish to do the same. The recipes are given on the following pages.

Orange Cake

¾ cup butter or shortening
1½ cups sugar
3 eggs
½ cup orange juice
Grated rind of 1 orange
2 tablespoons lemon juice, added to the orange juice
⅓ cup water
2¾ cups pastry flour
3½ teaspoons baking powder
¾ teaspoon salt

Cream the butter and sugar until fluffy. Add the eggs one at a time; beat briefly after adding each one. Add the orange rind. Sift the flour together with the baking powder and salt. Combine the orange juice with the water. Add dry ingredients alternately with the liquid to the creamed batter. If you have used an electric mixer up to this point, now complete the cake mixing by hand. Pour into 2 9-inch layer pans, greased and lined with wax paper. Bake at 350° in a preheated oven for 25 to 30 minutes.

Put layers together with orange marmalade or pineapple preserves. Frost with Orange Icing. Chocolate icing is also delicious on this Orange Cake.

Orange Icing

Measure 2 *cups confectioners' sugar*. Dilute this with *warm orange juice* and 2 *tablespoons melted butter* until nearly the right consistency to spread. Add *1 tablespoon Cointreau*. If the Cointreau does not bring the icing to the right spreading consistency, add a bit more orange juice. Place the bowl over boiling water for a few minutes to remove the raw taste (optional). Cool and spread over top and sides of cake.

Gateau à la Princess Louise

I've no idea who Princess Louise was, but this dessert in her name is a ravishing tribute. It is festive looking, easy to prepare, and your choice of filling will govern how rich it is to be.

THE GATEAU BATTER:
¼ *cup butter*
1 *cup sugar*
2 *eggs, separated*
1½ *cups pastry flour*
1½ *teaspoons baking powder*
½ *cup milk*
1 *teaspoon vanilla*
¼ *teaspoon salt, beaten with the egg whites*

Cream the butter and sugar; add the egg yolks one at a time, and beat after each one. Alternately add the flour (sifted with the baking powder) and the milk to the creamed mixture. Add the vanilla. Last, fold in the egg whites which have been beaten stiff, but not dry.

Pour into 2 buttered 9-inch layer pans lined with wax paper. Bake in a preheated oven (350°) for 25 to 30 minutes. Invert on cake racks, and cool.

When thoroughly cool, cut out the center of 1 layer, leaving a rim 1½ inches wide. Spread apricot jam or any jelly or jam of your choice on the bottom layer. Place the cake rim on top of it and pat down firmly to keep it in place. Fill the center with any of the following suggestions, and frost rim and sides of cake with a suitable icing.

A Chocolate Gateau

In the center pour *chocolate custard* flavored with *coffee liqueur or rum.* (Sliced bananas may be arranged on cake top before custard is poured on). Top with *whipped cream* and *slivered almonds or chocolate curls.* For icing, combine with an electric mixer: *1½ squares melted semi-sweet chocolate, 1 tablespoon boiling water, 1 egg yolk, 2 tablespoons softened butter* and *¼ teaspoon rum* (or use the same flavoring as in chocolate custard). Press slivered almonds against the sides of the cake for added glamour.

A STRAWBERRY GATEAU

In the center place *whole large strawberries*. Over them dribble *melted strawberry jelly* to serve as a glaze. Frost the rim and sides with an icing of *confectioners' sugar* mixed with *milk* and flavored with *Cointreau*.

A MACAROON GATEAU

Fill center with *crushed macaroons* folded into *whipped cream* slightly flavored with *almond extract or apricot brandy*. Glaze rim and sides of cake with *melted apricot jam*. Press *slivered almonds* against sides of cake.

I'm sure you can add to these variations, ad infinitum.

Another teacher of cooking whose career and cookbooks covered a long span was Sarah Rorer of Philadelphia. Her books ran from a slight 72 pages on sandwiches to a 541-page volume that covered every phase of cookery: *Mrs. Rorer's New Cookbook*. "Why should any woman be asked to stand for hours over a hot fire, mixing compounds to make people ill? Is this cookery?" she demanded, shrilly, I am sure. As an example of a non-dyspeptic dessert, her Banana Soufflé is superb.

Banana Soufflé

1½ *cups well-mashed ripe bananas (about 3 large bananas)*
⅓ *cup sugar*
1 *tablespoon lemon juice*
4 *egg whites (large)*
½ *teaspoon baking powder*

Set the oven at 375°; butter a 1½-quart soufflé mold, and have ready a pan of hot water in which to set the soufflé.

Combine the banana pulp with the sugar and lemon juice; set aside while you beat the egg whites. Beat them until they are stiff, but not dry. Blend the baking powder into the whites with a few strokes, and turn them into the bowl of banana pulp. Fold and cut in the whites with as few strokes as possible, but be sure to scoop under the pulp that falls to the bottom.

Pour into the buttered soufflé dish, and place the soufflé in the pan of hot water. Bake for 30 minutes. It's fairy-light, delicious, and really quite easy to make.

Even the durable, basic *Settlement Cookbook* was a school book in the beginning. It listed its twenty-four lessons at the back of the first edition, published in 1901. The purpose of such learning was shrewdly summed up on the white oilcloth cover and is still repeated on the thrice-as-thick edition today: "The Way to a Man's Heart." American women learned that lesson well.

As THIS ENGROSSING PROJECT comes to an end, I sit back and reflect on lessons I've learned while exploring my old and rare cookbooks. I started out thinking I knew quite a lot, but even on my own terrain, among those books I thought I knew so well, there was more to uncover. New doors opened each time I picked up another volume. History beckoned; cookbook authors became so alive I wanted to know them better; and the recipes, ranging from bizarre to mouthwatering, tempted me into the kitchen when I should have been at the typewriter—or perhaps it was vice versa. Above all, I learned that foods are like the letters of the alphabet: they can be arranged in limitless combinations.

There was so much material, so many recipes, so many books— some choices had to be arbitrary. If I have overlooked some favorite cookbook of the past, please excuse me. It wasn't possible to include all of them; even all that I own. And since this is really a book about cookbooks, I've even omitted such giants in gastronomy as Brillat-Savarin, though I own the two-volume first edition of his *La Physiologie du Goût*, published in 1826, and the first illustrated edition, which appeared in 1848.

Sometimes it was a wrench to exclude a book I loved. *New, Universal and Complete Confectioner* by Mrs. Elizabeth Price is one of my favorites, still in its original marbled paper wrappers, though

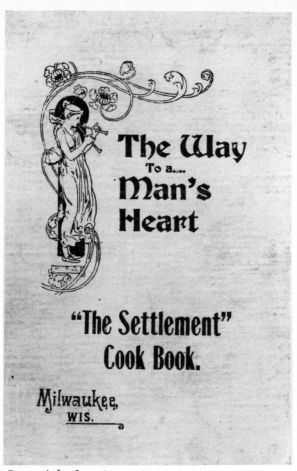

Cover of the first edition of The Settlement Cookbook,
by Mrs. Simon Kander. 1901.

it was printed in 1780. What a treasure for my collection, but unfortunately it had nothing to add in recipes.

Even recipes had to be curtailed so that all the centuries and their representative books could have a say. When I think of the many more there are to share, I long to start all over again. But at least I've pointed the way. Those who like old cookbooks (and the books need not be very old to be interesting) will find their own trails to follow. Those who like to invent will, I hope, be inspired to do even more of it. Perhaps this glimpse of the past will make the present even more delectable for those who like to cook well, eat well, and to read cookbooks.

An informal listing
of Books
in My Own Collection,
Consulted for

The Delectable Past

I seem to be following in the footsteps of Dr. Kitchiner (*The Cook's Oracle*) in publishing this list of books in my collection. The good doctor was the first author-collector to add such a list to his cookbook, and I have not in fact heard of another author who did so.

This is anything but a complete catalogue of my collection. I am neither an expert cataloguer nor a prompt one; over the years many books have entered my collection, but not my files. Someday an expert will put everything straight, but meanwhile I enjoy acquiring the books and go my own casual way about recording them. However, this list covers most of the high spots, including manuscript cookbooks—handwritten, private notebooks of the owners' favorite recipes—which are the most interesting of all to me.

I have not included the many German books; they begin with *Ein Koch und Erzen Buch*, Gratz, 1686. Nor my marvelous collection of Japanese cookbooks; they begin with 1730. Nor any of the cookbooks for children, though I must mention the handsome and charmingly illustrated *Cooking Garden* (1885), one of 250 limited copies.

Books after 1901 have been excluded from this list, although among them are many interesting and desirable items—*A Handbook of Cookery* by Mrs. Joseph (Jessie) Conrad, and Charles Nignon's *Plaisirs de la Table*, to name just two that are sought after by collectors.

Bibliographies have not been included, though my Vicaire is the original 1890 limited edition, and is signed by Georges Vicaire. (Any cookery catalogue, from Mrs. Elizabeth Pennell's impressive *My Cookery Books* to the auction catalogue of Claudia Q. Murphy's books, is an important acquisition for the would-be collector. I am happy to say I have these, and many more.)

Then there are non-recipe books about food, such as Ellwanger's *The Pleasure of the Table*; the books of Artemus Ward; Jeaffreson's and Kettner's books about the table; Hackwood's *Good Cheer*. All of them have been excluded because they are later than 1901, but all of them happily repose in my collection. And such books as *Coryat's Crudities*, in which Thomas Coryat describes his first sight of a fork being used in Italy—both the 1611 copy and the Glasgow reprint of 1905—are items to grace a cookbook collection even though they contain no recipes.

As you can see, the field of cookbook collecting reaches into many areas. Good luck to those of you who may be tempted to take up this fascinating hobby!

[The date and country of original publication are listed above each title. An author's name in square brackets indicates that the name does not appear on the title page of the book but has been otherwise verified. Editions and dates listed after the title refer to books in my collection. Unless otherwise specified, the first edition is in the author's collection.]

c. 1420 Latin
APICIUS, COELIUS—*De Re Coquinaria.* Latin ms.

Early fifteenth-century manuscript of the ancient cookery book attributed to Apicius. A superb example of handwritten books before printing began.

1475 Latin
PLATINA, pseud. (Bartolomeo de' Sac-

chi)—*De Honesta Voluptate.* [Printed in Venice by Lorenzo de Aquila and Sibyllinus Umber.]

The first printed cookbook. Also, the only book known to have been printed by Aquila and Umber.

An edition was printed around the same time in Rome by Ulrich Han and left undated.

My collection includes another edi-

tion: Rome, 1501. This edition unknown to Vicaire.

1494 Latin
GRAPALDI, FRANCESCO MARIO—*De Partibus Aedium.* Parma. *Second edition, 1516. This work describes how a perfect home should be planned and managed, and discusses the various foods and wines that should be on hand.*

1514 Greek
ATHENAEUS—The Deipnosophists. Aldine Press. *Original binding.*

1570 Italian
SCAPPI, BARTOLOMEO—*Cvoco Secreto di Papa Pio Quinto* (Cooking Secrets of Pope Pius V). Venice. *Original vellum binding. Includes 28 pages of copperplate illustrations. In addition to its many recipes, the book includes a pictorial documentary of Renaissance kitchens and cooking equipment.*

1581 Italian
CERVIO, VINCENZO—*Il Trinciante.* Venice. *A book on carving. Contains a large picture of a fork. (The only earlier picture of a fork that I know of is in Scappi's book.) Another edition, 1604.*

1588 Italian
CIACCONIUS, PETRUS—*De Triclinio Romano.* Rome. *Describes the feasts and eating habits of the ancient Romans.*

1588 English
The Good Hous-wives Treasurie. London: Edward Allde.

1597 English
A Booke of Cookerie. Otherwise called: The Good Huswives Handmaid for the Kitchin. London: Edward Allde.

1598 Italian
EVITASCANDALO, CESARE—*Libro Dello Scalco.* Rome. *1609 edition. Describes the duties of the various members of an aristocratic household.*

1599 English
BUTTES, HENRY—*Dyets Dry Dinner.* London. *The Henry Huth copy.*

1600 English
[PARTRIDGE, JOHN]—*The Treasurie of Hidden Secrets.* London. *Second edition, 1627. With the bookplate of Arnold W. Oxford, bibliographer of*

English cookbooks. (This work was originally issued in 1573, in somewhat different form.)

1608 English
[PLAT, SIR HUGH]—*A Closet for Ladies and Gentlewomen.* London. *With the Arnold W. Oxford bookplate.*

c. 1610 English
Manuscript Cookery Book. Includes a large medical section. Apparently belonged first to a William Daile, a butcher (?) in East-Cheape. Passed into the hands of the William Denny family in the eighteenth century (and finally into mine). A particularly interesting recipe for boiling a tench begins, "First kill him in the laike."

1615 English
[MARKHAM, GERVASE]—*The English House-wife.* London, 1668. *The eighth edition.*

1615 Italian
RABASCO, OTTAVIO—*Il Convito.* Florence. *How to plan feasts in private homes and for public occasions.*

1617 Spanish
MONTIÑO, FRANCISCO MARTINEZ—*Arte de Cocina.* Barcelona, 1763. *Thought to be the twelfth edition. (Montiño was chief cook to the King of Spain when Arte de Cocina appeared.)*

1620 English
VENNER, TOBIAS—*Via Recta ad Vitam Longam. Whereunto is annexed a necessary and compendious treatise of the famous Baths of Bathe.* London, 1628. *The third edition. A detailed discussion of all foods, and how they affect health.*

1651 French
LA VARENNE, FRANÇOIS PIERRE DE—*Le Vray Cuisinier François.* Paris. *1682 edition.*

1655 English
Manuscript Cookery Book. Dated, and inscribed, "Jose. Lovett."

1655 French
LA VARENNE, FRANÇOIS PIERRE DE—*Le Pastissier François.* Amsterdam. *The rare Elzevier press edition (1655). The book was originally issued in 1653 by Gaillard (Paris).*

1655 English
The Queens Closet Opened. London. 1668 edition. With the Faithorne portrait of Queen Henrietta Maria. Another edition: 1710.

1661 English
[RABISHA, WILL]—The Whole Body of Cookery Dissected . . . London.

1662 French
L'Escole Parfaite des Officiers de Bouche. Contenant Le Vray Maistred'Hostel; Le Grand Escuyer-Tranchant; Le Sommelier Royal; Le Confiturier Royal; Le Cuisinier Royal; Le Pastissier Royal. Third edition. Paris, 1676. The six sections of the book were sometimes published separately.

1669 English
DIGBY, KENELM—The Closet of the Eminently Learned Sir Kenelme Digby Kt. Opened . . . Published by his son's consent. Third edition. London, 1677.

1675 English
Manuscript Cookery Book. Dated and signed, "Chris, Maddison."

1678 English
Manuscript Cookery Book. Dated and signed, "Hopestill Brett."

1681 English
The True Way of Preserving and Candying . . . Made publick for the benefit of all English ladies and gentlewomen; especially for my scholars. Second edition. London, 1695. Apparently used in a cooking school.

1684 French
MARTIN, B.—Traité de l'Usage du Lait. Par B. Martin. Paris. The book deals with butter and cheese, as well as milk.

1685 French
DUFOUR, PHILLIPPE SYLVESTRE—Traités Nouveaux et Curieux du Café, du Thé, et du Chocolate. Lyon, 1688. Second edition.

1687 English
SHIRLEY, JOHN—The Accomplished Ladies Rich Closet of Rarities. London. The first edition, so far as I know. (Despite the "second edition" designation on the title page, no earlier edition has been recorded.)

1692 French
[AUDIGER]—La Maison Réglée et l'Art de Diriger la Maison d'un Grand Seigneur, et Autres. Amsterdam: Chez Paul Marret. 1697.

1692 French
[MASSIALOT, FRANÇOIS]—Nouvelle Instruction pour les Confitures . . . Paris. Also the 1737 edition, with many plates of richly set tables.

1695 English
SALMON, WILLIAM—The Family Dictionary: or, Houshold Companion. The fourth edition. London: Printed by H. Rhodes. 1710. Salmon was a "noted" quack doctor.

1698 English
Manuscript Cookery Book. Dated, and with Catherine Cotton's name on the covers of the book.

1699 English
[EVELYN, JOHN]—Acetaria. A discourse of sallets. London. The first book on salads.

1699 English
Manuscript Cookery Book. Dated; no owner's signature.

1702 French
LÉMERY, LOUIS—Traité des Aliments . . . Paris.

1704 English
LÉMERY, LOUIS—A Treatise of Foods, in General . . . London. The English translation of Traité des Aliments.

1705 English
LISTER, MARTIN, translator—Apicii Coelii: De opsoniis et condimentis sive arte coquinaria . . . Amsterdam. Second edition, 1709. Dr. Lister, Queen Anne's physician, based his translation of De Re Coquinaria on a fifteenth-century text.

1705 English
Manuscript Cookery Book. Dated and signed, "Dore Petry."

1708 English
KING, WILLIAM—The Art of Cookery (poem). Satirizes Dr. Lister's translation of De Re Coquinaria.

1710 English
HALL, T.—The Queen's Royal Cookery . . . London. Third edition, 1719.

1710 English
LAMB, PATRICK—*Royal Cookery* . . . London.

1714 English
KETTILBY, MARY, compiler—*A Collection of Above Three Hundred Receipts in Cookery, Physick and Surgery.* London. (*Also the extremely rare supplement issued to this book, still in its original paper covers.*)

1718 English
EALES, MARY—*The Compleat Confectioner* . . . London. *Fifth edition, 1753. Including also a Curious Collection of Receipts in Cookery, Pickling, Family Physic, etc. In this collection, under Receipts for Brewing, is "The Method of Brewing followed at Philadelphia, in Pensilvania." First published with the title Mrs. Mary Eales's Receipts.*

1723 English
SMITH, ROBERT—*Court Cookery* . . . London.

1724 English
Manuscript Cookery Book. Dated and signed, "Mary Statham."

1727 English
SMITH, ELIZA—The Compleat Housewife . . . London. *Fourteenth edition, 1750.*

1730-44 English
Manuscript Cookery Book. Two volumes, dated as above, and signed, "J. Bedingfield."

1734 English
MIDDLETON, JOHN—*Five Hundred New Receipts in Cookery* . . . London.

1736 English
BAILEY, NATHAN—*Dictionarium Domesticum* . . . London.

1737 English
Manuscript Cookery Book. Dated, and signed, "Ann Laurance."

1737 English
The Whole Duty of a Woman: or, An Infallible Guide to the Fair Sex. London.

1739 French
[MARIN]—*Les Dons de Comus.* Paris. *1750 edition, three volumes.*

c. 1741 English
KIDDER, EDW.—*Receipts of Pastry and Cookery for the use of his scholars. Manuscript copy of Kidder's book: either his, or used by one of the students at his school.*

1741 Italian
[MALASPINA, ALESSANDRO]—*Bacco in America. Americans celebrated Bacchus by drinking chocolate, not wine, wrote Malaspina.*

1746 French
[MENON]—*La Cuisinière Bourgeoise* . . . Paris. *1767 edition.*

1747 English
[GLASSE, HANNAH]—*The Art of Cookery, Made Plain and Easy* . . . London. *1774 edition.*

1747 Spanish
MATA, JUAN DE LA—*Arte de Reposteria* . . . Madrid. *All editions listed by bibliographers are later than this one of 1747. The earliest cited is 1755 (Vehling).*

1749 English
MOXON, ELIZABETH—*English Housewifry.* Leeds. *Tenth edition, 1769.*

c. 1750 English
MRS. FISHER—*The Prudent Housewife* . . . London.

1758 English
PHILLIPS, SARAH—*The Ladies Handmaid* . . . London.

1758 French
Traité Historique et Pratique de la Cuisine. Le Cuisinier Instruit. Paris.

1761 Italian
[FERRARI, GIUSEPPE]—*Gli Elogi del Porco Capitol.* Modena. *A facetious eulogy to pork and sausage dating from the time of the ancient Greeks and Romans: Described as an "unprocurable work" in Ellwanger's Pleasures of the Table.*

1762 English
GELLEROY, WILLIAM—*The London Cook* . . . Dublin.

1766 Italian
Il Cuoco Piemontese . . . Turin.

1767 French
Dictionnaire Portatif de Cuisine . . .
Paris.

1767 English
[MENON]—*The Art of Modern Cookery
Displayed* . . . London.

1767 English
PECKHAM, ANN—*The Complete English
Cook; or, Prudent Housewife. The
fourth edition.* To which is added, a
supplement, containing forty-nine receipts, never before printed. Leeds,
1772.

1769 English
RAFFALD, ELIZABETH—*The Experienced English Housekeeper* . . . London. Tenth edition, 1786.

1769 English
TAYLOR, E.—*The Lady's, Housewife's,
and Cookmaid's Assistant* . . . Berwick upon Tweed.

1772 French
FREDERICK THE GREAT—*Épitre au Sieur
Noël Maître d'Hôtel. Par l'Empereur de
la Chine. À Pékin.* Poem to his cook, by
Frederick the Great. I know of no other
copy, although the poem is referred to
by Joseph Berchoux in La Gastronomie.

1775 English
MASON, CHARLOTTE—*The Lady's Assistant* . . . London. *Ninth edition,
1805.* Contains a recipe for "viper
broth."

1777 English
Manuscript Cookery Book. Dated 1777.

1780 French
PARMENTIER, A. A.—*Traité de la
Châtaigne.* Paris.

1780 English
[PEGGE, SAMUEL, editor]—*The Forme
of Cury, a roll of ancient English cookery, compiled, about* A.D. 1390, *by the
master-cooks of King Richard II* . . .
London. The English translation of the
fourteenth-century manuscript.

c. 1780 English
PRICE, ELIZABETH—*The New, Universal, and Complete Confectioner* . . .
London. First edition, in its original
paper wrappers.

1783 English
FARLEY, JOHN—*The London Art of
Cookery* . . . Dublin. Second edition,
1789.

1786 English
BRAIDLEY, A.—*The Complete English
Cook* . . . London. The subtitle and a
few remarks on "How to choose meats"
copied from Hannah Glasse; the recipes
are completely different. Not listed by
Oxford, Bitting and other standard bibliographers.

1788 English
[TRUSLER, JOHN]—*The Honours of the
Table* . . . London.

1789 English
[NUTT, FREDERIC]—*The Complete
Confectioner* . . . London.

1789 French
PARMENTIER, A. A.—*Traité sur la Culture et les Usages des Pommes de Terre*
. . . Paris. Discusses the cultivation of
potatoes. By the man who sponsored
their introduction to French dining
tables.

1791 Spanish
ALTAMIRAS, JUAN—*Nuevo Arte de Cocina* . . . Barcelona. 1822 edition.

1791 English
WARNER, RICHARD, compiler—*Antiquitates Culinariae* . . . London.

1792 American
BRIGGS, RICHARD—*The New Art of
Cookery* . . . Philadelphia. First American edition of this English cookbook.

1793 English
MENON—*The French Family Cook.*
London. English translation of Menon's
La Cuisinière Bourgeoise.

1796 American
SIMMONS, AMELIA—*American Cookery*
. . . Walpole, N. H. 1812. The copy
that once belonged to Mrs. D. A. Lincoln.

1797 English
BATTAM, ANNE—*The New and Complete Cook.* London. Other books by
Anne Battam are recorded, but this
work seems to be unknown to bibliographers.

1801 French
BERCHOUX, JOSEPH—*La Gastronomie, Poëme.* Paris, 1805. *The famed and oft-quoted poem on gastronomy.*

1802 English
WILLICH, A. F. M.—*The Domestic Encyclopedia . . . In four volumes.* London. *The first edition, so far as I can determine.*

1803-12 French
GRIMOD DE LA REYNIÈRE, pseud. (Alexandre-Balthazar-Laurent) — *Almanach des Gourmands ou Calendrier Nutritif . . .* Paris. *Complete set of the periodical Almanach.*

1803 French
ANTIGRIMOD, pseud.—*Almanach Perpétuel des pauvres Diables . . .* Paris. *A spoof on the Almanach des Gourmands. With Grimod de la Reynière's sense of humor, I wouldn't put it past him.*

1804 English
HUNTER, ALEXANDER—*Culina Famulatrix Medicinae: or, Receipts in Modern Cookery . . . The fifth edition, considerably enlarged.* York, 1807. *"Cookery worthy of the notice of those medical practitioners who ride in their chariots with a footman behind, and who receive two-guinea fees from their rich and luxurious patients."*

1806 English
[RUNDELL, MARIA ELIZA (Ketelby)]— *A New System of Domestic Cookery . . . By a lady.* London. (*Oxford gives 1807 as the first edition.*)

1806 French
VIARD, A. (with Fouret and Délan)— *Le Cuisinier Royal . . .* Paris, 1832. *This is the first edition of the book with this title; the work started out as Le Cuisinier Impérial and became Le Cuisinier Royal or Le Cuisinier National, depending on the government in power.*

1808 English
The British Guide; or, A Directory to Housekeepers and Innkeepers . . . Liverpool. *Not in Oxford. Author unknown.*

1808 American
EMERSON, LUCY, compiler—*The New-England Cookery . . .* Montpelier. *Bears this charming inscription: "This book was given to Anna Powers Dunsmore by her father, at her marriage to Samuel Dunsmore, June 21st 1808 [just 3 months after its publication]. It then was handed down to her eldest daughter Jane Dunsmore Jones, to her eldest daughter Clara Jones Staples, and last to her eldest daughter Minne Staples Davis."*

1808 French
[GRIMOD DE LA REYNIÈRE]—*Manuel des Amphitryons . . .* Paris.

1810 English
MRS. SMITH—*The Female Economist . . .* London.

1813 English
UDE, LOUIS EUSTACHE—*The French Cook; or The art of cookery developed in all its various branches. By Louis Eustache Ude, formerly cook to Louis XVI, King of France, and at present cook to the Right Hon. Earl of Sefton.* London: Printed by Cox and Baylis for the Author. *First edition.*

1814 French
BEAUVILLIERS, ANTOINE—*L'Art du Cuisinier.* Paris. *Two volumes.*

1815 French
CARÊME, ANTONIN—*Le Pâtissier Royal Parisien . . .* Paris. *Second edition, 1828. Two volumes, in the original paper wrappers.*

1815 Spanish
La Nueva Cocinera Curiosa y Económica . . . Madrid. *Second edition. Three volumes.*

c. 1816 English
[KITCHINER, WILLIAM]—*The Cook's Oracle. The original manuscript. Bound in are various notes to and from Dr. Kitchiner pertaining to the publication of the book.*

1817 English
[KITCHINER, WILLIAM]—*The Cook's Oracle* [*Apicius Redivivus*] *. . .* Cheapside. *Fifth edition, 1823. This edition contains a list of cookery books. To the best of my knowledge, no other cookbook—before or since Dr. Kitchiner—includes such a list.*

1818 French
[AUDOT, LOUIS EUSTACHE]—*La Cuisinière de la Campagne et de la Ville* . . . Paris. *1890 edition.*

1821 English
ACCUM, FRIEDRICH CHRISTIAN—*Culinary Chemistry* . . . London.

1821 French
MME PARISET—*Manuel de la Maîtresse de Maison* . . . Paris. *Second edition, 1822.*

c. 1823 American
Manuscript Cookery Book. The 75 recipes include a few medical recipes. (One for "polmonary disease" starts off with one quart of whiskey.)

1823 American
[RUNDELL, MARIA ELIZA (Ketelby)]—*The Experienced American Housekeeper* . . . New York. *American edition of this English book.*

1825 French
CARDELLI, pseud. (M. Querard)—*Manuel de la Jeune Femme. Par Mme la Comtesse Clémence de G.* . . . *Paris: Charles-B'ecket, Libraire, 1827. After the first edition appeared in 1825, M. Querard altered his pseudonym from Cardelli to Mme La Comtesse Clémence de G.*

1826 French
BRILLAT-SAVARIN, JEAN ANTHELME—*Physiologie du Goût* . . . Paris. *Two volumes. Other editions in my collection: 1842; 1868, one volume, the first illustrated edition (illustrated by Bertall); 1879, two volumes, the Jouaust edition.*

1826 French
MME GACON-DUFOUR—*Manuel Complet de la Maîtresse de Maison, et de la Parfaite Ménagerie* . . . Paris.

1828 American
LESLIE, ELIZA—*Seventy-five Receipts, for Pastry, Cakes, and Sweetmeats* . . . *By Miss Leslie, of Philadelphia. New York: Oliver S. Felt. 1865.*

1828 Spanish
Modo de Hacer Salar y Conservar la Manteca de Vacas. Madrid. (In original paper wrappers.)

1829 American
CHILD, LYDIA MARIA (Francis)—*The American Frugal Housewife. Twenty-first edition, enlarged and corrected by the author. New York: Samuel S. & William Wood; W. W. Allen, printer. 1838. Appeared first as The Frugal Housewife; "American" was added to title in 1830.*

1829 English
HUMELBERGIUS SECUNDUS, DICK, pseud.—*Apician Morsels; or, Tales of the Table, Kitchen, and Larder* . . . London. *A humorous pseudonym. Humelbergius was a fifteenth-century translator of an Apician manuscript.*

1831 American
The Cook Not Mad, or Rational Cookery . . . Watertown (N.Y.)

1831 English
NICOL, ROBERT—*A Treatise on Coffee* . . . London. *Second edition. Presentation copy signed by the author. Apparently unknown to bibliographers.*

1832 American
LESLIE, ELIZA—*Domestic French Cookery, chiefly translated from Sulpice Barué.* Philadelphia. *First edition.*

1833-35, 1844-45 French
CARÊME, ANTONIN, and PLUMEREY—*L'Art de la Cuisine Française au XIXme Siècle.* Paris. Chez MM. J. Reynouard et Cie, Tresse, Mansut [etc.]. *A 5-volume work, covering 7 books. The first 3 volumes were issued in the years 1833 to 1835. After Carême's death in 1833, Plumerey (first name unknown to me) prepared the remaining material for publication.*

1834 English
CARÊME, ANTONIN—*The Royal Parisian Pastrycook and Confectioner. Edited by John Porter. First English edition.*

1837 American
[McDOUGALL, FRANCES HARRIET (Whipple)]—*The Housekeeper's Book* . . . *By a lady.* Philadelphia.

c. 1838 English
CHAMBERS, WILLIAM, and CHAMBERS, ROBERT—*Cookery and Domestic Economy for Young Housewives. Thirtieth*

edition . . . London and Edinburgh: Printed by W. & R. Chambers. 1881. *Unknown, apparently, to bibliographers.*

1839 American
The American Housewife . . . By an experienced lady. New York. *Eighth edition, 1853.*

1840 American
LESLIE, ELIZA—*The House Book, or, Manual of Domestic Economy. By Miss Leslie* . . . Philadelphia: Carey & Hart.

1843 French
[AMÉRO, JUSTIN]—*Les Classiques de la Table* . . . Paris. *Second edition, 1844.*

1844 American
WEBSTER, MRS. A. L.—*The Improved Housewife* . . . Hartford. *1847 edition.*

1845 English
ACTON, ELIZA—*Modern Cookery for Private Families* . . . London. *1877 edition.*

1846 American
ABELL, MRS. L. G.—*The Skillful Housewife's Book* . . . New York. *1852 edition.*

1846 American
BEECHER, CATHARINE ESTHER—*Miss Beecher's Domestic Receipt-Book.* New York. *Third edition, 1857.*

1848 American
The American Family Keepsake: or People's Practical Cyclopaedia. By the Good Samaritan. Boston.

1849 English
SOYER, ALEXIS—*The Modern Housewife or Ménagère.* London. *Second edition. This is actually the first edition, so far as I can determine.*

1851 French
Manuscript Cookery Book. Originally the property of a Swiss chef named Hotz. Includes intricate, elaborate drawings of pièces montées that would do credit to Carême; also elaborate menus and recipes. Two volumes.

1852 English
HAYWARD, ABRAHAM—*The Art of Dining.* London. *1883 edition.*

1854 English
YONGE, C. D., translator—*The Deipnosophists or Banquet of the Learned of Athenaeus. Three volumes.* London.

1854 English
DORAN, JOHN—*Table Traits with Something on Them.* London.

1854 American
LESLIE, ELIZA—*New Receipts for Cooking.* Philadelphia.

1855 American
Cookery As It Should Be . . . By a practical housekeeper, and pupil of Mrs. Goodfellow. Second edition, revised and enlarged, with illustrations. Philadelphia. *No earlier edition has been noted.*

1855 American
AUNT MARY, pseud. (Mary Hodgson) —*The Philadelphia Housewife; or, Family Receipt Book. By Aunt Mary.* Philadelphia: J. B. Lippincott & Co.

1856 English
CLUTTERBUCK, LADY ` MARIA, pseud. (Mrs. Charles Dickens)—*What Shall We Have for Dinner?* London. *With this cookbook, Mrs. Dickens strove to assert her own importance.*

1856 French
URBAIN-DUBOIS, FÉLIX, and ÉMILE BERNARD—*La Cuisine Classique* . . . Paris. *Fifth edition, 1872. Two volumes. First published as a smaller work in one volume.*

1856 French
GOGUÉ, A.—*Les Secrets de la Cuisine Française.* Paris.

1856 American
THORNWELL, EMILY—*The Lady's Guide to Perfect Gentility* . . . New York.

1857 American
LESLIE, ELIZA—*Miss Leslie's New Cookery Book.* Philadelphia.

1859 American
[ANDREWS, JULIA C.]—*Breakfast, Dinner, and Tea* . . . New York. *Second edition, 1860.*

1861 English
BEETON, ISABELLA—*The Book of Household Management* . . . London.

1861 American
MANN, MRS. HORACE (Mary Peabody) —*Christianity in the Kitchen, A Physiological Cook Book.* Boston.

1863 American
BLOT, PIERRE—*What to Eat, and How to Cook It* . . . New York.

1865 American
[LEE, MRS. N. K. M.]—*The Cook's Own Book . . . By a Boston housekeeper.* New York.

1865 American
CROWFIELD, CHRISTOPHER, pseud. (Harriet Beecher Stowe)—*House and Home Papers.* Boston.

1865 American
What to Do with the Cold Mutton: A Book of Réchauffés. New York.

1866 American
SCOTT, SARAH—*Every-day Cookery for Every Family* . . . Philadelphia.

1867 French
GOUFFÉ, JULES—*Le Livre de Cuisine* . . . Paris.

1868 French
BARON BRISSE—*Les 366 Menus du Baron Brisse* . . . Paris. *1870 edition.*

1872 French
URBAIN-DUBOIS, FÉLIX—*Cuisine Artistique.* Paris. *Two volumes.*

1873 American
BEECHER, CATHARINE E., and STOWE, HARRIET BEECHER—*The New Housekeeper's Manual* . . . New York.

1873 French
DUMAS, ALEXANDRE—*Grand Dictionnaire de Cuisine.* Paris.

1883 American
LINCOLN, MRS. D. A. (Mary Johnson)—*Mrs. Lincoln's Boston Cook Book. By the First Principal of the Boston Cooking School.* Boston. *1898 edition.*

c. 1884 American
HARLAND, MARION, pseud. (Mary Virginia Hawes Terhune)—*Cookery for Beginners. A series of familiar lessons for young housekeepers.* Boston.

1885 American
[HEARN, LAFCADIO, compiler]—*La Cuisine Créole.* New York. *First issue of the first edition.*

1887 American
LINCOLN, MRS. D. A. (Mary Johnson) —*Boston School Kitchen Text-Book.* Boston.

1887 American
PARLOA, MARIA—*Miss Parloa's Kitchen Companion.* Boston.

1887 American
PFAU, C. F.—*A Book of Cooking and Pastry.* Quincy, Ill. *One of many books published by private cooking schools around this time.*

1890 American
POOLE, HESTER M.—*Fruits, and How to Use Them.* New York.

1893 American
SHUMAN, CARRIE V., compiler—*Favorite Dishes. A Columbian Autograph Souvenir Cookery Book.* Chicago. *Souvenir cookbook of the Columbian Exposition.*

1894 American
RANHOFER, CHARLES—*The Epicurean.* New York.

1895 French
COLOMBIÉ, AUGUSTE—*Nouvelle Encyclopédie Culinaire. Three volumes.*

1898 English
GARRET, THEODORE FRANCIS, et al.— *Encyclopaedia of Practical Cookery. Eight volumes.* London. *The Bitting bibliography calls it "a monumental work."*

1898 American
KELLOGG, ELLA EATON—*Every-Day Dishes and Every-Day Work.* Battle Creek, Michigan.

1901 American
[KANDER, MRS. SIMON (Lizzie Black)] —*The Way to a Man's Heart.* Under the auspices of "The Settlement." Milwaukee, Wis. *First edition of The Settlement Cookbook.*

INDEX TO COOKBOOKS

241

INDEX TO RECIPES

Index to Recipes

Vegetables (*continued*)
  Mushrooms
    Champignons Farcis, 63
    Champignons à l'Olivier, 64
  Parsnip(s)
    Balls, 219
    Crisped, 219
  Tomatoes, Stuffed
    à la Florentine, 145
    à la Provençale, 145
    à la Sicilienne, 145
Venison, Red Currant Jelly Sauce for,
    168

Violets (*see* Candied Blossoms)

Westphalia Loaves, 164
White Bread Crumbs, 156
Whole Fish, Broiled or Baked with
    Fennel, 121
Will Rabisha's Green Chicken, 88
Wow Wow Sauce, 166

Yorkshire Pudding, Perfect, Puffy, 124

ABOUT THE AUTHOR

Esther Aresty's twin enthusiasms for rare cookbooks and for cooking make a happy combination. Every new acquisition for her incomparable antique cookbook collection inspires her to interpret the old recipes—converting handfuls and pecks to modern measures, eliminating such items as "the braines of fower cocke sparrowes"—yet preserving the intention of the original. Mrs. Aresty lives in Trenton, New Jersey, with her husband and their two children, who have enjoyed sampling these delicious dishes from centuries past.

Par vn excez de friandise
Icy lon donne du ragoust;
Et lon y vend, pour plaire au goust,
Toute sorte de marchandise.

Chascun y trauaille à son tour,
Châcun met la main à la pa
L'vn fait des pastez à la hâ
Et l'autre les met dans le fo

A Paris, Chez Mcᵉˢ Tauernier, Graueur et Imprimeur du Roy pour les Tailles-douces.

The Pastry Cook, from a series called "The Trades."